Male Novelists and Their Female Voices

Male Novelists and Their Female Voices:

Literary Masquerades

by

Anne Robinson Taylor

The Whitston Publishing Company
Troy, New York
1981

For my mother, Helen Tomkinson Jeter.

Acknowledgments

I would like to thank Professors Masao Miyoshi and Thomas Flanagan for their many readings of this book in manuscript, for their invaluable criticism, and for their energetic encouragement of this work. Robin Lakoff made many useful suggestions, and her own lucid, interesting work is itself an inspiration. Others have helped in shaping my thinking over the years, and here I would mention Professor George Starr and Professor Richard C. McCoy. Willard Potts, Dorothy Brown, Margaret Comstock, Muriel Dance, Diana Ketchum, Cathy Evans, and Dennis Evans all read individual chapters and offered a great many useful suggestions. I would like to thank the College of Liberal Arts, the Research Council at Oregon State University and Professor Richard Astro for giving me time off from a heavy teaching load to complete this work. Thanks go to Shirley Neyhart for typing the manuscript. My friends and family, have helped, of course, immeasurably, and I think they know just how much.

Grateful acknowledgment is made to the following for permission to reprint previously published material:

Dover Publications, Inc. for permission to quote from Otto Rank's *Beyond Psychology*, copyright © by Estelle B. Rank, 1941.

Grove Press, Inc. for permission to quote from the translation of the Marquis de Sade's *Justine, or Good Conduct Well Chastised*, by Richard Seaver and Austryn Wainhouse, copyright © 1965.

Quotation from *Orlando*, copyright © 1928 by Virginia Woolf; renewed 1956 by Leonard Woolf. Reprinted by permission of Harcourt Brace Jovanovich, Inc. and the Hogarth Press.

Harper & Row for permission to quote from Henry James, *The Conquest of London, 1870-1881*, by Leon Edel published by J. P. Lippincott, copyright © 1962 by Leon Edel.

Viking Penguin Incorporated, Faber and Faber Ltd., and The Society of Authors for permission to quote from *Selected Letters of James Joyce,* ed. Richard Ellmann, copyright © 1957, 1966 by the Viking Press, Inc., copyright © 1966, 1975 by F. Lionel Monro, as Administrator of the Estate of James Joyce.

Viking Penguin Incorporated, The Society of Authors and Jonathan Cape as the literary representatives of the Estate of James Joyce for permission to quote from *A Portrait of the Artist as a Young Man,* copyright © 1916 B. W. Huebsch, 1944 Nora Joyce, copyright © 1964 by the Estate of James Joyce; "*Exiles, A Play in Three Acts,*" in *The Portable James Joyce,* introduction and notes by Harry Levin, copyright © 1947, copyright © 1916, 1918 by B. W. Huebsch, Inc., 1927, 1936, 1939 by James Joyce; 1918, 1919, 1920 by Margaret Caroline Anderson; 1944, 1946 by Nora Joyce. *Stephen Hero,* copyright © 1944 by New Directions. *Finnegans Wake,* copyright © by James Joyce, 1939, renewed 1967 by George Joyce and Lucia Joyce.

Viking Penguin Incorporated, Laurence Pollinger Ltd. and The Estate of the late Mrs. Frieda Lawrence Ravagli for permission to quote from *The Collected Letters of D. H. Lawrence,* ed. Harry T. Moore, copyright © 1962 by Angelo Ravagli and C. Montague Weekley, Executors of the Estate of Frieda Lawrence Ravagli. *The Fantasia of the Unconscious and Psychoanalysis and the Unconscious,* published by William Heinemann Ltd. Copyright © 1961 by Angelo Ravagli and C. Montague Weekley, Executors of the Estate of Frieda Lawrence Ravagli.

Table of Contents

List of Illustrations

Chapter VII
Henri Matisse, *Persian Nude with Fruit and Flowers*, 1923
by courtesy of
The Art Institute of Chicago

Masquerade in the Novel

When Virginia Woolf, in her well-known feminist essay *A Room of One's Own,* flipped through the card catalogue at the library, she was astonished to find how many books had been written about women, and how many of these had been written by men. Great female figures dot the literary landscape, in all literatures in all times, and attest to the male proclivity to recreate the woman in art. One should take note of the fact (and many have) that the woman so created, the "image" of woman, is likely to reflect her creator's preoccupations rather than her own. But then how would we know her own, since as Otto Rank said; "As far as we can see now, her real psychology, not the one furnished by man, consists of just that ability to take on any masculine ideology as a cloak for her real self."?[1]

At certain points in the history of fiction, male novelists have seen fit to take on the voice of a woman for a significant portion of the novel, have chosen to use the first person of a woman. This narrative form has not been used often, certainly more in French and British literature than in Russian or American, undoubtedly because it combines the difficulties of the "I" form with those of transposing one's gender. When it has been used the results have been rich, provocative, and often confusing. Rarely have critics taken serious note of the effect of the male origins on such female voices as Daniel Defoe's Roxana, Samuel Richardson's Clarissa, Charles Dicken's Esther Summerson, Henry James's governess in *The Turn of the Screw,* or even James Joyce's Molly Bloom.

When I say effect, I do not mean that no one notices the fact of male authorship; I mean that many confusing aspects of these female characters can be explained by examining the male author's choices and difficulties about adopting the female voice as his own. Woolf thought that men wrote so often of women because they needed a mirror, someone to reflect them back to themselves, but bigger and greater.[2] Certainly such a narrative pose offers the opportunity to observe men through female eyes, and we will find these female speakers more or less obsessed with the assorted powers that belong to men. Looked at in this light, writing as a woman becomes a narcissistic exercise. Charles Dickens was moved to remark sardonically that " 'Defoe's women . . . are terribly dull commonplace fellows without breeches; and I have no doubt he was a precious dry and disagreeable article himself. . . .' "[3] He felt that this famous early creator of the feminine consciousness had simply put skirts on his men and called them women; his women were the author himself engaged in a transparent, unconvincing masquerade. I share the Dickensian conviction that certain fictional women are primarily their male authors in disguise.

According to Oscar Wilde, a student of masquerades, we can expect to learn more about the author in this guise than we can expect to learn from his autobiography. "Man is least himself when he talks in his own person. Give him a mask, and he will tell you the truth."[4] The female mask is certainly an effective disguise, a voice through which much can be said that cannot be said through a male persona. The challenge of the disguise is clearly compounded when the woman is young, adult, and a candidate for heroic status. The essays that follow concern what the author says as a man, what as a woman—and how these things are said. The authors I have chosen: Defoe, Richardson, Dickens, Henry James, and James Joyce, are major figures in English literature, stylistic and thematic innovators whose female voices have spawned numerous imitations, who in fact have done much to create contemporary notions of women. In each case they have tried to create a young heroine of tremendous importance to the other characters in the drama, a heroine whose mind and feelings are revealed to us with precision and detail. Defoe's women influenced so modern a writer as James Joyce. On the continent and in America, Richardson's Clarissa became the very type of the beleaguered good women, even as some hundred years later Dickens's Esther showed young English women the way to happiness. Henry James's conception of the ardent young woman (seen at its most extreme in *The Turn of the Screw*) gave to other less "feminine" Americans a heroic female type. And no figure has been more influential than Molly Bloom, who continues to find herself awash in food and sex in the works of such disparate writers as William Faulkner, or Norman Mailer or John O'Hara. My concern is the revelations these so-called women actually make about their authors, the extent to which they are versions of their creators in skirts.

I invite you to think of this sexual transposition as a literary masquerade. The term comes from the drama; it involves disguise, pretence, and a false outward show. Such an imaginative act would be particularly necessary when writing in the first person. To create for the reader a world issuing from the mind of "I" necessitates adopting the voice, manners, clothing, and feelings of such a person. There is much evidence to suggest that these novelists all actually did feel an essentially dramatic relationship to their own characters. Dickens used to claim that he could hear the voices of his characters and, of course, went about dramatizing them later in his career. Samuel Richardson began his literary career by adopting the voices of young ladies and penning their love letters for them. Henry James's notebooks reveal his complete imaginative involvement in his own fictions; the very person who should tell the tale seemed to take hold of him and demand that his or her story be told. Hugh Kenner points out James Joyce's indebtedness to Defoe, who was "drawn, as in *Moll Flanders* and *Roxana*, to people who pass through roles and have multiple costumes, names, identities. By writing in the first person he himself impersonates them, his skills nearly indistinguishable from those of imposture."[5] Joyce rarely used what we recognize as conventional first-person form; nevertheless, the interior monologue involves the ability to imitate a characteristic voice turned into thoughts. With Molly Bloom Joyce ventured to play the game in much the same way that his eighteenth-century predecessor had.

Why would male novelists choose a female persona? For the same reason, undoubtedly, that Laurence Sterne chose the histrionic voice of Tristram Shandy or that Thackeray chose the voice of the disinterested, cynical puppeteer in *Vanity Fair*—the voice is a congenial one, one that is suited to stand in for the author, and that provides a role the author enjoys. Masquerade is a form of play, and adopting a female voice seems to have been play of a challenging, pleasurable sort. It is a conjuring trick, to raise oneself up before the world in another sex. I think it is important to recognize this element of play, the element of exploration that is central to storytelling. As John Gardner puts it; "What the writer understands, though the student or critic of literature need not, is that the writer discovers, works out, and tests his ideas in the process of writing."[6] The writers I am discussing here explore a female consciousness as they create it; much of what they do in this guise will be experimental.

Twentieth century philosophers of personality provide ample rationale for another motive in the female masquerade—that of identification. As early as 1905 Freud was speculating on the original bisexual psychical disposition, though he thought it always evolved into a unitary sexual identity. Further research led him in 1908 to affirm in man an innate bisexual disposition.[7] C. G. Jung went much further in this view and personified the female component of the personality as the *anima*. Recognition of the *anima* is essentially therapeutic. According to Jung the *anima* has a positive function "when a man takes seriously the feelings, moods, expectations, and fantasies sent by his *anima* and when he fixed them in some form— for example, in writing, painting, sculpture, musical composition, or dancing."[8] Jung considered the *anima* very much part of the man, oftentimes waiting in limbo to be expressed, waiting for a form. The use of the female voice in the novel would present an opportunity for such expression, for imaginative unity, strength, and wholeness. Simone de Beauvoir has written at length about the male artist's preoccupation with female characters and finds in it a confirmation of the ancient duality between self and other. According to de Beauvoir, man seeks qualities in the woman that he himself lacks. And "it is in seeking to be made whole through her that man hopes to attain self-realization."[9] She argues that the author's female characters exemplify an encounter with the author himself, as well as with someone distinctly alien. A fictional masquerade becomes then not only a pleasure, but a need, a therapeutic act.

Narrative poses can be, in and of themselves, liberating disguises. When William Faulkner writes as Benjy in *The Sound and the Fury* he is allowing himself to experience and recreate the world as a retarded boy. By that choice the author is released from the demands of a coherent ego or of any moral, adult considerations whatsoever. Fyodor Dostoyevsky adopted peculiar, almost mad personae in *Notes from Underground* and *The Dream of a Ridiculous Man*. In the first tale he begins; "I'm a sick man . . . a mean man. There's nothing attractive about me. I think there's something wrong with my liver." In the second he says "I'm a ridiculous man. Now they call me a madman."[10] Through these poses (in the first instance he takes pains to separate the authorial self from this voice) he may say a great deal that would destroy the adult male protagonist's condidacy for heroic status. Not so for a crank or madman for whom the act of writing is in itself heroic. The pose of the woman offers distinct artistic advantages as well for the male novelist. She is, first of all, outside the male power structure. The male hero has many choices and actions open to him to succeed in a world that he must make his own. A woman acts under restraints. Whatever way in which she exerts her power, she will do it under the disguise of weakness and passivity. In any age, a healthy dose of apparent helplessness must accompany her exertions, if she is to appear a socially acceptable female. A young woman is vulnerable, especially sexually. Her very femaleness will call up licentious thoughts in men and will force her into a protective mode. How different the horizon appears, as Henry James said, when it appears to a young woman confronting her destiny than when it opens to a young, male hero.

These two elements, powerlessness and physical vulnerability, would appear to be drawbacks to the use of the female voice, and yet the womanly situation resembles dilemmas of these male artists. All of these men, as we shall see in the essays that follow, felt vulnerable physically; some because of the actual dangers to which they were exposed, others because of illness, and others because of family history. Even the most robustly masculine novelist must feel isolated and separated from more "normal" masculine concerns. The writer is inevitably alone and seated for days on end. Passivity and retirement make his daily life more like that of a woman in the world than like a man. Even the most manly of these authors, Defoe and Dickens, felt on occasion miserably dependent on the whims of others; Defoe on his patron for a livelihood, Dickens on his need for love from a woman he could never find. Obviously every human being has such feelings, but for the artist the female voice appears a congenial mode through which to express them.

Women have traditionally been perceived as having fewer emotional constraints than men, and it is here that we would expect to see male authors taking full advantage of the female persona. Laughter, fears, fainting, teasing—there are a whole range of behaviors available in the female repertoire unavailable to a male hero. It would not do to have Robinson Crusoe weeping in terror for long periods of time when he learns of his abandoned state, but Roxana is in a state of terror a great portion of the time. This is a question of emotional range. Femaleness has conventionally been thought of as a richly defined state of mind—a mode of consciousness itself, much more than the category "male."[11] We are so used to seeing the male author taking advantage of the greater range of expressive modes available to women, that it hardly seems odd, but it is unusual for women novelists to speak in the first person as a man. Fanny Burney wrote epistolary novels, and she could have given over more time to her male speakers. Instead, she prefers to write most of her letters from the female point of view. Charlotte Brontë adopted the male voice in *The Professor*; that book is afflicted, as a result, with an almost painfully awkward tone. It would seem that for a woman to imagine herself a young, heroic male presents complex, rarely attempted difficulties. Joyce Carol Oates, a prolific novelist of the twentieth century, once remarked that whenever she took pen in hand and tried to create a believable male narrator, she faltered, because for her the male perspective restricts the angle of vision severely. Too much feeling and self-awareness must be sacrificed.[12]

The penchant of the male artist for using the female, as whatever form, whether as myth, symbol, character, voice, or point of view is so ancient that their creations have become embedded in culture. In the first century B. C. Ovid wrote a series of letters, called *The Heroides,* to classical heroes from women, most of whom. were lovelorn and who showed a remarkable willingness to do themselves in with swords. Women were depicted as thus suicidal; these images become yet another rule of female psychology. Can we say that Ovid pictures his own self-destruction with a pointed phallic object? That the sword represents his own fears of penetration or his own fears of the strength of men? Phyllis writes to Demophoon: "Oft do I long for poison; oft with the sword would I gladly pierce my heart and pour forth my blood in death."[13] Blood pours forth so

often from the sword, as Ovid pictures it, that we might well ask
whether or not this is a male act that he is picturing. It is most difficult to pry apart these images of woman herself from her masculine origins. As de Beauvoir said, " . . . there is an absolute human
type, the masculine."[14] That type so pervades literature and culture that its explication is extremely difficult; the image has itself
become normative.

The English language novelists I treat here have invested a
significant amount of energy and sympathy in their women narrators. The act of creating such a female voice makes many more demands on the author than the creation of a single female character,
although both characters and narrators may address the same issues.
The first person is a dramatic convention, and is related to the dramatic monologue or the soliloquy. The first person speaker addresses both herself and the audience; we *overhear* an ordinary character
speak to another character. The tone, the sound of the voice determines our response to the way she pictures her world. The author
must invest her with sufficient sincerity for the reader to attend to
her words. The use of "I" (whatever the narrative form in which it
appears) suggests an autobiographical impulse at work also. The
speaker wants to explain her life. Lionel Trilling remarks; "The subject of an autobiography is just such a self, bent on revealing himself
in all his truth, bent, that is to say, on demonstrating his sincerity."[15] But the narrative "I" must not only appear to mean what she
says, she must possess authority. This latter quality is dependent
upon the author's use of her as a stand-in for himself. She must represent for us the authorial presence in his soveriegnty over the tale;
otherwise the tale will founder. Such a collapse befalls Esther Summerson in Dicken's *Bleak House*. When she denies her own authority
as storyteller, we are forced to ask why Dickens has chosen her at all
to speak. We do not demand sincerity and authority from every character we meet in a fiction. These people are merely the cast. They
can and do represent different ways of approaching experience. But
the narrator carries with her a special burden, since her view will
shape the meaning of the story at every turn. Tolstoy's Anna Karen-
ina, if she herself were the speaker, would shed an entirely different
light on her history—and the author's objectivity would be compro-
mised. So too had Thackeray written *Vanity Fair* through the eyes of

Becky Sharp, he would have, *ipso facto,* revealed something crucial about himself and his commitments. The very choice of such a person represents an authorial announcement.

The first-person narrator has a dimensionality that no ordinary character does. He or she represents a sustained point of view— one that goes on for a long time. Though the author may occasionally let the mask drop in order to propel the story forward, essentially he commits himself to a believable human epistemology. The omniscient narrator is godlike in his ability to know motives and events and to inform us of them when he will. But the author commits himself to a realistic presentation of how and when one finds out anything at all when he writes as "I." Such a choice allies him to a slow pace and areas of incomprehension. As a result we often feel that, as readers, we are coming to know things when the narrator does. David Goldknopf calls this process the "confessional increment." "Everything an I-narrator tells us has a certain characterizing significance over and above its data value, by virtue of the fact that he is telling it to us."[16] How much we know often depends on the function of the narrator, as Wayne Booth has pointed out.[17] The narrator may be merely a frame through which the actions of the other characters are placed in perspective or may be a complete consciousness or character himself. Each of the women in this study is a detailed rendering of the female consciousness. She is a character about whom we think we know a great deal, and her effect accumulates as we read and grows larger than the sum of its parts. Small wonder that writing as a woman in the first person is a relative rarity, since to do so demands immersion in the inner life of the woman, in order for her to have what Goldknopf calls "the necessary weight and screening power."[18]

It should be apparent that I take the first-person speaker rendered in sufficient detail to indicate the intense involvement of the author with her. The New Critical preoccupation with denying connections between author and work had dropped this old-fashioned idea into a sort of neglect that has only recently been questioned. As Irvin Ehrenpreis says, in his brilliant essay "Personae," to assert that Marlow does not, in some sense, speak for Conrad or that (in our own case) Roxana does not speak for Defoe or Molly Bloom for

Joyce is to assume clinical detachment in the artist that probably better applies to a critic.[19] In our own time, distrust for the narrative "I" has to do more with modern epistemological doubts than it does with artistic creation. I do not mean to be simple-minded in an equation of artist-narrator, but I do want to insist on a connection between them intense enough to be felt in the pages of a novel. In the words of Ehrenpreis, "the primacy of meaning does not originate or end in the rhetorical persuasiveness of the speaker. It does not depend on our agreement or disagreement with him. Rather, it springs from the power of his case to arouse us to intense contemplation one way or the other."[20] The power of the case can be conveyed only when there is sufficient authorial sympathy with his narrator to go a long distance in her voice.

Apart from the more general motives for this masquerade to which I alluded earlier, Defoe, Richardson, Dickens, Henry James, James Joyce all share artistic purposes particularly suited to the use of the female voice; they are novelists of feeling, and they look to qualities of heart and mind if not to transform, then at least to change people. Consciousness itself is a vehicle for social reform. While the personnel varies slightly according to each critical scheme, these men have often been named as part of a specific humanistic tradition (by F. R. Leavis, W. Y. Tindall, and Ian Watt): ". . . they all seek by introspection and observation to build their own scheme of moral certainty. . . ."[21] In this sense they are didactic novelists. Molly Bloom is meant to redeem the deadness of Dublin and restore Leopold to his rightful place beside her. Dickens's Esther Summerson is engaged in a struggle to redeem the times in London, just as Clarissa is used as a tool against the rapacity of the aristocratic Lovelace. Much of the fascination of *The Turn of the Screw* involves our confusion as to whether James's little governess is really redeemer or devil. The tale itself is didactic, although like many Jamesian lessons, it is ambiguous. But there is no doubt that his finely tuned observers, depending on the rightness of their illusions, lead the way for other less prescient mortals. But what of Defoe? He always announces, rather self-righteously, his didactic purposes at the beginnings of his novels. His gamier stories (by the way, usually told by women) seem even more self-defensively framed by moralisms. Many readers see these as a sham, a justification for Defoe's plumbing the depths of evil while protesting loudly his innocence. I think that he really did have social motives in mind; to know Moll or Roxana intimately was to understand the problems of poor women driven to thievery and prostitution to survive. It was also to know Defoe himself, since the problems he allowed his female speakers to confront bore a close relationship to his own.

The readings that follow examine the form of the consciousness represented as female and its origins in the masculine concerns of her author. Susan Sontag once remarked that "The great task which remains to critical theory is to examine in detail the *formal* function of subject matter."[22] She objected to viewing works of art as statements, as the presentation of codified, coherent views. A work of art "is an experience of the qualities or forms of human consciousness."[23] Conceiving of the author's female voice as a masquerade helps us keep this crucial idea in mind. "I" as a woman is first and foremost a style; it controls every piece of information we know. Its sound is indissolubly linked to the meaning of things that happen to her. Critics have often been suspicious of the style of these ladies, finding in them a peculiarly androgynous quality. Ian Watt speculates that Moll Flanders, in "the essence of her character and actions is, to one reader at least, essentially masculine."[24] On the one hand we might think these creations some sort of androgynous ideal, answering to the American transcendentalist Margaret Fuller's challenge, " 'Will there never be a being to combine a man's mind and a woman's heart?' "[25] On the other hand, these creations, if viewed as "women" or representations of women (which is certainly what they assert) are grotesque, distorted figures, who have spawned other female characters in their own image.

The problem, of course, is that we do not think of them as particularly outrageous or strange—they *are* women. Let us look at the reverse of this narrative situation. Mary Shelley's *Frankenstein* is a particularly good place for us to watch a woman imagining herself fully and intensively as a man, as a young male hero. This simple horror tale has been replayed so often in films and popular literature that much of its success comes surely from the force of the psychological investment the author has in this masquerade. Amongst the male authors I am considering, only Clarissa has achieved a similarly mythic status. The most striking element in her masquerade is the degree to which she has invested her male voices, both Victor and the monster, with her own central concerns.

Shelley's imaginative fusion with her hero is only partially realized. Reflecting on men themselves, she considers their primary impulse the urge for power and domination. In wishing to best other men, in wishing to demonstrate their superiority to the category "average" or "normal," the hero ruthlessly pursues his ends. Power for Victor Frankenstein resides in knowledge, and the author makes Victor a demonstration of an explicit thesis: "learn from me, if not by my precepts, at least by my example, how dangerous is the acquirement of knowledge, and how much happier that man is who believes his native town to be the world, than he who aspires to become greater than his nature will allow."[26] But the kind of knowledge he seeks is at the very heart of life itself: "Whence, I often asked myself, did the principle of life proceed?" (p. 51). He is afflicted with a sort of womb envy and usurps the female role by creating a child of his own. Ruin results from the ruthless search for knowledge, as the forsaken, hideously ugly child endlessly importunes its parent to love it. Ellen Moers has written fascinating material on precisely how Shelley imagines herself a man, especially in Victor's relationship to his terrible child. Mary herself had a number of miscarriages and worried obsessively about these terrible losses—not surprisingly she felt herself at fault.[27] Much of the energy in the book comes from the haunting of the parent (now a man) by his child. We should recall here Dickens's remark about Defoe's women; they are merely "fellows without breeches," men dressed up as women but still transparently male. Here Shelley seems to be dressing herself up as a man, in fact several men. She does not manage to create a convincing narrative voice in any of them, and her male masquerade is afflicted with a dislocation of tone in the extreme. Victor, Walton, the monster—all speak with hyperbolic intensity. Victor says, "I have described myself as always having been embued with a fervent longing to penetrate the secrets of nature" (p. 39). Walton and the monster are similarly afflicted by tortuous motions of heat and light.

Mary Shelley solved some of her difficulties with the male voice by interpolating into her narrative several long passages on the psychological effects of the mountains, nature, and the sublime. The rhetoric of such material was easily available to her. She also had a model for male speech in her father's novel written in 1794, *Caleb Williams*. This work succeeds as thrilling, psychologically intense narrative in a way that Shelley's does not, but one can see her striving after effects and borrowing certain "manly" poses and attitudes from her father's book. Shelley's problems with narrative voice are mirrored in the difficulties encountered by women authors writing later in the nineteenth century. One can see that authors like George Eliot and both of the Brontës worked carefully to adopt an authoritative narrative voice, a person whose views would not immediately betray the sex of the author. George Eliot struggled with creating a neutral, almost sexless observer, one often given to moralistic pronouncements. Charlotte Brontë, on the other hand, is most successful when she creates an "I" that is essentially autobiographical, as she did on the case of Jane Eyre and Lucy Snowe. About artistic difficulties with male figures Brontë remarked: " 'In delineating male character, I labour under disadvantages; intuition and theory will not adequately supply the place of observation and experience. When I write about women, I am sure of my ground—in the other case I am not so sure.' "28

Male authors have for centuries had a guide to the range and quality of the female voice. The way a woman sounds, her tone of voice was very early in the history of the English language enshrined in epithets. Woman could be a shrew, a scold, a termagant, but if she is young and a romantic heroine such tones demean her hopelessly or even call into question her sex. In Shakespeare's *As You Like It*, that extended joke on sexual masquerades, Rosalind questions whether Silvius' shepherdess love could have penned a certain letter:

> Why, 'tis a boisterous and cruel style,
> A style for challengers; why she defies me,
> Like Turk to Christian: women's gentle brain
> Could not drop forth such giant-rude invention,
> Such Ethiop words, blacker in their effect
> Than in their countenance . . .29

Negative epithets for boisterousness originally applied to both sexes but came rather quickly to apply primarily to women. Loud tones, a brow-beating posture toward the male, and self-assertion of an unacceptable type do not favor the young heroine, who should take her tones from Cordelia: "Her voice was ever soft, Gentle and low, an excellent thing in woman."[30] This view is an ancient, persistent one, and Robin Lakoff, in a recent analysis of the language women use today reiterates the importance of a display of docility and resignation. According to this study, women continue to use words and patterns of words that indicate their subservience to men, and are enjoined from self-assertion: "women's speech is devised to prevent the expression of strong statements."[31]

Male authors, confronted with the problem of creating a female voice, have relied upon excessive marks of politeness to indicate the good woman. Clarissa Harlowe and Esther Summerson are particularly afflicted with a sense of decorum—it puts a burden on their speech, and they both tend to go on and on politely and in a self-denying fashion, often entirely contradicting the gross egotism of which they are an expression. When the woman is aspiring to a higher social class, and when she teeters on the edge of either goodness or badness, she has highly decorous moments, as do Moll Flanders and Roxana, but then lapses into bold, direct, racy speech patterns that better befit the career of a thief or a prostitute. Such contradictory ways of speaking appear also in the voice of James's governess. Decorum is continuously violated in the monologue of Molly Bloom, and the act of its being violated forms a datum about her character. James Joyce would have had plenty of models for this voice (not the least of which was his wife Nora) because Molly too represents an age-old adage about the way women speak. Her voice comes from the "misogynistic stereotypes in our culture that women cannot follow the rules of conversation: that a woman's discourse is necessarily indirect, repetitious, meandering, unclear, exaggerated. . . ."[32] It is no surprise that Joyce chose a woman to reflect the time between waking and sleeping, since women's speech has often been characterized as dreamy and rambling.

Male heroes created by women like Brontë's Rochester or Eliot's Will Ladislaw are regularly criticized for the outrageousness and unreality of their ways of speaking. These women speakers have

certainly not been dismissed as unreal, but they all have had a sing-
ular talent for creating a sense of unease, and often of downright
disbelief. The most drastic and obvious problem with these female
voices is their untrustworthiness. James Joyce explicitly avowed
that this was one of Molly Bloom's outstanding characteristics, but
it is true of Roxana, Clarissa, Esther, and certainly James's benighted
little governess. Several of these women have provided scholars with
their favorite examples of the unreliable narrator, and they certainly
all possess an extra ironic dimension. Though I have done no scien-
tific survey, it would not surprise me to find that the largest pro-
portion of studies of irony have been undertaken on female voices
created by men. But this is natural once we acknowledge that the
woman is both subject (the author himself) and object (the woman
herself as character). The sense of her words seems to be continuously undermined and, ever since Dr. Johnson expressed his distrust of
Clarissa, critics have questioned how intentional the artist was in his
creation of a persona who appears to be at best deluded, at worst a
liar. Roxana dissembles, Clarissa does not know herself, Esther pre-
tends not to know what her author unmistakably shows that she
must. And the governess: those who do, and those who do not believe her continue to wrangle. In the essays that follow I have taken
particular notice of the linguistic peculiarities of the female speaker,
especially in contrast to comparable male speakers. Even so, much of
what such an analysis will yield is impressionistic, simply because the
narrator of a novel must perform so many tasks and observe so many
events, in contrast, let us say, to the dramatic monologist of a poem.
In the novel her tonal effects accumulate, and the sense of her voice
encompasses not only individual sentences but prolonged exchanges,
and we remember what she has said at other moments in other situations. Her linguistic dimensions are accordingly vast. Where useful
I have placed an author's male and female speakers side by side—
often drastic differences appear, differences that indicate the stream
of ambiguous meanings that drop from a woman's tongue. Once we
take note of the pose itself, of the male masquerade, it is obvious
that her linguistic problems are rooted in her origins.

These readings attempt to penetrate her origins, if only spec-
ulatively, through a study of the biographical connections that may
exist between the author and his female speaker. One can hardly

expect to understand the women these authors create without understanding what in ther lives made this act of identification possible in the first place. Biographical criticism has many pitfalls, not the least of which is the leap from life (itself abstracted as "lives") to art. Fortunately all of the authors I discuss here have been the subject of extensive biographies, and the biographers of the two most "feminine," Samuel Richardson and Henry James have themselves speculated, Leon Edel in particular, on the parallels between the author's central dilemmas and their expression through female characters. My own major interest has been in the relations between author and mothers, lovers, wives, and friends—or whatever is left to us of these relations in letters or autobiographical works. But also I have been concerned to locate the author's fears, his worst feelings of vulnerability—those worries that would make him wish to write as the weaker sex. We do not make such disturbing leaps here, I think, since these men were enormously productive writers, and one certainly has enough fictional material to notice obsessive (or just repeated) patterns and themes. The working out of continuing anxieties and fears will be realized differently through the female voice, and it is at this point of difference that we can speculate on the act of a sexual transposition.

F. W. Dupee has called Henry James "the great feminine novelist of a feminine age in letters."[33] Certainly both James and Richardson were deeply feminized males whose identification with women must have come from their own sense of physical vulnerability—itself derived from psychic forces that one can only guess at. Whether really ill or only hypochondriacal, Samuel Richardson (especially after he started writing *Pamela* in 1740) felt himself on the brink of death. Though we know little of his relations with parents or even spouses, when he became a novelist we find him engaged in an extensive correspondence with numerous female friends who advised him on the problems of women and solutions to the quanary in which the unfortunate Clarissa found herself. Henry James's sense of physical vulnerability was epitomized by his back injury, sustained (and very mysteriously so) at a time in which he should have been maturing into manhood. That he remained feminine in his sexual identity—that is, passive and chaste (if not actually homosexual) is evident in his letters and late autobiographical works.

But we can make no such assertions about the innate feminity of the other authors in this study. Daniel Defoe had an extraordinary life, one that encompassed almost incredible activity and daring with an equally astonishing output of works of fiction, travel and conduct books, and pamphlets. Like Richardson, however, he did not begin his fictional narratives until well into his later years (he was probably about fifty-nine when he wrote *Robinson Crusoe*), and along with the risks he had taken as both journalist and spy, he had been pilloried and imprisoned in 1703. His continuous failures in trade appear to have been deeply humiliating to him, as was his dependence on the vagaries of political patronage. He died in hiding and destitution. Defoe's wish to write the stories of women thieves and prostitutes (stories that contrast rather dramatically with the noble self-sufficiency of the narratives of Robinson Crusoe or Colonel Jack) must have come from the real difficulties and downright failures which the author himself suffered. A woman was the person to whom such a story could be given.

Charles Dickens and James Joyce, though separated by years, religion, and nationality share a misogyny that pervades their work, a misogyny counterbalanced by a worshipful pose before the shrine of woman. The dislike and the idolization go hand in hand, one would think, and may have resulted from their guilt-ridden relationships with their mothers. Dickens was much more intransigent about his mother's failures of love than was Joyce, and he parodied her remorselessly in the mother of Nicholas Nickleby. It was a woman of this asinine sort who had hoped for his return to the hated, humiliating position in the blacking warehouse. Joyce, on the other hand, seems to have been haunted by his own failure to perform religious acts important to his mother, a failure that seemed even more unkind in the midst of his father's gross mistreatment of May Murray Joyce. Both of these authors seem to cast a cold eye on individual women, and yet seem entirely enthralled by the idea of Woman. No matter how different the lives of these authors are in many particulars, something in that life has induced them to write in the voice of a young female heroine, to create her voice and mind in detail and in rich dimensions. It is these dimensions that are of primary interest to us now. How does the world look to her and what is it she sees?

René Magritte, the twentieth century Belgian painter, in 1934 produced a painting he called *Le Viol* (The Rape), a picture that wittily dramatizes the masculine conception of woman. The painting shows the head of a woman, but her eyes are breasts, her nose becomes her navel, and her mouth becomes her vagina. Like many of his paintings the picture is a spoof of the imaginative transformations to which a man is prone, and this one too is very funny. The painting seems to say—"This is what he sees—not head or brain, but body. Everywhere upon you, he sees only the marks of your sex." The tendency to see woman as body alone is reflected in a number of ways in these narratives. Each of these women is more or less obsessed with sex and in turn sees every male as primarily body. As the male author views women, so he has her think of men. Where male narrators (and this is true for everyone but Richardson, though a case could be made here too) have only a cerebral interest in sex or none at all, female speakers seem to walk about in a sexual haze—they carry with them a physical, sexual presence that is clearly felt in the novel, if elliptically expressed by the author. Think for a moment of Esther Summerson, that representative of Victorian purity. Her self-conscious cringing and physical fastidiousness that serve to call attention to her purity, also call attention to her womanhood, her physical vulnerability, ultimately her fear of being raped. When Dickens introduces her suitor, Allan Woodcourt, he has her announce this man's presence in the most indirect way possible—she is so fearful of young, adult males that she can barely discuss them. Such fear and trembling is obvious in Richardson's Clarissa, whose fears about men are extreme. Roxana thinks of sex as a way to manipulate men, and Defoe dwells upon her narcissistic fascination with her own body. For other reasons James's little governess and Molly Bloom think about sex constantly; according to their authors, it informs their every thought. Like the ambiguous, ironic tone of the woman speaker, her preoccupation with sex is a constant, informing mode of consciousness that can barely be separated from other, more explicit themes. The preoccupation centers around fear, fear of physical vulnerability, but even more importantly awe at male strength. This element of awe is reminiscent of John Cleland's *Fanny Hill*, another first-person narrative written by a man as a woman. Here the celebration of the size, shape, etc. of the male organ is quite extraordinary, and Fanny is likely to fall into raptures at its sight.

Sexual awe pervades the narratives I am going to discuss; in the imagination of these women a man's sexuality is frightening indeed. Such
a point of view is indicative of a weird man-woman who displays her
author's fears and fantasies and his over-protectiveness and over-
valuation of male sexuality and the male body.

Sexual awe is merely a component, however, of the general
celebration, or at least aggrandizement, of the importance of men
themselves in these novels. When Virginia Woolf speculated on the
oversized figure of the male reflected by female characters, she could
certainly have been talking about that arch-male figure Lovelace,
whom Richardson has strutting about and gloating over his sexual
and economic powers. The prolonged incarceration of Clarissa,
scarcely credible even according to the manners of the mid-eighteen-
th century, serves to allow her to reflect continuously on the extraordinary range of masculine coercions. These become rapidly overdetermined, in the Freudian sense, and such powers take on eerie,
finally inordinate dimensions when reiterated in the mind of a
terrified young woman. In a similar sense other men in these narratives take on outsized strength in the female consciousness telling
us the tale. The Dutch merchant, who has shown himself an amazing-
ly benevolent soul in his dealings with Roxana, turns into a horrifying figure of vengeance as the story progresses. In either guise his
powers are reflected back to us as extraordinary. And the almost
grotesquely benevolent Mr. Jarndyce, or the alarming Mr. Quint,
or even the half-ridiculous figure of Leopold Bloom—the women
who picture them for us, picture them large, impressive, and think
about them constantly.

Men are certainly not alone in their exercise of power, as these
women see them, for through the voice of the woman the entire
world is made into a battlefield. Such dramatically different "women" as Roxanna and Esther Summerson are obsessed with the acquisition of power. These women are envisioned for us by their male
creators as engaged in a search for dominance over people and events,
that is by almost any standard invoked, extreme. Freud would have
said that fantasies of power and dominance suffuse the literature of
men the world over; they are daydreams of power. While women's
daydreams are for Freud primarily erotic, those of young men are

first and foremost dreams of the ego, of ambition (although they may have an erotic component also). Growing up is, for the young man, learning "to suppress the overweening self-regard he acquires in the indulgent atmosphere surrounding his childhood."[34] This act of suppression means that such dreams will recur, and for Freud they do dramatically in the invulnerable male heroes who move through all difficulties to victory in the end. "It seems to me, however, that this significant mark of invulnerability very clearly betrays—His Majesty the Ego, the hero of all daydream and all novels."[35] Life for the hero of the English *bildungsroman* is not without profound difficulties, but novels of the eighteenth and nineteenth century do often chronicle a movement from relative powerlessness to ascendance, or perhaps just the acquisition of one's rightful place (which often turns out to mean ascendance). Think of Fielding's Tom Jones, Thackeray's Dobbin (in *Vanity Fair*), and even Dicken's David Copperfield. According to Patricia Spacks masculine fictions of the eighteenth century display a positive "obsession with the attainment and preservation of power," and a concomitant terror of a loss of control or powerlessness.[36]

The female mask is in itself a disguise of weakness, vulnerability, relative powerlessness. Yet the will to power pervades the consciousness of these women—it seems central to the way which their character has been perceived. There is an element of painful constraint present, however, especially since women must be more passive than men. Weakness and fear accompany this will to power. In fact these women suffer heavily under the burden of the struggle, all perhaps, except Molly Bloom. They must fight with one hand behind their backs. Since women are more subject to the will of others than are men, their attempts to wrest power are usually addressed to manipulating people and to achieving ascendance through deviousness and indirection. Unlike male heroes, who are often manipulating inanimate objects (Robinson Crusoe) or abstract notions of power (Lovelace) or simply abstractions (Leopold Bloom), these women must control through sheer force of will and through the ability to persuade others. The portraits of this power-seeking are rich and complex, since limitations and fear are characteristic of a realistic, self-conscious approach to power and in some measure inimical to a fantasy of omnipotence. Yet the fantasy exists; it exists almost as a flame that consumes. When Roxana puts her maid to bed with her own paramour, she is forcing someone to become like herself. Esther Summerson's relationship to power is clouded by her self-abnegation; still, through her Dickens imagines himself the agent of social transformation. Richardson certainly explores a form of power in Lovelace, but Clarissa knows power beyond the limits of life itself. When Baudelaire commented on the character of Flaubert's Madame Bovary, he noted in her: "An unlimited urge to seduce and dominate, including a willingness to stoop to the lowest means of seduction, such as the vulgar appeal of dress, perfume and make-up— all summarized in dandyism, exclusive love of domination."[37] The character in search of control of the world, when clothed as a woman, takes on peculiar distortions and circumlocutions in order to help the author keep insisting that, yes, this is a real woman.

These authors differ, widely, of course, about the kind of power to be achieved by the heroic figure. For Defoe, it is economic self-sufficiency, for Richardson absolute spiritual integrity, and for James, we might say, the ability to make others believe one's story. The problematic presentation of this will to power in female speakers can become dramatically clear only in the context of the author's male heroes. Without a comparative sense of these, it is difficult to understand how the author's particular vision of the most desirable form of power and control is being expressed through the voice of a woman. Offhand one might claim that these authors simply picture the truth; that the heroic woman has a strong will and is capable of a conquest equal, at least in scope if not in sphere, to that of a man. What actually happens in these narratives is that the woman is released from definitions of success that belong to male figures and ascends to an even higher level of power, whether sexual or spiritual, that brings with it the attempt at an extraordinary degree of control over the lives of other people. And this of course would be a real triumph, were it to be achieved, more even than the remaking of an island, the finding of a mate or job, or the seduction of a young lady.

Not that these women are all expressions of success, for as a group they seem particularly prone to lose their minds, their bodies, or both. Whatever defined limits of self are set up by formal narrative constructs, they are dissolved in these female speakers. Mary

Ellmann suggests that the most universal category belonging to woman is that of formlessness and fluidity. In and of herself she embodies incoherence.[38] The authors under discussion here seem to spend a great deal of time imagining what it would be like to disintegrate, to obsess, to lose one's breath, to live in a nightmare or a dream, to babble. In the simplest sense we can see this as a punishment for all the bad acts these women have performed in order to gain control of others. Through them the authors have explored an illigitimate use of power, what Erich Fromm would call domination rather than potency; "power, in the sense of domination, is the perversion of potency. . . ."[39] But there seems to be a strong component of play here also, albeit masochistic play. There is hardly a more complete representation of powerlessness than the inability to distinguish between self and other—total loss of ego. To imagine oneself in this state is to imagine a form of death in life. Roxana loses her ability to distinguish between self and other—total loss of ego. To imagine oneself in this state is to imagine a form of death in life. Roxana loses her ability to distinguish herself from her maid and finally descends into a nightmare haze of paranoia. The volumes Richardson devoted to the death of Clarissa testify to his love for the pose of weakness and imminent loss of consciousness. The act of fading and dying was one that he found somehow pleasing to imagine. Dickens's Esther Summerson suffers the ravages of smallpox, and this is a way of wiping the slate clean of her "dirty" past. But her author actually seems to enjoy imagining a melting away of the features, and makes much of the experience of darkness and illness and then awakening to find oneself transformed. In *The Turn of the Screw* the intersection between imagination and reality is complete, as the governess sees a nightmare become real, for her anyway. Certainly James makes it impossible for the reader to discover the boundaries between fact and fiction as the strange goings on at Bly are reflected through this woman's eyes. And finally there is no fictional character more disintegrated (or more omnivorous at the same time) than Molly Bloom. In her dreamy reflections before bed, Joyce wallows in the process of her formlessness, as he was to do later with Anna Livia Plurabelle in *Finnegans Wake*. In one way or another all of these women are expressions of an altered form of consciousness.

What I have said so far obviously does not apply in all details to every female speaker to be discussed in the ensuing chapters. But these generalizations do hold, I think, despite differences in the narrative form in which the female "I" appears, some differences in genre, and the long span of time that separates Roxana (1727) from Molly Bloom (1922). The narrative form chosen by each of these men involves the imaginative act of perceiving the world through the eyes of a young, female protagonist. The history of various narrative forms seems to be closely connected, as Ian Watt has pointed out, to social and economic conditions and to the value placed on individualism at any given time.[40] Daniel Defoe wrote using the pseudo-biographical form, and he seems to be completely immersed in the consciousness of the speaker he presents. Samuel Richardson's use of the epistolary form introduced competing voices into the novel. Even so, the tendency is for one speaker to dominate. Though Lovelace's voice is bombastic and certainly "dominant" in one sense, most of his letters, and those of Anna Howe, reiterate positions Clarissa has taken, address issues she has raised. Ultimately her voice sets the terms of the discourse and determines the value to be placed on others' actions. An apparent autobiographical mode, whether in letters or in pseudo-biography, became much less popular during the nineteenth century. Most novelists (that we continue to read, at any rate) adopted narrative conventions similar to those introduced by Henry Fielding; an idiosyncratic, omniscient authorial presence given to announcing his control over what we are going to know and hear of the story. Hence Anthony Trollope's invasions of his stories, a blatant demonstration of the artificiality of fiction that Henry James deplored. The third-person form was used to assert distance from the characters in the tale. During an age of repression, it was important not to appear to be confessing anything about oneself, the author. As Hillis Miller has said; "In most Victorian novels there is relatively little detached self-consciousness, the self-consciousness of a single person becoming aware of himself in separation from other people."[41] The romantic Charolotte Brontë risked serious excursions into the first-person form, while her sister Emily and the incredibly prolific Wilkie Collins used various narrators to frame a story. Their minds were not explored; they were often used to define the limits of propriety and to measure observed events against this standard. Charles Dickens's attempt to write as Esther Summerson for half of *Bleak House* is that much more interesting because it is a rarity of its time.

Confining my remarks to the first person speaker forces me to neglect the work of other English authors deeply interested in women, like Thomas Hardy or George Meredith and to speak only briefly about D. H. Lawrence and his view of the redemptive, primitive female consciousness. Such a choice demands also that I take up the controversial governess of *The Turn of the Screw* and forego much discussion of the many fine young ladies with whom Henry James was so deeply in tune. But I want to insist that through the first person we are given the author's sense of the voice and character of woman realized to its fullest extent, and a study of the male imagination logically begins here. The governess, of course, narrates for us a ghost story. Such a genre has conventions of its own and rhetorical and physical postures unlikely to appear in another kind of story. To a lesser extent the work of Samuel Richardson, in the minute dissection of character, seems to have been influenced by Puritan devotional literature, as was undoubtedly Defoe.[42] But whatever the modes of discourse a genre may suggest or allow, I take the very act of masquerading as a woman to be far more important than generic considerations in determining what is said and how it is said.

Many years separate these texts, and I am well aware that by conflating them, historical differences receive only brief consideration. When looking at the phenomenon of woman one can often solve the historical problem by arguing as Mary Ellmann and Simone de Beauvoir have, that there are certain immutable qualities that male artists always assign to women. In whatever age, in whatever fiction, these traits (woman as fleshly, natural, poetic, good at mediation, immanent, and *other*) will be recreated by the male author.[43] A great deal of important work of this kind has already been done, viewing the female character from the outside as the expression of an archetype or a stereotype. In Chapter Four I do consider the development during the nineteenth century of what we think of as stereotypes, and the effects these had on narrative choices of both male and female artists. I also address the question of the authentic female voice, to dramatize the distortions present when male authors take up the pen as a woman. Certain of these distortions, the sexualization of the field of vision, the obsession with power, the fascination with a disintegrated consciousness, clearly recur in these "fellows without breeches" and become even more obvious when a woman and a "woman" narrator confront similar situations and choices.

We might be tempted to call these preoccupations immutable propensities of the male mind, if our aim were not the particularity of the vision at work here. My own readings concentrate on the personal history of the author and on the text as a peculiar expression of that history. The female voice becomes a kind of psychic shorthand that leads us to the inner life of a male artist and to *his* fears and fantasies often in a more direct way than do his male narrators, who might be taken very quickly for the artist himself. Thus disguised, the woman that results is an odd fellow, a man-woman whose richness and complexity have long been confounding her readers.

When I saw *A Midsummer Night's Dream* with an all-male cast (admittedly not very dainty ones) the audience laughed whenever one of these men-women appeared. The play's female characters were not real, and every line they uttered took on a double meaning, as each speech became both itself and a parody of itself. There actually seemed to be more characters present in the play than were explicitly admitted to. A novel acts upon us differently, of course, and we tend to have less sense of the artificiality of the medium and more sense of the "reality" of novel characters and narrators. But we do well to retain a lively sense of the doubleness of the male author's women characters and speakers. To call these authors expert psychologists of women is to understand but half the story. Leslie Fiedler called Richardson's insights into "the complexities of the female mind," "terrifyingly acute."[44] If there are complexities here, surely a great many of them belong to the author himself. I would not deny that Richardson, or the other men in this study, spent much time observing the behavior of a woman (although he claimed that the aim of his fiction was to *form* their behavior, not reflect it). But so formidable a "female" as Clarissa Harlowe, beneath her voluminous petticoats and her notorious stays, hides the odd little figure of her author, cowering before the mighty forces of masculine sexuality, wishing to conquer the world in spirit and in the process to cast off his own flesh. For Richardson, as for Defoe, Dickens, James, and Joyce, the female voice was a form of self-knowledge, as well as a portrait of the other. We should not forget who shapes her tones and moves her limbs, no matter how many times she is said to capture the essence of womanhood.

Notes

[1]Otto Rank, *Beyond Psychology* (New York: Dover, 1941), p. 255.

[2]Virginia Woolf, *A Room of One's Own* (New York: Harcourt, Brace, 1957) p. 35.

[3]Quoted by John Forster, *The Life of Charles Dickens*, ed. J. W. T. Ley (London: Cecil Palmer, 1928) p. 611. He was referring to Robinson Crusoe's wife, however, and not specifically to Moll Flanders or Roxana, although no doubt he found them suspiciously hardened also.

[4]Oscar Wilde, "The Critic As Artist," Part II in *The Artist As Critic, Critical Writings of Oscar Wilde*, ed. Richard Ellmann (New York: Vintage, 1969) p. 389.

[5]Hugh Kenner, *Joyce's Voices* (Berkeley: Univ. of California Press, 1978) p. 94.

[6]John Gardner, *On Moral Fiction* (New York: Basic Books, 1978) p. 107.

[7]Sigmund Freud, See *Three Essays on the Theory of Sexuality*, (New York: Journal of Nervous and Mental Disorders Publishing Company, Monograph Series # 7.) The later view is found in "Hysterical Phantasies and Their Relation to Bisexuality," in *Sigmund Freud*, Collected Papers, Vol. 2, trans. under supervision of Joan Riviere (New York: Basic Books, 1959) p. 58.

[8]Quoted by M. L. von Franz in C. G. Jung's *Man and His Symbols* (Garden City: Doubleday, 1964) p. 186.

[9]Simone de Beauvoir, *The Second Sex*, trans. & ed. H. M. Parshley (New York: Knopf, 1957) p. 142.

[10]Fyodor Dostoyevsky, *Notes from Underground, White Nights, The Dream of a Ridiculous Man* and selections from *The House of the Dead*, trans. Andrew A. MacAndrew (New York: Signet, 1961) p. 90, p. 204.

[11]See, for instance, Mary Ellmann's fine work, *Thinking About Women* (New York: Harcourt, Brace, Jovanovich) 1968.

[12]Joyce Carol Oates, Panel Discussion on Androgyny in Fiction, Modern Language Association Convention, Chicago, 1975.

[13]Ovid, *The Heroides*, Letter II, trans. Grant Showerman (London: Heinemann, 1914) p. 13.

[14]de Beauvoir, p. XV.

[15]Lionel Trilling, *Sincerity and Authenticity* (Cambridge: Harvard Univ. Press, 1972) p. 25.

[16]David Goldknopf, *The Life of the Novel* (Chicago: Univ. of Chicago Press, 1971) p. 38. In many of my remarks on the primacy of first-person narration, I am indebted to this work.

[17]Wayne Booth, *The Rhetoric of Fiction* (Chicago: Univ. of Chicago Press) 1961.

[18]*The Life of the Novel*, p. 77.

[19]Irvin Ehrenpries, "Personae" in *Literary Meaning and Augustan Values* (Charlottesville: Univ. Press of Virginia, 1974). See p. 53.

[20]*Ibid.*, p. 59.

[21]Ian Watt, *The Rise of the Novel* (Berkeley: Univ. of California Press, 1965) p. 85.

[22]Susan Sontag, "On Style," in *Against Interpretation and Other Essays* (New York: Delta, 1966) p. 20.

[23]*Ibid.*, p. 27.

[24]Ian Watt, *The Rise of the Novel*, p. 113.

[25]Quoted by Ann Douglas, *The Feminization of American Culture* (New York: Avon, 1977) p. 350.

[26]Mary Shelley, *Frankenstein, or The Modern Prometheus,* ed. M. K. Joseph (London: Oxford Univ. Press, 1971) p. 53. all subsequent references will be to this edition of the novel.

[27]Ellen Moers, "Female Gothic: The Monster's Mother," *The New York Reivew of Books,* March 1974, pp. 24-29.

[28]Quoted by Elaine Showalter, *A Literature of Their Own, British Women Novelists from Brontë to Lessing* (Princeton: Princeton Univ. Press, 1977) p. 133.

[29]William Shakespeare, *As You Like It*, IV, iii, 31-36.

[30]William Shakespeare, *King Lear*, Act V, iii, 272-273.

[31]Robin Lakoff, *Language and Woman's Place* (New York: Harper and Row, 1975) p. 19.

[32]*Ibid.,* p. 75.

[33]F. W. Dupee, *Henry James* (New York: Delta, 1956) p. 97. Dupee is referring here to the so-called predominance of feminine values and literature in American culture during the second half of the nineteenth century.

[34]Sigmund Freud, *On Creativity and the Unconscious, Papers on the Psychology of Art, Literature, Love, Religion* (New York: Harper and Row, 1958) In "The Poet and Day-Dreaming," p. 48.

[35]*Ibid.,* p. 51.

[36]Patricia M. Spacks, "Early Fiction and the Frightened Male," *Novel 8*, No. 1 (1974), p. 14.

[37]Charles Baudelaire, "*Madame Bovary* by Gustave Flaubert," in Gustave Flaubert, *Madame Bovary* ed. and trans. Paul de Man (New York: Norton, 1965) p. 340.

[38]Mary Ellmann, *Thinking About Women,* p. 74.

[39]Erich Fromm, *Escape from Freedom* (New York: Rinehart & Company, 1941) p. 162.

[40]Ian Watt, *The Rise of the Novel*. See especially Ch. III, "*Robinson Crusoe*, Individualism and the Novel," pp. 60-92.

[41]J. Hillis Miller, *The Form of Victorian Fiction* (Notre Dame: Univ. of Notre Dame Press, 1968) p. 5.

[42]See Cynthia Griffin Woolf, *Samuel Richardson and the Eighteenth-Century Puritan Character* (Hamden, Conn.: Archon Books) 1972.

[43]Simone de Beauvoir, *The Second Sex*, p. 248.

[44]Leslie Fiedler, *Love and Death in the American Novel* (New York: Dell, 1960) p. 46.

Chapter 2

This Beautiful Lady Whose Words He Speaks:
Defoe and His Female Masquerades

When he was in his sixties, Daniel Defoe created two extra-ordinary fictions written from the point of view of a relatively young sexual woman. All too often *Moll Flanders* (1722) and *Roxana* (1724) are lumped together critically and the fact of the sex of the author and that of the protagonist ignored. It is true that a number of the same concerns animate those fictions presented to us by male speakers; but his masquerades as a woman involve, in the most direct and intense way, a consciousness distinctly *other* from the one we encounter in Crusoe. And we are asked to reside in that conscious-ness for a long period of time and through a multiplicity of events. Defoe imaginatively experiences the world very differently through female eyes, and it is on the surface at least surprising that this dis-senting would-be merchant (dramatically unsuccessful in trade), a man who was imprisoned in Newgate in 1703 and who went on to become a government spy, should have wanted to write narrative fictions as a woman. Both Charles Dickens and James Joyce, while noticing the fascinations of Defoean women, responded to them with some bewilderment. Who or what were they? James Sutherland, Defoe's first authoritative biographer noted Moll Flanders' "jolly facetious air" and speculated on the good deal of the author obvious in her character.[1] Their jolliness, however, is by no means their most outstanding characteristic. These women are allowed to express fear, guilt, and in Roxana's case ultimate madness. Unlike Robinson Crusoe, they do not manage to recreate their worlds, although they try rather ferociously. In their struggles and failures they resemble the author himself, and it is clear that Defoe found the female mask a most congenial one.

Why did Defoe write as a woman, and in what ways are *Moll Flanders* and *Roxana* different from those fictions written from a male point of view? Of course, we immediately hit upon innumerable difficulties in finding a way even to approach the matter. Some of these difficulties have to do with the personality of the artist. Almost all of what we know of him concerns his public life. What we know about his personal life is spotty at best, and how he felt about much of what happened to him we can only guess. Information on the women in his life is minuscule.[2] Defoe tells us virtually nothing about the role of fiction in his life and the nature of his fictional choices. Secondly, as Bonamy Dobrée has noted, to separate out his novels from his other works can sometimes be an artificial exclusion.[3] Editorializing that appears in his nonfiction prose appears in the novels, as do scenes from the conduct books. Hence to say where Defoe the journalist or moral instructor and Defoe the narrator begin and end becomes complicated. And Defoe caused considerable trouble for himself when he published *The Shortest Way With the Dissenters*, presenting a satirical persona so believable that he went to jail. Ever since that time readers and critics have been fascinated by the assorted masks he saw fit to adopt. So, when I choose to discuss this author as creator of a first-person narration as a woman, I should be more specific. Defoe gives us a fictional world, insofar as he conceived of one, through the eyes of a woman. In projecting himself through the "I" that belongs to a Moll Flanders or to a Roxana, he explores what it would be like to be inside a female consciousness. We do not need to ask at this point what he thought was or was not true, or where he allows us to know more about her motives than the speaker allows. We need to ask instead, what is this female consciousness like and what use does the author make of it?

   We know from a number of clues in his nonfiction prose that Defoe had a lively interest in the economic problems women faced, was distressed that their talents were wasted through underdevelopment, and was concerned that they make wise marriages or none at all. His views on women sound remarkably progressive for the times, although we cannot make him out a confirmed feminist. He did say in the *Essay on Projects*: "God had given to all Mankind equal Gifts and Capacities, in that he has given them all *Souls* equally capable; and that the whole difference in Mankind proceeds either from Accidental Difference in the Make of their Bodies, or from the *foolish Difference* of Education."[4]

Perhaps what concerned him most were the difficulties of marriage for an independent woman. Marriage should not be a form of bondage and the duties between man and wife demand:

> . . . that of Love, in the Government of Affection, and the Obedience of a complaisant, kind, obliging Temper; the Obligation is reciprocal, 'tis drawing in an equal Yoke; Love knows no superior or inferior, no imperious Command on one hand, no reluctant Subjection on the other.[5]

This rather even-handed approach was balanced by his sense that a single woman really is in charge of her own life and sacrifices much when married:

> Now take a married Life, with all its Addenda of Family Cares, the trouble of looking after a Household, the hazard of being subject to the Humours and Passions of a churlish Man, and particularly of being disappointed, and matching with a Tyrant, and a Family-Brute; with still the more apparent hazard of being ruined in Fortune by his Disasters if a Tradesman, by his Immoralities if a Gentleman, and by his Vices if a Rake: I say, what Woman in her Senses would tie herself up in the Fetters of Matrimony, if it were not that she desires to be a Mother of Children, to multiply her Kind, and, in short, have a Family?[6]

He recognized female genius and considered that merely because of lack of education women had been made to look inferior and silly:

> The Capacities of Women are suppos'd to be greater and their Senses quicker than those of the Men; and what they might be capable of being bred to, is plain from some Instances of Female-Wit, which this Age is not without.[7]

In *Applebee's Journal* he wrote that it was cruel to deny women the benefits of education and that the proper kind of early learning would make them "equal, if not superior in all manner of science and even more capable of all possible Improvement than the men."[8] It is obvious that Defoe's written statements on women were the kind that would permit him to sympathize with them, to think carefully about them, and to accord them minds as worthy to be written about as those of men.

In fact, Roxana stands as one of the author's most complicated, most fully realized speakers. Both she and Moll Flanders are
more human, more real, resonant, and hence more problematic than
his male speakers. They seem to partake richly of a central element
in Defoe's genius, what Dobrée has called: "that most distinctive
mask; that capacity so to enter into the being of a person he is portraying as seemingly to become that person, to have that person's
emotions, to speak with his or her authentic voice . . . It is the creative imagination working on actuality raised to the highest pitch; it
seems almost to be the complete transference of Defoe's self into his
Creature."[9] We may read *Robinson Crusoe* for the fun of the adventure, for delight in the triumphs of middle-class economic man, but
Moll Flanders and Roxana, I think, hold many more of the pleasures Dobrée describes. Their lives contain more self-conscious introspection than do the male narratives. It is the quality of consciousness itself that still interests modern readers in his women, rather
than any adventures per se.

Defoe usually discussed this "transference of the self" in the
prefaces to his novels. To the beginnings of Crusoe and Colonel Jack
he appended straightforward notice of the tales's primary purposes:
to instruct and to delight. In the preface to *Moll Flanders*, however,
Defoe ascribes to himself a greater role as an agent of intervention.
There is more material that an alleged editor needs to clean up, and
a gap between the content of the tale and the way it is expressed
becomes an issue. He says:

> The author is here supposed to be writing her own history, and in the
> very beginning of her account she gives the reasons why she thinks fit
> to conceal her true name, after which there is no occasion to say any
> more about that.

> It is true that the original of this story is put into new words, and the
> style of the famous lady we here speak of is a little altered; particularly
> she is made to tell her own tale in modester words than she told it at
> first, the copy which came first to hand having been written in language
> more like one still in Newgate than one grown penitent and humble, as
> she afterwards pretends to be.[10]

Aside from the titillating tone of this preface, Defoe seems
somewhat uncomfortable in his role. He is both intermediary and

translator, and thus he tries to account for difficulties in the tone of voice of his speaker. With Roxana's tale the author draws the issue more specifically:

> *The History of this* Beautiful Lady, *is to speak for itself: If it is not as Beautiful as the Lady herself is reported to be; if it is not as diverting as the Reader can desire, and much more than he can reasonably expect; and if all the most diverting Parts of it are not adapted to the Instruction and Improvement of the Reader, the Relator says, it must be from the Defect of his Performance; dressing up the Story in worse Cloaths than the Lady, whose Words he speaks, prepar'd it for the World.*[11]

The story stands alone, Defoe seems to say, but then if there are faults, he is to be blamed. He speaks her words, but dresses them up; it is fundamentally his performance. In this preface Defoe has alerted us to his own awareness of the problem of masquerade. While he and the lady are to be very closely connected in the reader's mind, Defoe acts to make her story more attractive and accessible.

Why he should have to raise the question of his role at all involves the kinds of lives Moll and Roxana lead. And here we come to the first point of departure with his male speakers. Defoe's women narrators inhabit worlds more like the author's own. Islands and plantations offer a milieu whose dimensions can be constructed by the protagonist himself. They lend themselves to idealized visions of self-sufficient man. Not so for the women in Defoe's work. They face financial, moral, even sexual choices in a social world that is oftentimes hostile. The world for Crusoe and Jack is filled with objects to be manipulated. Except for the early thief narration of Colonel Jack, these two speakers are primarily concerned to create a hierarchy of control and value that is cut loose from social definitions of failure. In particular, the relative absence from their worlds of two items, money and sex, is a source of relief. And Defoe explicitly allows them to feel pleased that they can avoid such conflicts Crusoe makes the oft-noted statement: " 'O drug!' said I aloud, 'what art Thou good for? Thou art not worth to me, no, not the taking off of the ground; one of those knives is worth all this heap; I have no manner of use for thee, e'en remain where thou art, and go to the bottom as a creature whose life is not worth saving.' "[12]

Colonel Jack, even in the early stages of his career, finds money more a hindrance than help: "And now as I was full of Wealth, behold! I was full of Care, for what to do to secure my Money I could not tell, and this held me so long, and was so Vexatious to me the next Day, that I truly sat down and cryed."[13] Here follows a funny scene in which Jack cries first because he has the money and then because he does not, having dropped it down a tree trunk.

But for Defoe's female speakers, having or not having money is of critical importance. Moll shows a fascination with gold from the very beginning: "As for the gold, I spent whole hours in looking upon it; I told the guineas over and over a thousand times a day" (p. 30). Pleasure in money also has to do with the very real role it plays in survival. Moll considers what her behavior should be with men in the future: "The case was altered with me: I had money in my pocket, and had nothing to say to them. I had been tricked once by that cheat called love, but the game was over; I was resolved now to be married or nothing, and to be well married or not at all" (p. 69).

Like Moll Flanders, Roxana faces destitution repeatedly. The threat of ruin, emphasized by the business failures of her brother and then her first husband, is dramatized by her sitting on the floor in a heap of rags with numbers of hungry children and no money. She feels "like one of the pitiful Women of *Jerusalem*, I should eat up my very Children Themselves" (*Roxana*, p. 18). The image is appropriately desperate, and even when she finally does get enough money, indeed when like Moll Flanders she is wealthy, she still appears rapaciously greedy. Her question, why am I a whore now—like Moll's continued accumulation of wealth—can be translated into "Why am I always desperately fearing ruin?" Jack and Crusoe certainly hoard their goods and delight in elaborate inventories. But through Moll and Roxana Defoe imagines the threat of imminent loss of goods and money, a loss that will plunge the woman into tremendous difficulties and will force her into illicit procuring. The drama may be similar (how does one get enough of anything to ensure survival?), but for women narrators it takes place in a fictional world that mimics the difficulties of the author himself.

Anxiety centering around money would have been quite natural to Defoe, since he himself was one of the tribe of unfortunate bankrupts. In the *Essay on Projects* he contended that the bankruptcy laws "contrive all the ways possible to drive the Debtor to despair."[14] He went on to admit that "I may be a little warmer on this Head, on account that I have been a larger Sufferer by such means than ordinary."[15] He wrote of his own financial difficulties to his patron Harley in ways that may enlighten us as to his sympathy for Roxana. To him he described his "Large and Promiseing Family, a Vertuous and Excellent Mother to Seaven Beautifull and Hopefull Children, a woman whose fortunes I have Ruin'd, and with whom I have had 3700£, and yet who in the worst of my afflictions when my Ld.N. first Insulted her Then Tempted her. . . ."[16] As a result of all his business failures, Defoe was hounded by his creditors and never really escaped the shadow of persecution and imprisonment. His difficulties with money led also to his complete dependence on his patron, Robert Harley. Political patronage supported many writers during this period; still, for a man of Defoe's reckless and buoyant temperament, this absolute dependency must have been humiliating. Most of the letters we have from Defoe to Harley are informational epistles, newsletters that become often pedagogical, occasionally importunate. Defoe was always apologetic about begging for money but explained his tone by saying, "The Miserable are allways full of Their Own Cases and Think Nothing Impertinent."[17] After six years of working for Harley as an intelligence gatherer, Defoe saw himself as "a Man Entirely Given up to, and I had almost Said Ruin'd in her Majties Service."[18] His female disguise allows him to express his fears about money, allows him to imagine desperation and destitution.

The female world that Defoe allows himself to inhabit also contains within it much more sex, much more eroticism than the male worlds of Crusoe and Jack. Just how much anxiety this holds for Defoe is evident, for instance, in Crusoe's narrative. This hero is pleased to be on his island, away from the lusts of the flesh (*Crusoe*, p. 139). The world of Colonel Jack is mainly a male one, with a section on the trials and tribulations of marriage involving a series of wives. This wife section of the novel, while it has some references to how these women look and their assorted coquetries, has only the most indirect references to sex. These experiences serve to fill out Jack's career; thief, plantation slave, then owner, husband, soldier. And Defoe's main interest is to show how Jack achieves dominance over slaves, plantation owners, and wives.

Both Moll Flanders and Roxana make their way through the world by sex—being a woman involves using sex to survive. Virginity has cash value, and Moll is acutely aware that the loss of it lowers her earning power. But the author also explores what it would be like to be a sexual person through the female voice. Certainly, with Moll, there is little *love* to the sex. She can be "warmed" by one of her early lovers (p. 29), and Defoe has her fantasize about sex with her first lover (while married to his brother). Once Defoe presents a rather prurient scene with Moll and one of her prospective husbands lying in bed together naked, in order to prove their mutually chaste intentions. This tempting activity is doomed to failure, but for our purposes it is important to make two notes. First, the scene is indeed prurient, asking the reader to fantasize about Moll having sex:

> It was one night that we were in bed together warm and merry, and having drunk, I think, a little more wine that night, both of us, than usual, though not in the least to disorder either of us, when, after some other follies which I cannot name, and being clasped close in his arms, I told him (I repeat it with shame and horror of soul) that I could find in my heart to discharge him of his engagement for one night and no more. (p. 134)

And Defoe explicitly encourages erotic imaginings, in part because Moll does possess her own erotic desires: "for I own I was much wickeder than he, as you shall hear presently" (p. 134). Defoe does not explore at length this alleged sexual wickedness. Instead he devotes the second half of the book to her career as a thief (since she is now too old to make a living with her body).

Roxana, written two years later than *Moll Flanders*, explores much more fully an erotic consciousness. Eroticism of this kind was intensely frightening to Defoe, as is obvious in *Conjugal Lewdness*, written also near the end of his career (1727). This book contains a number of lengthy discussions about sex, women, and marriage. It is such a strange book for us to read now, undoubtedly because the conduct book is a didactic public performance. Much of the work is taken up with the control of that "corrupt Principle inbred and indwelling, taking a kind of Possession. . . ."[19] Defoe is concerned in this work with the problem of discussing sex at all. He is at pains to know how to open the discussion and calls his book a "modest portrayal of immodesty."[20] Even so, he adopts the view that marriage is useful mainly for procreation, and interestingly enough, grounds his work in the female perspective; that is, he sees marriage as too frequently a sexual tyranny over women. It is certainly true here, as everywhere else in his work, that Defoe adopts an economic perspective. But his bias leads him inevitably to champion women, who find themselves in a weakened position. In sympathizing with their position he fears humiliation in the sexual practices demanded by men and even approaches the question of sexual perversion. The author feels so strongly about the dangers of a loveless marriage that he envisions misshapen, monstrous children who will result from such unions. Without affection, love for him becomes a form of legal prostitution. Sexuality is talked about as if it were a dangerous, brutal force (even substance, one might say) that could erupt at any moment. It must be contained and controlled.

In *Roxana*, Defoe chooses to see the world through the eyes of a woman who lives by her body. Much more than *Moll Flanders*, this work reveals his anxieties about sex. The fact that there is so much essentially forbidden material in *Roxanna* in part explains its tone, often almost hysterical. The book breaks off perhaps because of insoluble narrative problems, as Dobreé suggests, and perhaps also because of the nature of the material discussed.[21]

Like Moll Flanders, Roxana is well aware of the cash value of sex, and in fact much discussion in the novel is given over to this fact. When considering the emotional elements connected to physical desire however, she disavows any interest. Considering whether or not to sleep with her landlord, she says: "the Jade [Amy] prompted the Crime, which I had but too much Inclination to commit; that is to say, not as a Crime, for I had nothing of the Vice in my Constitution; my Spirits were far from being high; my Blood had no Fire in it, to kindle the Flame of Desire. . ." (p. 40). She does not like it

when a "person of Honour" "began to talk of the old Game, Love
and Gallantry, and to offer at what was rude enough; things as
nauceous to me now, as if I had been married, and as virtuous as
other People" (p. 185). But in *Roxana* we are treated to a couple of
real seduction sequences replete with good food, fine wine, a prince,
and a barely clothed lady. Defoe wants us to know what kind of life
she leads and wants us to experience her as a bad, sexual woman.
Hence he must give us what he gives in *Conjugal Lewdness* also—
apparently modest means of portraying immodesty.

Let us look at one of these seduction scenes in detail to see
if the author endows his narrator with any sensuality of her own.
The prince arrives at Roxana's room and calls out:

> *Au Boir, says he*; upon which, his Gentleman immediately brought up
> a little Table, cover'd with a fine Damask Cloth, the Table no bigger than
> he cou'd bring in his two Hands; but upon it, was set two Decanters, one
> of Champaign, and the other of Water, six Silver Plates, and a Service of
> fine Sweet Meats in fine *China* Dishes, on a Sett of Rings standing up
> bout twenty inches high, one above another; below, was three roasted
> Partriges, and a Quail; as soon as his Gentleman had set it all down, he
> order'd him to withdraw; now, *says the Prince*, I intend to Sup with you.
> (p. 62)

Note the dramatic speech effects given to the prince, and note also
the damask cloth, decanters, and pieces of silver, and finally the
sweet meats. Luxury, richness, profusion—all signs of the ensuing
debauch.

The prince's announcement of an intent to sup with her sig-
nals another, no less obvious, intent. As his tone grows more intimate, she recounts; "I stood up, and offer'd to wait on *his
Highness* while he Eat, but he positively refus'd, and told me, No,
To-morrow you shall be the Widow of Monsieur—the Jeweller,
but to-Night you shall be my Mistress; therefore sit here, *says he* and
Eat with me, or I will get up and serve" (p. 62). Even though she is
restating the prince's words, the tone suggests physical closeness and
acquaintance between the two, showing her to be acquiescent and
docile, a stance that is really quite foreign to Roxana. Defoe emphasizes the luxuriousness of their feelings:

> It is only a loose Habit, my Lord, *said* I, that I may the better wait on *your Highness*; he pulls me to on the Bed-side, *says he*, Now you shall be a Princess, and know what it is to oblige the gratefullest Man alive; and with that, he took me in his Arms,—I can go no farther in the Particulars of what pass's at that time; but it ended in this, that, in short, I lay with him all Night. (p. 64)

This sequence outdistances anything else in Defoe's fiction by virtue of the erotic consciousness ascribed to the speaker. True, we are not given sensuous detail in the narrator herself—she merely relates the scene as if a viewer at a play. But Defoe surely wants us to feel her involved in a sensual process and that she herself possesses the taint of sensuality. Not only are prurient scenes longer and more developed in this novel, but costume, so important in Defoe's work to signal the state of being of a character (Crusoe's Skins), is explicitly sexual. Roxana's Turkish habit and her *deshabille* are costumes that she delights in describing. She enjoys showing them off, and through them demonstrates her ability to control others with her body:

> When all the Dress was put on, I loaded it with Jewels, and in particular, I plac'd the large Breast-Jewel which he had given me, of a thousand Pistoles, upon the Front of the *Tybaia*, or Head-Dress; where it made a most glorious Show indeed; I had my own Diamond-Necklace on, and my Hair was *Tout Brilliant*, all glittering with Jewels. (p. 247)

She becomes famous for the Turkish costume and even when in danger of exposure by her daughter, loves to hear her triumphs (dancing with the king) recounted, triumphs linked to her ability to dazzle the world with her body:

> I cannot help confessing what a Reserve of Pride still was left in me; and tho' I dreaded the Sequel of the Story, yet when she talk'd how handsome and fine a Lady this *Roxana* was, I cou'd not help being pleas'd and tickl'd with it; and put in Questions two or three times, of how handsome she was? and was she really so fine a Woman as they talk'd of? *and the like*, on purpose to hear her repeat what the People's Opinion of me was, and how I had behav'd. (p. 287)

Her "*Deshabille*" is her second favorite costume, again an explicitly sexual one: "This Morning-Vest, or Robe, *call it as you please,* was more shap'd to the Body, than we wear them since, showing the Body in its true Shape, and perhaps, a little too plainly. . . ." (p. 283). The delight she experiences in describing herself, and even more in hearing herself described, indicates something very close to our modern notion of narcissism. Defoe impresses upon us this narcissism by giving us a certain kind of touching. Roxana demonstrates to the prince that her beauty is natural: "With this, I put a Handerchief into his Hand, and taking his Hand into mine, I made him wipe my Face so hard, that he was unwilling to do it, for fear of hurting me." Amy, her maid, brings her some hot water and "I immediately wash'd my Face all over with it." The demonstration excites the prince and "he kiss'd my Cheeks and Breasts a thousand times . . ." (all on pp. 72, 73). Defoe, I think, tries two things with this episode: first, he wants us to get a sense of how her body feels; and second, he underscores her self-love, even the sensual feelings she has for herself. In the seduction scenes he wants her to be sexual, because her sexuality is part of her badness; but not knowing how to make this inherently part of her consciousness, he locates it instead in the objects that surround her (as indeed Defoe has trouble with emotion in general). Feelings do not seem to be part of action—they appear to be tacked on to people and situations, almost as if they were excess baggage. In the "touching" scenes he verges on experiencing an erotic consciousness. We can almost hear him wondering aloud through his female persona, what would it be like to experience the world through my body, through my sex?

I said earlier that the tone in this work is often noticeably like that of *Conjugal Lewdness*. In imagining what it would be like to be a whore, Defoe explores forbidden, certainly "bad" feelings of his own. This accounts for the intense self-criticism, one might even say, self-loathing that the author allows Roxana to express:

> I, that knew what this Carcass of mine had been but a few Years before; how overwhelm'd with Grief, drown'd in Tears, frighted with the Prospect of Beggary, and surrounded with Rags, and Fatherless Children; that was pawning and selling the Rags that cover'd me, for a Dinner, and sat on the Ground, despairing of Help, and expecting to be starv'd, till my Children were snatch'd from me, to be kept by the Parish; I, that was after this, a Whore for Bread, and abandoning Conscience and Virtue, liv'd with another Woman's Husband; I, that was despis'd by all

my Relations, and my Husband's too; I, that was left so entirely deso-
late, friendless, and helpless, that I knew not how to get the least Help to
keep me from starving; that I should be caress'd by a Prince, for the
Honour of having the scandalous Use of my Prostituted Body, common
before to his Inferiours; and perhaps wou'd not have denied one of his
Footmen but a little while before, if I cou'd have got my Bread by it.
(p. 74)

Here she portrays herself dramatically, points to herself as an object,
as an example. "Look at me. I'm an icon of sin," she seems to say.
The tone, though highly melodramatic, manages to be moving in its
build-up, in its rhythmic recital of self-hatred. Speeches of exactly
this quality are sprinkled throughout the novel and become pro-
gressively more shrill and hysterical. Despite all the mitigating fac-
tors in her situation, she never has a good word for the reasons she
does something. This harsh self-criticism contrasts rather vividly
with her other pose as witty conversationalist. Defoe allows her to
confide in the reader, but then forces that person to judge her, to
draw back and see her as an abject, despicable object. George Starr
has examined, in one episode, Defoe's seesawing between identification with her and loathing for her—this movement toward and
away from her as an index of the anxiety she arouses in the auth-
or.[22] Robinson Crusoe and Colonel Jack criticize themselves also,
but their reflections are for the most part progressive, optimistic.
We know that theirs is the consciousness of self-improvement, of
redemption. But Roxana's agonized reflections never lead anywhere
but down. From the outset of her narration, there is little hope of
improvement, only the consciousness of failure in herself and in
others.

Defoe addresses even more directly through his women speakers the problem of being involved in a master-slave relationship, in
all his work the paradigmatic relationship. The idyllic and uncompli-
cated Crusoe and Friday mirror the many patrons, benefactors,
teachers, and tutors of Colonel Jack. These relationships depend on
the two people knowing their place, receiving useful things from each
other, and being able to part with no regrets. The pattern is essentially that of the good father and the erring but ultimately good-
hearted son. With older men Colonel Jack presents himself in a submissive posture, plays on their gratitude, and finally induces the men

to help him with his ill-gotten gains. When Jack is transported to the colonies, the book becomes a rather schematic assertion of the virtues of duty and gratitude to good patrons. The planter speaks to his slaves and recommends:

> . . . that they ought to look upon the Life they were just a going to enter upon, as just beginning the World again; that if they thought fit to be diligent, and sober, they would after the time they were order'd to Serve was expir'd, be encourag'd by the Constitution of the Country, to Settle and Plant for themselves, and that even he himself would be so kind to them, that if he liv'd to see any of them serve their Time faithfully out, it was his custom to assist his Servants, in order to their Settling in that Country, according as their Behaviour might Merit from him . . . (p. 120).

Defoe casts human beings into hierarchical relations on the one hand, and identity relations on the other. The hierarchical elements need little explanation; Friday will do as he is told. On the other hand, Defoe makes it seem that the will of Friday is identical to that of Crusoe—he and his master are aspects of the same personality. Such being the case, there is little opportunity for conflict.

When Defoe writes as a woman, he writes as a dependent. He can no longer gloat and glory in his virtual kingship of an island, the way he allows Crusoe:

> My island was not peopled, and I thought my self very rich in subjects; and it was a merry reflection which I frequently made, how like a king I looked. First of all, the whole country was my own meer property; so that I had an undoubted right of dominion. 2dly, my people were perfectly subjected: I was absolute lord and lawgiver; they all owed their lives to me, and were ready to lay down their lives, if there had been occasion of it, for me. (pp. 240-241)

This fantasy of complete control contrasts sharply with the realities of Defoe's life. I spoke earlier of this author's difficulties with money. A problem that went beyond finances was his perpetual dependence on the will of his patron, "Robin the Trickster" (Robert Harley), and this would have been annoying, even enraging to a man of Defoe's reckless independence.[23] Harley would appear to have kept Defoe in a perpetual state of uncertainty by refusing him permanent employment. James Sutherland quotes a contemporary description of Defoe's benefactor: he loved " 'tricks even where not necessary, but from an inward satisfaction he took in applauding his own cunning. If any man was ever born under a necessity of being a knave, he was.' "[24] Sutherland goes on to suggest that when Defoe called *Robinson Crusoe* an allegory of his own life, then Crusoe was Harley and Defoe, Friday.[25] How must Defoe have felt about the man to whom he wrote: "I Confess my Own Pressures which are Sometimes Too heavy and Apt to Sink the hopes I conceiv'd from your Goodness Force me to Importune you, but I Can not but believ you Resolve to help me without my so Frequent sollicitations."[26]

The problematic nature of Defoe's relations with his benefactor is evident in an intriguing letter written in 1712:

> God and your Lordship are witnesses for me against this generation, in that your goodness to me was founded on no principles of bribery and corruption, but a generous compassion to a man oppressed by power without a crime, and abandoned even then by those he sacrificed himself to serve. The same witnesses are a testimony for me that my services (however small) are founded rather, and indeed entirely, on a deep sense of duty and gratitude for that early goodness, than on any view that I can merit what may be to come. You have always acted with me on such foundations of mere abstracted bounty and goodness that it has not so much as suggested the least expectation on your part, that I should act this way or that, leaving me at full liberty to pursue my own reason and principles, and above all enabling me to declare my innocence in the black charge of bribery.
>
> Whatever you have done for me, you never yet so much as intimated (though ever so remotely) that you expected from me the least bias in what I should write, or that his Majesty's bounty to me was intended to guide my opinion . . .
>
> This, my Lord, gives me room to declare, as I do in print every day, that I am neither employed, dictated to, or rewarded for, or in, what I write by any person under heaven; and I make this acknowledgment with thankfulness to your Lordship, and as a testimony to your great goodness to me, that you never laid the least injunction on me of one kind or another, to write or not to write this or that, in any case whatsoever.

Denying that he wrote in *The Review* as Harley's paid hack, he
asserted that he gave his services on the basis of gratitude rather than
coercion; Harley himself acts only on principles of "abstracted bounty and goodness"; but, significantly, the letter ends: ". . . as I am
driven by the torrent, upon a more entire dependence upon your
Lordship, so I have no human appeal but to yourself. . . ."[27]

At the very moment that he claimed independence, he once
again became the poor importuning employee. Even a cursory look
at Defoe's narrations written as a woman shows him champing at the
bit of the supplicant. Through Moll Flanders, and in a more extensive way through Roxana, Defoe explores the problems of someone
placed in a dependent, precarious position but who is acutely conscious of her superiority to those around her. The issue of Moll's
sexuality, for instance, is almost completely subsumed under the
problem of dependence. Most of Moll's career as a young woman is
taken up with the problem of exerting her will in such a way as to
become safe and secure. Some of her speeches on this subject make
her sound very much the feminist.[28] The excitement and energy of
her assorted romances, especially the imbroglio with the two brothers early in the novel, comes not from any sexual or romantic content, but from Moll's energetic attempts to exert her superior gifts of
mind and body without alienating those about her.

Speaking as Roxana, Defoe allows hatred of benefactors, on
the one hand, and wishes to kill them on the other. Roxana's own
master-slave relationship reverses itself; the murderous Amy becomes
her director, and the last quarter of the book almost obsessively
hums around terror at a loss of control over others and guilt about
her successful manipulations. Defoe allows Roxana to be highly
conscious and assertive of her own superiority. She announces the
fact in the opening pages of the novel: "I was (*speaking of myself
as about Fourteen Years of Age*) tall, and very well made; Sharp as
a Hawk in Matters of common Knowledge; quick and smart in Discourse; apt to be Satyrical; full of Rapartee, and a little too forward
in Conversation; or, as we call it in *English*, BOLD, tho' perfectly
Modest in my Behaviour." (p. 6) Financial ruin devastates those
around her. Her brother fails in business and goes to prison; her
brewer husband leaves her in rags. Everywhere around her exists

financial chaos. In order to survive, she has to use her "Carcass," as she calls it. In the early parts of the novel Defoe makes us sympathize with her plight; her sex is all that she can muster for survival. Later on however, once she really has all she needs, he has her ask herself why she is still a whore. The kind of dominance she exerts becomes particularly sinister when she puts Amy to bed with her landlord benefactor: *"Here*, says I, *Try what you can do with your Maid* Amy: She pull'd back a little, would not let me pull off her Cloaths at first, but it was hot Weather, and she had not many Cloaths on, and particularly, no Stays on; and at last, when she see I was in earnest, she let me do what I wou'd; so I fairly stript her, and then I threw open the Bed, and thrust her in" (p. 46). Roxana explains her own behavior: "as I thought myself a Whore, I cannot say but that it was something design'd in my Thoughts that my Maid should be a Whore too, and should not reproach me with it" (p. 47). An important part of Roxana's sense of superiority is that whenever she does something bad, she has to make those around her do the same. Amy must either think well of her or be as bad as she is.

Her wish to dramatize her superiority becomes successively more problematic in her three extended involvements with benefactors. Each involvement is characterized by movement from extreme gratitude to extreme dislike. There is suspicion, mistrust, and an almost constant effort to wrest control away from these men. Her first patron, the jeweller-landlord, rescues her from poverty and (since her husband has deserted her) sets up a contract to "legalize" their relationship. Despite all the goodness of this patron, Roxana feels that out of sheer gratitude she has destroyed herself:

> . . . by this wicked Course, all the Bounty and Kindness of this Gentleman, became a Snare to me, was a meer bait to the Devil's Hook; I receiv'd his Kindness at the dear Expence of Body and Soul, mortgaging Faith, Religion, Conscience, and Modesty, for (as I may call it) a Morsel of Bread; or, if you will, ruin'd my Soul from a Principle of Gratitude, and gave myself up to the Devil, to shew myself grateful to my Benefactor. (p. 38)

This is the man Roxana has forced to sleep with Amy, and who has led her into evil courses. In a dream, she imagines his death: "I

star'd at him, as if I was frighted, for I thought all his Face look'd
like a Death's-Head; and then, immediately, I thought I perceiv'd his
Head all Bloody; and then his Cloaths look'd Bloody too; and immediately it all went off, and he look'd as he really did; immediately,
I fell a-crying, and hung about him. . ." (pp. 52-53). Shortly thereafter, he is actually set upon and killed, and his death releases her
from a humiliating relationship.

Successive relationships find Roxana achieving even more power and control but feeling ever more anxious about her achievements.
Toward the prince, her most lavish protector Roxana asserts utter
devotion, although she still decries the gratitude and now the vanity
that again propels her into this course, and even begins to fear him:

> . . . for tho' Poverty and Want is an irresistible Temptation to the
> Poor, Vanity and Great Things are as irresistible to others; to be courted
> by a Prince, and by a Prince who was first a benefactor. . . (p. 64).

When he gives her a necklace, she fears the feeling of his hands about
her neck: ". . . at last he leads me to the darkest Part of the Room,
and standing behind me, bade me hold up my Head, when putting
both his Hands round my Neck, as if he was spanning by Neck, to
see how small it was, for it was long and small; he held my Neck so
long, and so hard, in his Hand, that I complain'd he hurt me a little
. . ." (p. 73). It is only the gift of a necklace, but Defoe gives the incident sinister resonance. Later when the prince engages an old woman
to look after the pregnant Roxana, she suspects her of being hired
to kill her. Such a fear conflicts with the avowedly idyllic quality
of the relationship, and suggests that the prince's beneficence has
another side—murderousness. Friday and Colonel Jack look up to
their protectors as fathers, and perhaps Defoe felt this way toward
Harley—sometimes. Roxana represents another constellation of feeling altogether. For Defoe's female narrators gratitude leads to
corruption, dependence to slavery.

The force of the final section of the book comes from the
enormous anxiety around exposure, and hence loss of the benefact-
or's favor. Even though the Dutch merchant has shown himself a
paragon of understanding and benevolence, he now becomes a

bogey—his finding out about her past will mean abandonment and destitution. Roxana moves from house to house, adopts a series of disguises, and becomes a virtual prisoner of these fears;

> ... in truth, I cou'd not have been perfectly easie at living in *England*, unless I had kept constantly within-doors; lest some time or other, the dissolute Life I had liv'd here, shou'd have come to be known; and all those wicked things have been known too, which I now began to be very much asham'd of. (p. 249)

Her world is not a colony, an island, an object to be toyed with, but people—people whom she needs the more because she has deceived them.

Clearly structured hierarchies of relationship make the personal worlds of Crusoe and Colonel Jack relatively safe as a social milieu. The most serious threats come from nature, not from other men. In a sense the ease with which these protagonists manipulate others marks their elect status. But Moll and even more so Roxana have uneasy relationships with subordinates. The governess is Moll's bad benefactor, helping her into a life of crime—she simply appears to do whatever Moll would like her to do, and then disappears. Roxana and her maid Amy become, after awhile, indistinguishable. Defoe shows Roxana disintegrating under the pressures of secrecy, becoming engulfed in a haunting wretchedness that narrows her vision to a pinhole. This portion of the novel is an extraordinary *tour de force* in which we experience the nightmare world of the profoundly guilty. As in most relationships in his work, Defoe asserts initially an identity between the maid and the mistress; Roxana calls her "a cunning Wench, and faithful to me, as the Skin to my Back . . ." (p. 25) As Roxana's fear of dependence on men grows, Amy takes over the active, malevolent ego of the heroine. Defoe allows Roxana to become the passive observer of a murder that she herself wills. The pursuit of the abandoned daughter (perhaps wreaking the symbolic revenge of a whole host of Moll and Roxana's abandoned children) drives Roxana into madness—into murderous madness. Finding out that her daughter knows more than she and her mistress think, Amy "starts up, and runs about the Room like a distracted body; I'll put an end to it, that I will; I can't bear it; I must murther

her; I'll kill her B—" (p. 272). Roxana professes to be frightened
by these feelings, but her fear of murder is second only to her fear
of discovery:

> It is true, I wanted as much to be deliver'd from her, as ever a Slick-
> Man did from a Third-Day Ague; and had she dropp'd into the Grave by
> any fair Way, *as I may call it*; I mean had she died by an ordinary Dis-
> temper, I shou'd have shed but very few Tears for her: ... But, *as I
> said, Amy* effected all afterwards, without my Knowledge, for which I
> gave her my hearty Curse, tho' I cou'd do little more; for to have fall'n
> upon *Amy*, has been to have murther'd myself. (p. 302)

Defoe makes Roxana self-consciously aware of the close connection
between herself and her maid. The fear of discovery and horror at
relentless pursuit must have been as familiar to the author as uneasy feelings about benefactors. Six years after the creation of Roxana he ended his life in hiding, being pursued by a woman about
debts over forty years old. Such a situation merely repeated the terrors and isolation of a significant part of his life. Ironically, he was
also deeply concerned about betrayal by one of his own children. His
last letter shows him a fearful recluse:

> I was sorry you should say at the Beginning of your Letter, you were
> debarred seeing me. Depend upon my Sincerity for this, I am far from
> debarring you. On the contrary, it would be a greater Comfort to me
> than any I now enjoy, that I could have your agreeable Visits with Safe-
> ty, and could see both you and my dear Sophia, could it be without
> giving her the Grief of seeing her Father *in tenebris*, and under the Load
> of insupportable Sorrows. I am sorry I must open my Griefs so far as to
> tell her, it is not the Blow I recd from a wicked, perjur'd, and contempt-
> ible Enemy, that has broken in upon my Spirit; which as she well knows,
> has carried me on thro' greater Disasters than these. But it has been the
> injustice, unkindness, and I must say, inhuman dealing of my own Son,
> which has both ruin'd my Family, and, in a Word, has broken my Heart;
> and as I am at this Time under a weight of very heavy Illness, which I
> think will be a Fever, I take this Occasion to vent my Grief in the Breasts
> who I know will make a prudent use of it, and tell you, that nothing but
> this has conquered or could conquer me. *Et tu! Brute*. I depended upon
> him, I trusted him, I gave up my two dear unprovided Children into his
> Hands; but he has no Compassion, but suffers them and their poor, dying
> Mother to beg their Bread at his Door, and to crave, as if it were an

Alms, what he is bound under Hand and Seal, besides the most sacred
promises, to supply them with; himself, at the same Time, living in a
profusion of Plenty. It is too much for me. Excuse my Infirmity, I can
say no more; my Heart is too full. . . .

I have not seen Son or Daughter, Wife or Child, many Weeks, and
kno' not which Way to see them. They dare not come by Water, and by
Land there is no Coach, and I kno' not what to do.[29]

Disguise, assumed names, hiding—these were all a function of continuous necessity for Defoe. His heroes and heroines always are forced
to start anew and shirk off the past. But Moll and Roxana experience
this shirking off with more pain and with greater difficulty—they
have deceived others to gain their good opinion. Revelation will lead
to the loss of every possession, every friend, I might almost say, all
life.

Defoe's readers have long wanted to know what he really
thought about the fictions he created. What did he think he was
doing? The question has been most often posed around disjunctions
between what the character knows and what we think we may know.
Defoe either is or is not directing us to these disjunctions. I want to
pose the question differently. What are the dimensions of the female
consciousness when Defoe writes as a woman? We no longer inhabit
the fantasy world of Crusoe and Jack, worlds that bend with formu-
laic ease to the arms of the protagonist. In *Roxana* certainly, and to a
lesser extent in *Moll Flanders*, Defoe uses the female disguise to
approach the real anxieties of his own life. He peeps through the keyhole at both Moll and Roxana, thinks about watching them have sex.
Compared to James Joyce and D. H. Lawrence, his indulgence in
these fantasies seems restrained; but when Roxana washes her own
face, when she feels the prince's hand around her neck, when she
feels her body in her dress, these gestures are clearly sexual. The
female mask is also appealing to Defoe because it allows him to express an even more pervasive anxiety in his work: the rage of a dependent, the rage of someone always anxious about money and in
need of others' help to get it. His women narrators are greedy—their
hunger for money and security can never be satisfied. As a man Defoe knew what it meant to be at the mercy of those toward whom he
felt superior, but on whose bounty he also depended. His fictions

allow him to explore these anxieties at the same time that they allow him to disguise them.

The female voice is the most congenial disguise through which Defoe can take extremely personal risks, risks not congruent with his ideal of masculinity. As Crusoe and Colonel Jack he felt a social pressure to present to the world a thoroughly idealized male. At the rhetorical level the male voice is primarily a means of asserting the necessity of moral, practical, and spiritual choices. The will is everything. Defoe's women are much more clearly vehicles for self-exploration, exploration of both wishes and fears. Less constrained by their sexual identity, he has created more interesting, more complex human beings when he writes as a woman. These women sound much more tentative and exploratory, less rigidly conceived than their male counterparts. For Defoe it is not good to be greedy and constantly hungry for money, to be sexual and yet haunted by what to do with this sexuality, to be dependent on someone else for a livelihood and to hate and fear this person. Writing as a woman he can take these risks and as a man deny that he has taken them.

This reading of Defoe's work raises another important question—are there themes that are consistently addressed through female speakers, themes that in fact transcend the personal situation of the author? Roxana is certainly very like her male counterparts in the urge to dominate her world. Both Crusoe and Colonel Jack are almost hymns to a self-created universe, one in which the dominance of the hero is not really in doubt. For Roxana, maintaining her own position demands intense struggle. People are so much less tractable than islands, especially when one is highly conscious of her sins while wishing also to be in control. Many of Roxana's more mysterious acts and speeches make sense only when we see Defoe exploring through her a difficult, frustrating search for complete dominance. This search most often takes the form of manipulating others' good opinion, so that she will be reflected back favorably. Roxana loves the power that her singleness and her money give her:

> I return'd, that while a Woman was single, she was a Masculine in her politick Capacity; that she had then the full Command of what she had, and the full Direction of what she did; that she was a Man in her separated Capacity, to all Intents and Purposes that a Man cou'd be so to him-

self; that she was controul'd by none, because accountable to none, and was in Subjection to none; so I sung these two lines of Mr.'s.
> O! 'tis pleasant to be free,
> The sweetest MISS is Liberty. (pp. 148-149)

It is subjection itself that she fears, and so she works to subject others.

The way in which Roxana shows her will to dominate confuses us sometimes because it causes her to say things that, either she cannot possibly mean, or that her author simply interpolates as something *he* wants to say. Some of these contradictions are resolved, however, when we look closely at the uses to which the character of Roxana is being put. Surely one baffling moment occurs when, even though involved romantically with the prince, Roxana launches into extended praise of his wonderful wife:

> He had a Princess, a Wife, with whom he had liv'd several Years, and a Woman (*so the Voice of Fame reported*) the most valuable of her Sex; of Birth equal to him; if not superiour, and of Fortune proportionable; but in Beauty, Wit, and a thousand good Qualities, superiour not to most Women, but even to all her Sex; and as to her Virtue, the Character, which was most justly her due, was that of, not only the best of Princesses, but even the best of Women. (p. 107)

This woman, according to Roxana, is so good and generous as to excuse her lord's foibles and Roxana occasionally urges that he should return to her, even if it means her loss: "*Not for any other Favourite*, my Lord, said I; *That wou'd break my Heart*; but *for Madam, the Princess!* said I, and then I could say no more, Tears follow'd, and I sat silent a-while" (p. 108). Because of a touching deathbed scene, the prince repents and leaves Roxana, who for her part, is upset but, "Now I was at Liberty to go to any Part of the World, and take Care of my Money myself" (p. 111).

In front of the prince the game has become all generoisity, kindness, and refinement. Roxana always wants to look good, to appear a lady in every sense of the word. But what she really wants is her freedom, and this she takes by telling him to go back to his wife. Roxana, quite simply, would rather "be a *Man-Woman*; for as I was born free, I wou'd die so" (p. 171). Sometimes these impulses appear sinister, as when she puts Amy to bed with her landlord husband. At other times Defoe seems to support wholly the rational wish to be free and independent. As Maximillian Novak has commented, *Roxana* is doubtless "both morally and artistically his most complex work."[30] It is indeed because of the difficult issues Defoe explores through he female speaker.

However problematic the female search for power, even more intensely realized is her loss of consciousness. In later writers we will see that whatever psychological boundaries the narrator has, the author shows her losing them. We have some difficulties with Defoe here because he seems to confuse clear boundaries of character in his work. Who is to say where Crusoe begins and Friday leaves off? Roxana and Amy do indeed become indistinguishable, even down to the pronouns, but then Amy has not been given a discrete identity apart from Roxana from the very beginning. However Defoe certainly does explore a loss of mind through the female voice. Roxana comes obsessive, frantic, almost mad—and this process comprises the end of her narrative. Everett Zimmerman has remarked that "*Roxana* is Defoe's most extreme expression of the isolation, the diminishing sense of external reality, that is experienced by all his characters."[31] Clearly Defoe allows this narrator to explore frightening aspects of the human personality. Their exploration is much richer than the narrations of Crusoe and Colonel Jack, both of which display the strong generic influence of the spiritual autobiography form, as George Starr has described it, and are thus more schematic.[32] *Roxana*, in many ways a confusing work, bears the mark of a strange and strained identification on the part of the author. She is certainly not a dull figure. First a portrait of the realities that drive women to prostitution, she is also a portrait of the artist himself expressing some of his deepest fears. The same sympathies that lead Defoe to champion the female sex also lead him to invest her with the distaff side of his own personality. Understandably, she is a creature of contradictions, and we may also feel an understandable ambivalence about the use to which she is being put.

Notes

[1]James Sutherland, *Defoe* (London: Methuen, 1950), p. 245. See also Samuel L. Macey, "The Time Scheme in Moll Flanders," *N&Q*, 16:9, Sept. 1969, pp. 336-37. Mr. Macey asserts that much of Moll's actual life concurs closely in time with Defoe's. Curt Hartog discusses Moll Flanders in terms of a hierarchy of Oedipal and pre-Oedipal drives. This is the only other specific reading known to me, of female narrators in Defoe. See "Aggression, Femininity, and Irony in *Moll Flanders*," L&P, 22:121-38.

[2]Defoe married Mary Tuffley in 1683 or 84, and she figures most prominently in the correspondence with Robert Harley as the long-suffering mother of seven children and wife to a man in perpetual financial difficulties.

[3]Bonamy Dobrée, *English Literature in the Early Eighteenth Century, 1700-1740* (London: Oxford University Press, 1959), p. 398.

[4]Daniel Defoe, *An Essay Upon Projects* (London: Cockerill, Facsimile Edition 1697), p. 299.

[5]Daniel Defoe, *Conjugal Lewdness: or, Matrimonial Whoredom. A Treatise Concerning the Use and Abuse of the Marriage Bed*, Intro. M. E. Novak (Gainsville: Scholars' Facsimile Reprints 1967) p. 26.

[6]*Ibid.*, p. 129.

[7]Daniel Defoe, *An Essay Upon Projects*, p. 286.

[8]William Lee, *Daniel Defoe: His Life and Recently Discovered Writings* (London: Hotten, 1869) A. J., Aug. 8, 1724, p. 291.

[9]Bonamy Dobrée, *Daniel Defoe* (Facsimile Edition, Groningen, Batavia, 1946), p. 10.

[10]Daniel Defoe, *The Fortunes and Misfortunes of the Famous Moll Flanders* (London: Oxford University Press, 1961), p. 3. All subsequent references will be to this edition of the text.

[11]*Roxana, or the Fortunate Mistress* (London: Oxford University Press, 1964), p. 1. All subsequent references will be to this edition of the text.

[12]Daniel Defoe, *The Life and Adventures of Robinson Crusoe* (Penguin: Baltimore, 1965), p. 75. All subsequent references will be to this edition of the text.

[13]Daniel Defoe, *The History and Remarkable Life of the Truly Honourable Colonel Jacque* (London, Oxford University Press, 1965), p. 23.

[14]Daniel Defoe, *An Essay Upon Projects*, p. 192.

[15]*Ibid.*, p. 225.

[16]George Healey, *The Letters of Daniel Defoe* (Oxford: Clarendon Press, 1955), May-June, 1704 (?), p. 17.

[17]*Ibid.*, May-June 1704 (?), p. 18.

[18]*Ibid.*, 2 September 1710, p. 274.

[19]Daniel Defoe, *Conjugal Lewdness*, p. 60.

[20]*Ibid.*, p. 7.

[21]Bonamy Dobrée, *English Literature in the Early Eighteenth Century, 1700-1740*, p. 425.

[22]George Starr, "Sympathy vs. Judgement," *The Augustan Milieu, Essays Presented to Louis Landa*, F 48: 59-76.

[23]G. M. Trevelyan, *England Under Queen Anne, Ramillies and the Union with Scotland* (London: Longmans, 1932), p. 83.

[24]James Sutherland, *Defoe*, p. 149.

[25]*Ibid.*, p. 233.

[26]*Letters*, May-June 1704 (?), p. 14.

[27]Quoted in James Sutherland, *Defoe*, p. 190.

[28]See Joan C. Foster, *Daniel Defoe and the Position of Women in*

Eighteenth Century England: A Study of Moll Flanders and Roxana, DAI, 33:5677A (NM).

29*Letters*, 12 August, 1730, p. 474.

30Maximillian Novak, "Crime and Punishment in Defoe's *Roxana*," *JEGP*, 65, (July, 1966), pp. 445-465.

31Everett Zimmerman, *Defoe and the Novel* (Berkeley: Univ. of California Press, 1975) p. 180.

32George Starr, *Defoe and Spiritual Autobiography* (Princeton: Princeton University Press) 1965.

Chapter 3

An Odd and Grotesque Figure:
Samuel Richardson and Clarissa

It is rare to see a serious attempt to link the work of Defoe and Richardson. Theirs are worlds that seem vastly unlike: the external world of action and adventure in contrast to the internalizing, psychologically dramatic. Yet Defoe engaged in serious psychologizing, through his female protagonists, at least. These two authors are indeed alike in their creation of complicated female speakers who bear a direct relationship to themselves. They share also a religious tradition that provided a rationale and some formal properties of their work. Cynthia Griffin Woolf has written extensively on Richardson's debt to Puritan devotional literature, especially in his minute detailing of the "dynamics of character under stress."[1] Certainly Richardson everywhere displays a greater sense of pace, drama, and form than does Defoe. Yet they both claimed to see their work as didactic; literature for them was conceived as a humanizing instrument and the female consciousness was central to the enterprise. When Defoe writes as a woman, he presents us with a flawed, even bad, human being who nevertheless struggles to gain ascendancy over her world. Clarissa's psychological complexities are notorious, though Samuel Richardson claimed to be presenting to us a female model who was meant to be emulated. His avowal of her goodness has not gone unchallenged, however, and this physically debilitated printer, who like Defoe began his career in fiction late in life, managed to create a female voice and figure so powerful that she influenced the way women were to appear in the novel up until the end of the nineteenth century. As Leslie Fiedler puts it; "she flees through two hundred years of fiction, hounded by father and lover, brother and fiancé. . . ."[2] This woman is certainly the greatest of Richardson's creations—she seems to have captured her creator's most profound artistic energies. Through her the author can make inordinate claims for the power of the individual consciousness; this

woman can transform others as well as she can transform herself.
But these rather astonishing achievements take place within a woman
who loses both her mind and her body. Richardson explores through
her the disintegration of the self as we know it. He manages to create a mythic figure, yes, but one who is surely terrible and frightening. How the stout, hypochondriacal little printer should have
created so "odd and grotesque" a figure as his Clarissa will be the
subject of our explorations in this chapter.

Richardson's art was based on his love for masquerade.
Throughout his life Richardson liked to pretend to be other people,
especially women. In 1735, after a long career in printing (he was
Master of the Stationer's Company and printer to the House of
Commons) and a prolific one as a writer, Richardson bemoaned his
illnesses and his loss of inspiration: " 'O that I could carry myself
out of myself, into *other* characters, as in Times past! I am not
pleased with *my own*; and Want Amusement that I could be fond
of.' "[3] Those he carried himself into were, from the very beginning,
female. His writing career began when he was asked by some neigh-
borhood ladies to write their love letters. His description of this
task shows delight in the masquerade:

> 'I was not more than thirteen when three of these young Women,
> unknown to each other, having a high Opinion of my Taciturnity, re-
> vealed to me their Love Secrets, in order to induce me to give them
> Copies to write after, or correct, for Answers to their Lovers Letters:
> Nor did any one of them ever know, that I was the Secretary to the
> others. I have been directed to chide, and even repulse, when an Offence
> was either taken or given, at the very time the Heart of the Chider or
> Repulser was open before me, overflowing with Esteem and Affection;
> and the fair Repulser dreading to be taken at her Word; directing *this*
> Word, or *that* Expression, to be softened or changed. One, highly grati-
> fy'd with her Lover's Fervor and Vows of everlasting Love, has said,
> when I have asked her Direction; I cannot tell you what to write; But
> (her Heart on her Lips) you cannot write too kindly: All her Fear only,
> that she should incurr Slight for her Kindness.'[4]

Richardson's tone here is characteristic; he finds delight in choosing
this word or that work, in marking the minute progress of a courtship. When Richardson wrote his *Letters Written To and For Par-*

ticular Friends, On the most Important Occasions, Directing not only the Requisite style and Forms to be observed in Writing Familiar Letters; But how to Think and Act Justly and Persistently, in the Common Concern of Human Life, he wrote a number of letters discussing courtship, love, and marriage, and often from the point of view of a woman.

In his fifties, when Richardson began to write novels, he wrote from what must have been the most congenial point of view, and that was as the beleaguered little servant girl. He wrote the novel *Pamela* (at 51) in a creative burst, two volumes in two months. The character and voice that Richardson creates in her seems cloying and hypocritical to us now, I think, although her author clearly thinks her sincere and believable, a model even. Pamela is interesting (briefly, I might add) when she is being assaulted by the laughable Mr. B and when her author pictures her in an attitude of fearful surprise and bewilderment. Richardson proceeds in her through hyperbole and declaration, letting his heroine gush unashamedly:

> Thus, my dearest parents, is your happy, thrice happy Pamela, at last married; and to whom?—Why to her beloved, gracious master! the lord of her wishes! and thus the once naughty assailer of her innocence, by a blessed turn of Providence, is become the kind, the gracious protector and rewarder of it.[5]

Though *Pamela* was published anonymously, Richardson's friend Aaron Hill recognized the work of his friend. He was ecstatic about the book and wrote to the author:

> Yet, I confess, there is *One*, in the World, of whom I think with still greater Respect, than of PAMELA: and That is, of the wonderful AUTHOR of *PAMELA*.—Pray, Who is he, Dear Sir? and where, and how, has he been able to hide, hitherto, such an encircling and all-mastering Spirit? He possesses every Quality that ART could have charm'd by: yet, has lent it to, and conceal'd it in, NATURE,—The Comprehensiveness of his Imaginaion must be truly prodigious!—It has stretch'd out this diminutive mere *Grain of Mustard-seed* (a poor Girl's little, innocent, Story) into a Resemblance of That *Heaven*, which the Best of Good Books has compar'd it to![6]

He later wrote to a friend to say that he recognized the author " 'by the resembling turn of Pamela's expressions, weigh'd with some which I had noted, as peculiar in his letters. . . .' "[7]

The author is detected through his female voice, not through that of Mr. B. Pamela may be laughable, but Mr. B is surely ludicrous. Mr. B has neither force nor grace, and appears to capture little of the author's creative strength. Eaves and Kimpel, Richardson's biographers, comment on the source of his failure: "Most readers have felt that Fielding's expansion of that unfortunate initial into Booby is an apt summation. Austin Dobson points out that he is really two characters, both of them dull, " 'a rake derived from the play-book and a reformed husband derived from the copy-book'."[8] Mr. B is a derivative figure, one who issues less from the creative genius of the author than from models Richardson could find elsewhere. He is an excuse for the assault, really, a foil to the anguished cries of little Pamela. Later in his writing career Sir Charles Grandison, who was to be a portrait of the good man, failed utterly. Richardson was much more interested in his women letter-writers and let the correspondence of Harriet steal the scene from the ponderous, legalistic Sir Charles. Eaves and Kimpel comment on his dreadful effect whenever Sir Charles does appear: "When he is absent, the novel stirs to life. When he appears, it freezes."[9] In their view, Richardson could barely imagine himself inside Sir Charles at all: "But it is futile to think about Sir Charles's 'real' passions. We are never at any time allowed inside his mind—indeed his mind has no inside, because he must do what virtue requires."[10] Surely Richardson did not really want to be inside his hero's mind. Clarissa (created when the author was fifty-eight) is a model of virtue too, but she springs to life with amazing force. As a creator of fictions, it seems, Richardson had little to invest of himself in his male figures.

There is Lovelace, however. Where does he figure as a character, as an evocation of the author? It is important to note first that Lovelace is very much a derivative creation also. As Leslie Fiedler puts it, "Lovelace stands at the end of a tradition, Clarissa at the beginning."[11] He is of course an evocation of Milton's Satan, the arch-fiend, the shape-changer. Richardson reiterates his Protean qualities; he is infinitely changeable, all variety. His delight in chaos, movement, in just action itself, bears a heartily Satanic quality. When Richardson shows Lovelace refusing to violate the country girl Rosebud he shows us a restoration rake who loves plots and intrigue and who thrives on the war between the sexes. Richardson was himself concerned at the sympathy his readers might have felt for his villain and in subsequent revisions of the novel kept blackening his character.[12] Usually it is this dark side of Lovelace's character that is plumbed for its relationship to the unconscious drives of the author; unfortunately it is this side that is most contrived and artificial. Balzac commented on the difference in the art needed to create a Clarissa as opposed to a Lovelace: " 'Lovelace has a thouand forms, since social corruption takes on the colours of all the environments in which it develops. Clarissa, on the contrary, that lovely image of ardent virtue, has lines so pure as to make one despair!' "[13]

In many important ways Lovelace was an easier character to create. Like Mr. B., his words and actions had been replayed a thousand times. One has only to examine his letters to see that he speaks in Miltonic inversions and hyperbole and that he adopts the rhetorical flourishes of a stage villain. Lovelace also functions as a foil, an excuse. He is that force that drives the heroine to her triumph. He exists to propel her into heroism. Lovelace's most authentic, if I may use this word, moments come when he is commenting critically on Clarissa, analyzing her character. In these moments he is closest to his creator, since Richardson's main interest throughout the novel is to contemplate Clarissa's true nature. Richardson has his villain comment: "But had the same soul informed a masculine body, never would there have been a truer hero."[14] And we might say, on the other hand, that it is a masculine soul, Richardson's, that inhabits a female body. Richardson reserves his creative genius for Clarissa; hers is the generative consciousness that gives shape and meaning to the novel, hers is the voice closest to the author in sympathy and energy.[15]

Why he should have felt this way is evident in Richardson's life. He spent a good deal of his time, certainly when he was writing *Pamela* and afterwards, in company with women who he felt appreciated his work best. His volumes of letters are primarily concerned with social chit-chat; in fact these questions take up a good deal of his time. The minutiae of the letters and the deep pleasure the author took in social arbitration is characteristic also of his Clarissa. Richardson was in general a champion of the female sex. Speculating on female nature was one of his favorite topics, and for him they possessed finer motives, finer minds, finer sensibilities than men. To Miss Collier he wrote, "Who, my dears, shall vindicate the honour of a sex, the most excellent of which desert themselves?"[16] And to Lady Bradshaigh, "You must see that the tendency of all I have written is to exalt the sex.[17] Richardson prided himself that the circle of ladies who surrounded him were the best and the brightest. He wrote to his Dutch translator, "I think, Sir, we in England may glory in numbers of women of genius. I in particular may—I could introduce you, Sir, to such a circle of my own acquaintance."[18] Women, while performing their wifely duties, should not hide their light and "If a woman has genius, let it take its course, as well as in men; provided she neglect not anything that is more peculiar of her province."[19] Richardson proved his admiration of women by encouraging many to write, to utter opinions on subjects not thought suitable for them, and above all to confide in him their deepest wishes. And he often drew a clear distinction between himself and other men, since most men were quite dangerous: "Writing to your own sex I would principally recommend; since ours is hardly every void of design and makes a correspondence dangerous."[20]

Richardson actually liked, in his own correspondence, to appear more as a woman than a man. He was constantly cautioning his female correspondents (his letter-writers were mostly female) to guard themselves from the predations of the male. He carried on a strange epistolary flirtation with someone revealed to him as Lady Bradshaigh, and when the time came for them to meet, he wrote her this description as a means of identifying him:

> Short, rather plump than emaciated, notwithstanding his complaints: about five foot five inches; fair wig; lightish cloth coat, all black besides; one hand generally in his bosom, the other a cane in it, which he leans upon under the skirts of his coat usually, that it may imperceptibly serve him as a support, when attacked by sudden tremors or startings, and dizziness, which too frequently attack him, but, thank God, not so often as formerly: looking directly foreright, as passers-by would imagine, but observing all that stirs on either hand of him without moving

his short neck; hardly ever turning back: of a light-brown complexion; teeth not yet failing him: smoothish faced, and ruddy cheeked: at sometimes looking to be about sixty-five, at other times much younger: a regular even pace, stealing away ground, rather than seeming to rid it: a gray eye, too often over-clouded by mistiness from the head: by chance lively; very lively it will be, if he have hope of seeing a lady whom he loves and honours: his eye always on the ladies; if they have very large hoops, he looks down and supercilious, and as if he would be thought wise, but perhaps the sillier for that: as he approaches a lady, his eye is never fixed first upon her face, but upon her feet and thence he raises it up, pretty quickly for a dull eye; and one would think (if we thought him at all worthy of observation) that from her air and (the last beheld) her face, he sets her face, he sets her down in his mind as *so* or *so*, and then passes on to the next object he meets; only then looking back, if he greatly likes or dislikes, as if he would see if the lady appear to be all of a piece, in the one light or in the other. Are these marks distinct enough, if you are resolved to keep all the advantages you set out with? And from this odd, this grotesque figure, think you, Madam, that you have any thing to apprehend? Any thing that will not rather promote than check your mirth?[21]

Here he appears very safe indeed. He "steals away ground" and leans upon his cane. He gives the sense of someone who at times can barely stand. His weakness is no great hindrance to his relationship with the ladies, "his eyes always on the ladies," and look how judging this eye is. He appraises them candidly, putting them we may guess, into his special categories. They are objects, after all. This lover of ladies is also, however, an odd and grotesque figure who will not harm in any way the proper Lady Bradshaigh. Laughable, yes (and he must be laughing a bit at himself), but this self-portrait probably yields more by way of explanation than the volumes of letters that he wrote. Also, note how coy the tone; Richardson sounds as if he were masquerading as a woman right here.

Whatever else we may say about the author as he described himself, Richardson wanted his women to think of him as old, sick, and safe. He was not like other men whom they knew; in fact he was their champion and might even be one of them. He was not, after all, really a man. Richardson disliked men in part for their habitual mistreatment of women, for real abuses that he observed in the aristocracy, for the predations that men wreaked on a sex he loved.

Dislike for men comes undeniably in this author from a closely held feminism. But there are much murkier elements to his feelings, among which may be a fascination with weakness and death, a fascination that resulted from family events and from his own persistent illnesses or hypochondriasis.

Over his lifetime Richardson suffered greatly from a number of deaths in his family. Between 1722-1732 six of his children died, as did his wife.[22] One year eleven deaths in his family and circle of friends proved very debilitating. Richardson himself was ill from the 1740's on and the letters from Dr. George Cheyne show the author to be an anxious man, suffering fears, fits, and faintings. He seems to have complained to Cheyne pretty regularly, and to his patient Cheyne minimized the danger: "not for the Danger of it. . .but for the Pain, Anxiety, and Discouragement your symptoms give you, which, I most sacredly assure you, are merely nervous and hysterical."[23] These were simply "Startings, Twitchings, and Cramps that make you so uneasy and apprehensive but without any Foundations from real Danger."[24] Cheyne saw the great danger from all this as "Despondency which is its most severe sympton."[25] "I think Lowness of Spirits in its extremest Degrees is the only Misery in Life. If any thing in Purgatory or Hell be worse I would prefer annihilation to it if possible. . . ."[26]

We cannot now really know what part of Richardson's illnesses were real and what part he imagined.[27] But there is little doubt that he saw himself as weakened and in danger, and, I might add, on the verge of death for a number of years. Clarissa, of course, demonstrates an endless preoccupation with the status of her health and afflictions. That Richardson saw himself as ill suggests why he would write from the point of view of someone who is in a weakened physical state, a woman. Rape is one of the most serious physical violations a woman can suffer and Richardson's preoccupation with his own physical state must have led him to find the female voice a congenial one.

Both Defoe and Richardson are intensely concerned with dominance and submission. Both explore a central dynamic of control: the struggle to get it, the agonies of keeping it. In the female voice for Richardson that struggle is more masked than in Lovelace, but it is present all the same. How this struggle is realized has to do in great measure with Richardson's personal sense of illness and debility. The consequences of domination for Defoe are survival and beyond that, self-sufficiency. But for Richardson this matter of dominance leads to the issue of something larger—for purposes of argument I will call it transformation. Richardson fears changes, especially those of the body. For both Lovelace and Clarissa the contest is one of dominance that will result in the other's being permanently changed. And that change is explicitly pictured as physical. Lovelace thinks that if he can just get into bed with Clarissa, she will be changed into a sensual woman. He persists in this plan until he sees that she is practically dead. Like Clarissa, a spiritual reformer, Lovelace wishes her to become what all women are fundamentally, sexual. Clarissa has similarly violent and transformative impulses toward Lovelace, again involving reformation about which I will talk at length later.

For all the verbiage in this novel, for all the endless elaborations of matters of the social code, of the minute distinctions of punctilio, Richardson manages to create a drama of what Henry James would call that which is "hideously behind." For a very long novel, *Clarissa* is taut with struggle and tension—if it were not so, no one would now read the book. This struggle is realized almost wholly through the body, one might say through the gut, of a woman. The drama centers around one physical fact and one physical event, virginity on the one hand, and rape on the other. We have to understand, I think, the significance of virginity for Richardson. If we do not, we will have to see this as a silly story of its loss, merely as an economic setback, since it lowers her value on the marriage market. Virginity means integrity; it means wholeness of mind and of spirit. It is as much a state of mind as it is a physical state. Richardson's over-emphasis of this element is directly related to his fears about the body. A woman is a perfect stand-in for a neurotic fear about the author's wholeness, just as a physical fact.

Virginity is a state of mind in which the body is imagined as completely intact and closed. This is a state that Richardson celebrates. On the other hand, he is obsessed with the fear of violation, of being penetrated and as a result losing consciousness. A number of critics have noted this persistent obsession, this feeling that Clarissa is a lamb being prepared for the sacrifice.[28] In her incoherent letter to Lovelace after the rape she says, " 'O Lovelace! if you could be sorry for yourself, I would be sorry too—but when all my doors are fast, and nothing but the keyhole open, and the key of late put into that, to be where you are, in a manner without opening any of them —O wretched, wretched Clarissa Harlowe!' " (Vol. 3, pp. 210-11) Lovelace has opened the door of her body when she was drugged—he has penetrated her without her knowledge. Rape means physical invasion, knowledge without acquiescence.

The wholeness of body that he realizes through Clarissa, Richardson reverses in Lovelace. The villain is the principle of excess, superfluity, abundance, even generosity—hence overflow. Richardson sees him as continuously ready to expand, even to explode. The perennially retiring behavior of Clarissa contrasts sharply with the figure of the man throwing open his cloak, falling upon his knees, bearing the scars on his arm. Lovelace's moments of restraint (however rare they are) are pictured as the withholding of some physical force. The long, strange exhortations to his friend about not assaulting the country girl whom he calls Rosebud are a case in point: "O Jack! spare thou therefore (for I shall leave thee often alone with her, spare thou) my Rosebud!. . . Unsuspicious of her danger, the lamb's throat will hardly shun thy knife! O be not thou the butcher of my lambkin!" (Vol. 1, p. 171). Thus Richardson imagines the male principle, graphically, biologically, as the central impulse in Lovelace. The conflict between the two is highly sexualized because Richardson imagines it as a struggle between two male and female bodies. For our purposes it is important to recognize that Richardson imagines himself in the position of the female body. His own sense of physical vulnerability is at the heart of his taking on the role of a woman being raped almost from start to finish in the novel. Even in this aspect of the book Lovelace appears as a schematic formulation, while Clarissa's is the fully explored, fully realized consciousness.

Clarissa as a novel is certainly a drama of conquest. The drama centers around a number of people trying to force violation upon Clarissa, trying to force her to marry someone she does not love.

Daniel Defoe had some interesting remarks on the battle for control being waged by parents who try to force their children to marry:

> . . . if the Parent commands his Child to marry such or such a Person, and the child either cannot love the Person, or at the same time declares he or she is engaged in Affection to another, the Command of the Parent cannot lawfully be obeyed, because it is unlawful for the Child to marry any Person he or she cannot love. . . .[29]

To do so is to enforce an act of violence, it is "a Rape upon the Mind; her Soul, her brightest Faculties, her Will, her Affections are ravished. . . .[30] We tend to forget, I think, that the contest here is also decidedly parental, and that there is real violence attempted in the plots, strategems of a family that wishes to marry off Clarissa to the odious Solmes in order to improve its economic position. While this sort of conflict is common enough in other eighteenth-century novels (In *Tom Jones* Squire Western thinks little of fobbing off poor Mr. Blifil onto Sophia, although it is impossible to imagine that he would persist in this effort), it is in *Clarissa* clearly overdetermined, in the Freudian sense. There are a number of choices, of compromises open to all concerned parties, but none is ever taken. Like everything else that happens in the book, this is a conflict beyond the realities of the situation. Force is being applied against the will of Clarissa, and she is offering a counterforce. It is a contest beyond the facts or issues, beyond personalities; it is a sort of war of the wills. In this sense Richardson and Defoe interest themselves in a similar realm of feeling, that of protagonists agonizingly seeking power over all the opposition forces in the world of the novel.

What about Lovelace? He obviously is a figure obsessively concerned with dominance and control. In the first place he is richer than everyone else in the novel and his economic superiority, in a world so concerned with possessions, is undisputed. Lovelace is physically in control of the situation. He grabs Clarissa, and off they go. Henceforward he becomes her jailer; he watches her every movement. Richardson creates very strongly the feeling of being watched, being imprisoned (through Clarissa's eyes), and Lovelace is the watcher—he is more powerful than she—in his body. His physical strength is also evident in the games he plays—those of disguise and drama. I do not think we need to belabor Lovelace's interest in conquest and domination, except to point out its dimensions, for these dimensions are explored even more fully in Clarissa. It is important to understand the extent to which Lovelace and Clarissa share this obsession. Lovelace has the wit to say that he is no sensual man, and certainly his depredations against the body of Clarissa have little to do with sexuality as we would define it. Richardson gives Lovelace innumerable speeches, charged with the rhetoric of the evil genie, that are meant to pass for sexual interest:

> All my fear arises from the little hold I have in the heart of this charming frost-piece: such a constant glow upon her lovely features: eyes so sparkling: limbs so divinely turned: health so florid: youth so blooming: air so animated—to have an heart so impenetrable: and *I*, the hitherto successful Lovelace, the addresser—how can it be? Yet there are people, and I have talked with some of them, who remember that she was *born*. (Vol. 1, p. 148)

Here Lovelace is really a sort of set-piece, meant, I think, to express certain attitudes, but in any case the feeling here could hardly be described as erotic. She is really just a sort of wax doll for Lovelace, and his sexual feeling is a way of getting possession of her. Rape for him is a form of thievery, and he says in remembering the act; ". . . my *light*, my momentary ecstasy [villainous burglar, felon, thief, that I was!] " (Vol. 4, p. 263).

In a very strange letter Lovelace pictures his conscience taking control of him, and conscience here is a thinly-veiled Clarissa:

> While I was meditating a simple robbery, here have I (in my own defense indeed) been guilty of murder! A bloody murder! So I believe it will prove. At her last gasp! Poor impertinent opposer! Eternally resisting! Eternally contradicting! There she lies, weltering in her blood! Her death's wound have I given her! But she was a thief, an imposter, as well as a tormentor. She had stolen my pen.

[He goes on]

> Thus far had my *conscience* written with my pen; and see what a recreant she had made me! I seized her by the throat—*There!*—*There*, said I, thou vile impertinent! Take *that*, and *that*! How often have I given thee warning! And now, I hope, thou intruding varletress have I

done thy business!

> Lie there! Welter on! Had I not given thee thy death's wound, thou wouldst have robbed me of all my joys. Thou couldst not have mended me, 'tis plain. Thou couldst only have thrown me into despair. Didst thou not see that I had gone too far to recede? Welter on once more I bid thee! Gasp on! *That* thy last gasp, surely! How hard diest thou! (Vol. 3, pp. 145-47)

Even given the silly rhetorical flourishes of the arch villain, Richardson wants us to feel in Lovelace (and he surely wants us to feel this almost too much) his ability to inflict death, if he wills it. Much has been made of the fact that Clarissa sees rape and death as synonymous, but so does Lovelace.

No matter how dramatically Richardson tries to present Lovelace, he is, after all, merely a foil, a force against which the central female consciousness of the novel is meant to react. I want to consider instead how Richardson explores through his *female* voice what it would be like to control the world. The kind of power that Richardson envisions through Clarissa is total, it is omnipotence, and I do not think that I exaggerate. When he writes as a woman Defoe seems frightened of the results—he has to jump away from what he is saying. Richardson seems to invest himself completely in Clarissa— she is the good, the beautiful, the superior, the pure. She decides on the morality of others, and when they are bad she transforms them into the good. What would it be like to shape the world, according to one's own will? This is the role Richardson tries on when he writes as a woman.

I talked briefly about the matter of changing narrative form in the first chapter, but I would like to reiterate the extent to which Clarissa is the central narrative voice and the extent to which this itself is an element of her domination. Though there are a number of other voices who write letters in the novel, they act in the main to redefine the personality of the central speaker. In her own letters Clarissa focuses sharply on herself, on the implications of her own actions. Everyone else in the novel directs his or her letters to questions of Clarissa's behavior also. What does it mean? How should it be changed? How might she do better? Other speakers repeatedly reflect back for us the voice of Clarissa—they respond in writing to the central question of the book: what is Clarissa's true nature? Clarissa's behavior is really the sole topic of conversation. Roxana's narrative is open-ended, devoid of any modifying force, and the "I" seems to speak directly to the reader. Defoe seems to ask, "If I were looking through a window at the world as Roxana, what would the world be like?" In the epistolary novel someone is always being spoken to. The "I" is repeated through the implied presence and then the questioning of others. However, there is still one speaker who sets the terms and provides the substance of this discourse—and she is Clarissa.

In the letters of those who are not Clarissa, the central female speaker is held up as an object of contemplation. Clarissa then responds to people watching her think and act. As a result the narrative takes on an obsessional quality, since we are concerned with an endless series of people watching her, and then again her watching herself. The kind of concentration, narrative focus I should say, is much more extreme than that which Defoe manages, and this focus supplies the energy needed to impel an otherwise tedious form. Having structured his novel this way (and looking at another epistolary novelist like Fanny Burney shows us that it does not have to be so obsessional) as a long meditation on the nature of Clarissa, we can see how form here becomes very much part of her perceived strength. Her consciousness is the normative one. It provides the source of all "activity," all thought in the novel.

Clarissa's formal dominance of the narrative is emphasized in Richardson's *Hints to a Preface* of the novel. Here he states that she is the heroine of a Christian tragedy, and her conduct should be imitated by other young ladies. His aim is to "exalt the Sex," whereas in matters of virtue, women "are thought too meanly of, and depreciated."[31] He articulates here quite clearly the nature of the struggle that she must undergo:

> He has made his Heroine pass thro' many Persecutions from her Friends, and ardent Trials from her Lover; yet in the first to keep her Duty in her Eye, and in the latter to be proof against the most insidious Arts, Devices, and Machinations of a Man, who holds, as Parts of the Rake's Credenda, these two Libertine Maxims; That no Woman can resist Opportunity and Importunity, especially when attacked by a Man she

loves; and, That, when once subdued, she is always subdued; and who sets out with a Presumption, that in the Conquest of such a Lady he shall triumph over the whole Sex, against which he had vowed Revenge for having been used ill, as he thought, by one of it.[32]

Like Chaucer's patient Griselda, she is being tried in affliction by a man, and it is a contest that she wins:

> The Lady's Sufferings and Distresses are unequalled. Like pure Gold, tried by the Fire of Afliction, she is found pure. She preserves her Will inviolate, her Sincerity unimpeachable, her Duty to those who do not theirs by her, intire—Is patient, serene, resigned; and, form the best Motives, aspires to a World more worthy of her, than that she longs to quit.[33]

Through her Richardson endeavors to recommend what he calls the Christian system and her triumph within it.

This conception of her character as a model explains much of the verbosity of the novel, as long passages are given over, either by her or by others, to forms of behavior that should be imitated by young ladies. It makes clear also that she is to be perceived by the reader as the central, normative consciousness. In avowing his championship of her cause, Richardson articulates his loyalties from the first. And he also labels an important element in her domination over others; she is good. In one of Pamela's rare, interesting moments, she comments on the power of virtue: "O! What a godlike power is that of doing good! I envy the rich and the great for nothing else" (Vol. 1, p. 279). A godlike power indeed, as Richardson explores through Clarissa mental, physical, and spiritual domination over others.

I want to return at this point to the element of metamorphosis. Change is the great fear for Richardson, and it is change imagined through the body. For this author the body and the self are indissolubly connected. Through Clarissa, Richardson makes an insistent effort to imagine oneself beyond change. Through closure of oneself (emotional and physical), through containment of the passions of others, one can achieve wholeness, what Richardson would call integrity. It is finally integrity of self, imagined at the physical and spiritual level, that will triumph over people and over time. This triumph is accomplished at tremendous cost, however, and that is death. Clarissa is an exploration of an inordinately powerful state of consciousness. It will not do to see all the aggressions against her as particularly real, for as many have pointed out, no real situation like this could have continued very long. These are trials of the will, as Richardson himself stated in his *Hints to a Preface*. We have to understand that these trials are lived out over and over again in the mind of Clarissa. She is obsessed with dominance, distance, controlling herself, controlling others. Richardson has Lovelace comment on the female love for sexual intrigue:

> But the sex love busy scenes. Still-life is their aversion. A woman will *create* a storm, rather than be without one. So as they can preside in the whirlwind, and direct it, they are happy. But my beloved's misfortune is, that she must live in tumults; yet neither raise them herself, nor be able to control them. (Vol. 3, p. 106)

Lovelace here puts Clarissa at the center of chaos. Surely the world of this novel, for all the insistence of decorum, is a violent one. Passions are for the most part out of control. Richardson sees the social realm as a thinly veiled contest for survival of the most profound sort and chooses the voice of Clarissa as the vehicle for an attempt at its control.

The significance of the rape for Clarissa tells us crucial information about why Richardson adopts the role of a woman. The fact of virginity is a convenient shorthand for intactness of self. It is meant to stand as a sign of wholeness. In one of the many scenes in which she rails at her captor, she says: "Cheated out of myself from the very first! A fugitive from my own family! Renounced by my relations! Insulted by you! Laying humble claim to the protection of yours!" (Vol. 3, p. 135). His aggressions are designed to get at her *self*, rather than the more tangible elements of family or even revenge. When she relates the rape to Miss Howe, the incident is figured in terms of loss of self:

> O MY DEAREST MISS HOWE!—Once more have I escaped—but, alas! *I*, my *best self*, have *not* escaped! Oh, your poor Clarissa Harlowe! *You* also will hate me, I fear! Yet you won't, when you know all!

But no more of my self! My *lost* self. You that can rise n the morning to be blessed, and to bless; and go to rest delighted with your own reflections, and in your unbroken, unstarting slumbers, conversing with saints and angels, and the former only more pure than yourself, as they have shaken off the encumbrance of body; YOU shall be my subject, as you have long, long been my only pleasure. And let me, at awful distance, revere my beloved Anna Howe, and in *her* reflect upon what her Clarissa Harlowe once was!

O my best, my dearest, my *only* friend! What a tale have I to unfold! But still upon *self*, this vile, this hated *self*! I will shake it off, if possible; and why should I not, since I think, except one wretch, I hate nothing so much? Self, then, be banished from *self* one moment (for I doubt it *will* for no longer), to inquire after a *dearer* object, my beloved Anne Howe!—whose mind, all robed in spotless white, charms and irradiates—. but what would I say? . . . (Vol. 3, p. 321)

The self aspires to absolute ascendancy and integrity. The threat involves, on either side, the taking away of the self by another.

Not only is Clarissa engaged in trying to control those around her, but she is also out to reform Lovelace, to change him into something else. Probably the most obvious form of control that Clarissa exerts is that of language. As I said earlier the very form of the novel (letters that repeat, in slightly altered form, Clarissa's words and acts) makes her language the central form of discourse. That is, her view of events is always uppermost in our minds: "For what are *words*, but the *body* and *dress* of *thought*? And is not the mind strongly indicated by its outward dress?" (Vol. 2, p. 226). What kind of mind does the heroine display in her letters? In her first letter, she writes to Anna Howe:

How you oppress me, my dearest friend, with your politeness! I cannot doubt your sincerity; but you should take care that you give me not reason from your kind partiality to call in question your judgment. You do not distinguish that I take many admirable hints from you, and have the art to pass them upon you for my own. For in all you do, in all you say, nay, in your very looks (so animated!) you give lessons to one who loves you and observes you as I love and observe you, without knowing that you do—so pray, my dear, be more sparing of your praise for the future, lest after this confession we should suspect that you secretly intend to praise yourself while you would be thought only to commend another. (Vol. 1, p. 3)

Stylistically she is a hopeless prig. What is she saying? Do not praise me so much; it sounds as if you are praising yourself. Here she gingerly steps around or perhaps on the ego of another person. Her friend must take care, must use good sense, must not let herself be suspect in any of her motives, and must above all observe the wishes of Clarissa. Clarissa always sounds as if she is a victim of verbal constipation. Rarely addressing an issue directly, rarely saying what she means, we can see her here drawing into her own frame of reference acts performed by others. She is the measurer, the judge. She gives the world her shape, her color, her will. It is interesting the way the will of the two girls becomes confused in this letter. One cannot really tell when Clarissa and her friend are to be separated. How can we wonder at Richardson's lament that everyone preferred Lovelace over Clarissa? While Lovelace speaks in tones of naked (to risk *double-entendre*) aggression, Clarissa's controlling temperament masquerades as small corrections, quibbles, slight hints, anything but what they are, the shaping of another person's behavior. Lovelace's instrument is the sword, and as Richardson was fond of saying, Clarissa wields the proper feminine instrument, the pen.

This power of words that everyone in the novel remarks upon is what keeps her separated from her family during a good part of her trials. We are asked to believe that her manipulations of language will lead to their relenting; therefore she has actually to be sequestered. Clarissa explains her not being able to plead before them; "I depended, they said, upon *Their* indulgence, and my *own power* over them: they would not have banished me from their presence if they had not known that their consideration for *me* was greater than mine for *them*. And they *would* be obeyed, or I never should be restored to their favour, let the consequence be what it would" (Vol. 1, p. 193). Clarissa's use of words is thus part of her character; it is recognized as a significant talent by others in the novel, and it is also central to her control.

If we were to subject her letters to a comprehensive analysis of the kind that Stanley Fish recommends and applies to useful purpose in his reading of Milton, we would come to the conclusion that control and its loss are their primary dynamic.[34] It would be impossible, in a work of so many words, to do for *Clarissa* what one may do for a poem. But there is a characteristic speech pattern that manifests itself over and over again, enough so that without being linguistically rigorous, we can still isolate a predominant movement or direction, if you will, in the way she speaks. To her brother, who is trying to force her to marry Solmes:

> Let me take the liberty further to observe, that the principal end of a young man's education at the university is to learn him to reason justly, and to subdue the violence of his passions. I hope, brother, that you will not give room for anybody who knows us both, to conclude that the toilette has taught the *one* more of the latter doctrine, than the university has taught the *other*. I am truly sorry to have cause to say that I have heard it often remarked, that your uncontrolled passions are not a credit to your liberal education. (Vol. 1, p. 138)

On the one hand, "the principal end," "to learn him," "taught," "conclude;" on the other, "give room," "take the liberty," "uncontrolled passions." Granted, the situation itself generates such talk; force is always being applied against her to do something, but the way she talks about the situation at the very basic level involves control and its loss. Hers is the language of containment, repression, relearning and its opposite—anarchy.

Her second predominant linguistic trait is her concern for position. She is frequently searching out her own location in a hierarchy of closeness. Let me illustrate. When Lovelace first proposes to her, she says:

> Would he have had me catch at his first, at his *very* first word? I was *silent* too—and do not the bold sex take silence for a mark of favour? Then, *so lately* in my father's house! Having also declared to him in my letters, before I had your advice, that I would not think of marriage till he had passed through a state of probation, as I may call it. How was it possible I could encourage, with *very* ready signs of approbation, such an early proposal? Especially so soon after the free treatment he had provoked from me. If I were to die, I could not. (Vol. 2, pp. 28-29)

The motions in the language are almost physical. She will move closer, she will back away. These movements are themselves an indication of her control or lack of it in any situation. And of course as she moves between withdrawal and affirmation, she implies internal stress around her own physical location and creates doubts in others about her intentions.

Her own concern is mirrored, though in a different direction, in the speech of Lovelace. He is of course obsessed with subduing her, and whenever he exults in his own powers, he sees himself growing taller:

> How it swells my pride to have been able to outwit such a vigilant charmer! I am taller by half a yard in my imagination than I was. I look *down* upon everybody now. Last night I was still more extravagant. I took off my hat as I walked, to see if the lace were not scorched, supposing it had brushed down a star; and, before I put it on again, in mere wantoness, and heart's ease, I was for buffeting the moon. (Vol. 1, p. 515)

This comparison is particularly inviting. On a biological level we can again see these two as sexual opponents—one obviously phallic, the other (is there a word for it?) vaginal. At any rate, concern for position vis-a-vis others is central to the speech patterns of both male and female.

There is another physical component to Clarissa's strength, and it is that of withdrawal. In protesting her separation from her parents to her sister Bella, she says, "I will claim the protection due to a child of the family, or to know why I am to be thus treated, when I offer only to preserve to myself the liberty of *refusal*, which belongs to my sex. . ." (Vol. 1, pp. 226-27). One primary manifestation of her power is in her determined *no* in the face of a series of opposing forces. Richardson adopts the female voice in order to allow this power of negation and denial to be fully expressed. Others are cast in the role of trying to control her, but actually she controls them through a determined lack of mobility—she will not move.

When she does move, it is to move away. Clarissa cannot

really stand strong emotion, and she is always retiring to her closet or in general hiding herself away. Recrimination usually brings on faintness and so does conflict of most kinds. This tendency to withdraw cuts off every conversation midstream and leaves people in the middle of strong feelings with no way of expressing them. Her imprisonment in Mrs. Sinclair's house becomes merely a second stage in her withdrawal and does not, in the text, give the feeling that life has changed much for her. She has in fact been imprisoned since the early pages of the novel. Now she simply *must* retire. The great ceremony surrounding the ordering of the casket simply gives her a smaller closet in which to be imprisoned. Though she is the central figure in the drama, she is often not present to witness the consequences of what she says or does.

> "Oh, that I could say—that it were in my *power* to say—I never will see thee more! Would to Heavens I never were to see thee more!
>
> I speak, though with vehemence, the deliberate wish of my heart. Oh, that I could avoid *looking down* upon thee, mean groveller, and abject as insulting! Let me withdraw! My soul is in tumults! Let me withdraw!" (Vol. 3, p. 261)

To be absent is to be safe, to be whole. She cannot stand the conflicts that she creates, and she is best off incarcerated.

These elements completely interweave the text and make themselves felt as the meaning of Clarissa's world. She also derives an immense amount of strength from a view of herself as morally superior. As Cynthia Griffin Woolf puts it; ". . . she cannot be 'good'; she can only be 'better than.' "[35] The problem for Richardson is one of presenting the strength of a sex that in his view does not normally display it adequately. Lovelace offers the view that Clarissa is being torn apart by internal contradictions. Her strength of will wars with the female side of her, with a female weakness:

> Yet what a contradition! *Weakness of heart*, says she, with *such a strength of will*. O Belford! she is a iron-hearted lady, in every case where her honour, her punctilio rather, calls for spirit. But I have had reason more than once in her case, to conclude that the passions of the gentlest, slower to be moved than those of the quick, are the most flaming, the

most irresistible, when raised. Yet her charming body is not equally organized. The unequal partners pull two ways; and the divinity within her tears her silken frame. But had the same soul informed a masculine body, never would there have been a truer hero. (Vol. 2, p. 384)

Her undisputed spiritual superiority is undermined by her sex. Richardson asserts that Clarissa has a special vision of herself; it is one of moral, intellectual, and emotional superiority. The source of this strength is in large measure the wish to overcome the inherent weakened position of being a woman. When Clarissa says "I am afraid I shall not be thought worthy" (Vol. 1, p. 221), she is showing loyalty to her own standards, and very exacting ones they are indeed. Clarissa aspires to sainthood, the first in a long line of novelistic Saint Theresas. Richardson envisions the search for this status as demanding, as a form of hunger, as tortured as that which impels the most driven Renaissance overreacher. The rape is meant to show that at least on earth she will not be able to maintain control, primarily because of physical weakness. She is, as she herself says, punished for the vanity of wanting to be an example to her sex. But, as we shall see later, in her dying is Richardson's final ascription of omnipotence. *He* has the vanity to show her as an example to her sex.

In the struggle for control waged between Lovelace and Clarissa, the conditions for victory become clear. Richardson sees Clarissa as having to transform herself, draw herself out of her own nature, remake herself in order to triumph. In her ravings after the rape Clarissa jots down her thoughts and particularly noteworthy is her parable of the lady and the wild beast: "She fed it with her own hand: she nursed up the wicked cub with great tenderness; and would play with it without fear or apprehension of danger: and it was obedient to all her commands. . ." (Vol. 3, p. 206). This creature turns and tears her apart. The parable of course mirrors the situation with Lovelace, and it also shows the kind of control that interests her. Clarissa is to be the mother, the nurturer, to be obeyed. But then comes the question of who acts unnaturally: "For what *she* did was *out* of nature, *out* of character, at least: what it did was *in* its own nature" (Vol. 3, p. 206). As mother to the wild beast ("a reformed rake does not make the best husband") she calls herself unnatural. The beast is inherently destructive, but the lady should have bowed before the essential wildness of the male. The violence of her urge to reform Lovelace is destructive—Richardson sees her as more appropriately transforming herself, forging her warring elements into wholeness.

From the very beginning of the novel Richardson sees relations between the sexes as having little to do with love. When Richardson allows Clarissa to say in volume two of the novel, "Love, sir! who talks of *love*? . . . Have I ever professed, have I ever required of *you* professions of a passion of that nature?" (Vol. 2, p. 301), he is speaking to a view that Moll or Roxana would have subscribed to. The two founders of the English novel are unconcerned with anything approaching nineteenth century notions of love. Even that paragon of virtue, Sir Charles Grandison, sees relations between the sexes as fraught with difficulty:

> Most young women, who begin a correspondence with our designing sex, think they can stop when they will. But it is not so. We, and the dark spirit that sets us at work, which we sometimes miscall love, will not permit you to do so. Men and women are devils to one another. They need no other tempter.[36]

To be involved with men at all is for Richardson a dangerous compromise.

From the outset the choice of a man for Clarissa has involved, in her mind, the problem of domination, or more specifically loss of control:

> Let me assure you [Anna Howe], that if I see anything in Mr. Lovelace that looks like a design to humble me, his insolence shall never make me discover a weakness unworthy of a person distinguished by your friendship, that is to say, unworthy either of my sex or of my *former self*. (Vol. 2, p 45)

Most of her family's subsequent opposition derives from her refusal to allow herself to look bad. For instance, why not draw Solmes in by being friendly, creating an ally, and then getting him to leave off or try her sister? Such activities would of course be compromising and Richardson would have it that Clarissa chooses death over any loss of face.

The contest of wills is to lead to marriage, in which the author sees women coming under the fearful power of male sexuality:

> At *every* age on this side of matrimony (for then we come under another sort of protection, though that is far from abrogating the filial duty) it will be found that the wings of our parents are most necessary and most effectual safeguard from the vultures, the hawks, the kites, and other villainous birds of prey that hover over us with a view to seize and destroy us the first time we are caught wandering out of the eye or care of our watchful and natural guardians and protectors. (Vol. 2, p. 125)

Even in marriage male predators inspire fear in the hearts of their wives. After the rape she wonders "who now shall provide the nuptial ornaments, which soften and divert the apprehensions of the fearful virgin?" (Vol. 3, p. 207). Charlotte Grandison comments (and a good woman here marries a good man) that "After all, Lady L--, we women, dressed out in ribands, and in gaudy trappings, and in virgin-white, on our wedding days, seem but like milk-white heifers led to sacrifice" (*Sir Charles Grandison*, Vol. 5, p. 337). Richardson pictures marriage as extremely dangerous, both for the loss of control that it entails, and also because loss of virginity and submission to the sexual male involve loss of self. For women love and marriage are synonymous with debasement. Clarissa says, "he is for breaking my spirit *before* I am his; and while I am, ought to be [Oh, my folly, that I am not!], in my own power" (Vol. 2, p. 277).

Once again the problem of domination (imagined now as a physical event) becomes one of spiritual thievery. It is an invasion of the soul as well as of the body. Clarissa thinks that she can control this beast and attempts to do so through reforming Lovelace. In this attempt, at least on earth, Richardson shows her to be doomed to failure. All her complaints about his breaking her spirit have to be understood in connection with her own attempts. She will try to make him into a good man. As her mortifications increase she sees herself "above temptation from his sex," "for I have vanity to think my soul his soul's superior." "Let me wrap myself about in the mantel of my own integrity, and take comfort in my unfaulty intention!" (Vol. 2, pp. 167-68). Richardson very clearly agrees with her; she is better than everyone else, but she is going to have to prove it another way.

I quoted earlier Clarissa's dreams after the rape of the beast and the lady, and it is clear from these that she fancies herself the moral mother. It is primarily the passions that impel us forward—self-control is essential to reformation:

> The first step to reformation, as I conceive, is to subdue sudden gusts of passion, from which frequently the greatest evils arise, and to learn to bear disappointments. If the irascible passions cannot be overcome, what opinion can we have of the person's power over those to which bad habit, joined to *greater* temptation, gives stronger force? (Vol. 1, p. 326)

Clarissa has herself been guilty of a failure of *self*-control in even engaging in a correspondence with Lovelace:

> You know, my dear, that your Clarissa's mind was ever above justifying her own failings by those of others. God forgive those of my friends who have acted cruelly by me! But their faults *are* their own, and not excuses for mine. And mine began early: for I ought not to have corresponded with him.

> O the vile encroacher! how my indignation, at times, rises at him! Thus to lead a young creature (too much indeed relying upon her own strength) from evil to evil! This last evil, although the *remote* yet *sure* consequence of my first-my prohibited correspondence! by my father *early* prohibited.

>   .   .   .   .

> I supposed it concerned *me, more than any other, to be the arbitress of the quarrels of unruly spirits*—punished, as other sins frequently are, by *itself*! (Vol. 1, p. 486)

Richardson never stopped telling his numerous female correspondents that to engage even in writing to a man posed a threat. Clarissa must learn to subdue her own passions, for they have led her into her predicament. She counsels Anna Howe on the subject:

> Learn, my dear, I beseech you learn, to subdue your own passions. Be the motives what they will, excess is excess. Those passions in our sex which we take no pains to subdue, may have one and the same source with those infinitely blacker passions which we used so often to condemn in the violent headstrong of the other sex; and which may be only heightened in *them* by *custom*, and their *freer education*. Let us both, my dear, ponder well this thought; look into ourselves, and fear. (Vol. 2, p. 236)

Clarissa's own attempts at reform have a more suspect source; she herself has a reserve of passion. Richardson implies that Clarissa has let herself be betrayed by a physical attraction. As Dorothy Van Ghent has pointed out, she has a lively sense of Solmes's body, especially when she sits in a chair he has just vacated.[37] To her mother Clarissa comments, "Dearest Madam, forgive me: it was always my pride and my pleasure to obey you. But look upon that man—see but the disagreeableness of his person" (Vol. 1, p. 73). Physical appeal means something to her, or why would she prefer Lovelace? She likes him better than she "ought" to like him, and to Anna Howe confesses: "In a word, I will frankly own (since you cannot think anything I say too explicit) that were he *now* but a moral man, I would prefer him to all the men I ever saw" (Vol. 1, p. 203). But what is there to prefer about Lovelace—his wit, his charm, and what is decorously called his person? Even while he is contemplating the rape she is acknowledging all of his appealing characteristics, despite the bad company he keeps, "For he has, besides, an open, and, I think, an honest countenance" (Vol. 2, p. 230). She later laments "That had not my foolish eye been too much attached, I had not taken the pains to attempt, so officiously as I did, the prevention of mischief between him and some of my family. . ." (Vol. 2, p. 277).

Richardson pictures here the greatest threat to her security, her own sexual feelings for Lovelace. When I say sexual, I use the term cautiously. For Richardson even to admit to such feelings at all makes his heroine extremely vulnerable to attack. The most direct way we have access to her feelings is through the stabbing and ripping imagery she associates with sex. In another dream:

> Methought my brother, my Uncle Antony, and Mr. Solmes, had formed a plot to destroy Mr. Lovelace; who discovering it, and believing I had a hand in it, turned all his rage against me. I thought he made them all fly into foreign parts upon it; and afterwards seizing upon me, carried me into a churchyard; and there, notwithstanding all my prayers and tears, and protestations of innocence, stabbed me to the heart, and then tumbled me into a deep grave ready dug, among two or three half-dissolved carcasses; throwing in the dirt and earth upon me with his hands, and trampling it down with his feet. (Vol. 1, p. 433)

These fears lead her to shrink from physical contact of any kind and show also that such contact will inevitably lead to sex. Thus Richardson places her in a pronounced sexual milieu while she appears to fear sex to the point of terror. During the fire scene in volume two she assumes that when Lovelace comes to sit on the bed he has come to rape her. I am going to discuss this scene at length in chapter four, and so I will only say here that we are treated in her to constant cerebral violation. Her deepest fears are of physical penetration leading to a violation of her spirit.

I should repeat that Clarissa and Lovelace share the view that sex is potentially death-dealing. Pondering a number of projected sexual adventures, Lovelace always pictures them as the giving or taking away of life. In *Fanny Hill*, also a first-person narrative written from the point of view of a woman, that hearty eighteenth century writer John Cleland ascribes fantastic sexual powers to the male.[38] Defloration becomes a horrendous event surrounded by a great deal of blood and pain. The male organ is everywhere referred to as a weapon, a sword which is being rather frequently unsheathed. Fanny confesses to Phoebe that the size of the penis appears "at least to my fearful imagination, less than my wrist, and at least three of my handfuls long, to that of the small tender part of me which was framed to receive it, I could not conceive its being possible to afford its entrance without dying, perhaps in the greatest pain. . . ."[39] The first sexual experience is likened very much (as it is in *Sir Charles Grandison*) to a kind of blood sacrifice. As Fanny loses her virginity to the beloved Charles, she says:

> At length, the tender texture of that tract giving way to such fierce
> tearing and rending, he pierced somewhat further into me: and now,
> outrageous and no longer his own master, but borne headlong away by
> the fury and over-mettle of that member, now exerting itself with a
> kind of native rage, he breaks in, carries all before him, and one violent
> merciless lunge sent it, imbrued and reeking with virgin blood, up to the
> very hilt in. (p. 59)

Thoughts of just this sort animate the lengthy volumes of *Clarissa*,
and I might add that Richardson constantly has his female speaker
refer to men as "the sex." In *Fanny Hill* "the sex" means the phallus
(as "the sex" when applied to women means the clitoris). The phys-
icality of the vision, in a supposed Christian tragedy, is striking.

By volume three of the novel Clarissa admits that what she
earlier had called a conditional liking was in fact love. To Captain
Tomlinson she says, "*If I had never valued him, he never would have
had it in his power to insult me . . .*" (Vol. 3, p. 137) The rape has
"Ruined me in my *own* eyes; and that is the same to me as if *all the
world* knew it!" (Vol. 3, p. 232). This love has been a form of torment but also now the vehicle for her triumph, the transformation
of both herself and others. The rape is only a momentary recognition of physical weakness, and it is also a setback for Clarissa in her
power struggle. She tells Mrs. Howe that she has begged God to
giver her a "truly broken spirit, if it be not already broken enough
. . ." (Vol. 3, p. 324). Clarissa's extraordinary meditation in volume
four (p. 140) shows that she sees herself in some particular destroyed by Lovelace. She has been "smitten . . . down to the ground,"
she is "withered like grass." Clearly then, she feels at least a part of
herself destroyed. Is it because her prospects for an economically
advantageous marriage have been ruined? Hardly, since she had
planned to live single. No, Clarissa feels shattered because she knows
herself guilty of a failure of control.

We here come to an extraordinary fantasy that the author
allows himself to indulge in as a woman. Clarissa's superiority is
affirmed by her disintegration and death. On the one hand Clarissa's
view of death is an old one, especially the picturing of herself as the

bride of Christ. She is, after all, the heroine of a Christian tragedy. But Richardson explores longing for death through her, and even more emphatically lives out through her the process of dying. This death takes up much of a volume and exacts the obeisance and submission of others. Even taking into account the popularity of graveyard poetry at the time, this rapturous longing is suspicious and frightening, even as contemplated by such opponents as Anna Howe and Lovelace.

Richardson never shrinks from the fact of physical dissolution—in fact he dwells upon it. The sight of her coffin, the thought of her lying in it—all call up visions of the awful disintegration of her body. But this rude violation is greeted with joy by Clarissa:

> . . .I shall be happy! I *know* I shall! I have charming forebodings of happiness already! Tell all my dear friends, for their comfort, that I shall! Who would not bear the punishments I have borne, to have the prospects and assurances I rejoice in! Assurances I might *not have had*, were my own wishes to have been granted to me! (Vol. 4, p. 301)

Undoubtedly a significant element in the joyous tone comes from the fact that through loss of mind and body she triumphs. But the fight over her heart and the argument over whether or not to embalm her are grotesque. And Richardson insists on lingering over her loss of consciousness. Clarissa loses the ability to write: "But I am very ill—I must drop my pen—a sudden faintness overspreads my heart. Excuse my crooked writing! Adieu, my dear! Adieu!" (Vol. 4, p. 200) Clarissa comes to herself a number of times, regains her old lucidity, but then Richardson treats us to scenes of lingering weakness and debility; "I must lay down my pen. I am very ill. I believe I shall be better by and by. The bad writing would betray me, although I had a mind to keep from you what the event must soon—" (Vol. 4, p. 273) And still she goes on and on barely at the edge of consciousness, still using the voice of the legal manageress. On her death bed she seems to die again and be revived: each breath is catalogued very carefully. At the same time that Richardson asserts that she is destined for a better place, that her spirit remains intact, he insists on her physical deterioration, on the death of the conscious self.

In the midst of this loss of consciousness, Richardson confirms her spiritual integrity and absolute superiority to every one around her. She points out that whatever has happened, her *"will too unviolated"* (Vol. 4, p. 59). To Dr. Leuwen Clarissa explains that the rape,

> . . . has not tainted my mind; it has not hurt my morals. No thanks indeed to my wicked man that it has not. No vile courses have followed it. My will is unviolated. The evil (respecting *myself*, and not my *friends*) is merely personal. No credulity, no weakness, no want of vigilance, have I to reproach myself with. I have, through grace, triumphed over the deepest machinations. I have escaped from him. I have renounced him. The man whom once I could have loved, I have been enabled to despise: and shall not *charity* complete my triumph? And shall I not *enjoy* it? And where would be my triumph if he *deserved* my forgiveness? Poor man! He has had a loss in losing me! I have the pride to think so, because I think I know my own heart. I have had none in losing him! (Vol. 4, pp. 185-186)

By maintaining her spiritual integrity she has triumphed over Lovelace. She has not managed to reform, but has *Transformed* him. In the last volume he alternates between skulking bravado, depression, and made peculiarity. Lovelace himself recognizes this and says, "A *jest,* I call all that has passed between her and me; a mere jest to die for—for has not her triumph over me, for first to last, been infinitely greater than her sufferings from me?" (Vol. 4, p. 261) It is inconceivable that he should turn into a Sir Charles Grandison; he instead becomes a cast-out wanderer who dies proclaiming the expiation of his crime. Clarissa reforms a number of others, Belford in particular. Anna Howe sees the light and will marry Hickman. Her whole family forgives her. While not specifically reformed, they are at least changed and many are the protestations at the end of the book as to Clarissa's good influence. Thus the last volume becomes a testament to her transformative power. She of course is not the least of her own converts. She signs her letters to Arabella as one "who NOW, made perfect (as she hopes) through sufferings, styles herself, The happy CLARISSA HARLOWE" (Vol. 4, p. 364).

There can be little doubt that Richardson sees death as his heroine's triumph. Through her he wants us first of all to learn how to die properly. Her death also is by no means unaccountable. Unlike popularized versions of Clarissa cast in a domesticated form, Richardson insists upon the cause of his heroine's demise. Rape is a violation so threatening that it does inevitably lead to death, as both Lovelace and Clarissa attest:

> I am persuaded, as much as that I am now alive, that I shall not long live. The strong sense I have ever had of my fault, the loss of my reputation, my disappointments, the determined resentment of my friends, *aiding* the barbarous usage I have met with where I least deserved it, have seized upon my heart: seized upon it, before it was so well fortified by *religious considerations* as I hope it now is. Don't be concerned, my dear. But I am sure, if I may say it with as little presumption as grief, that God will soon *dissolve my substance;* and *bring me to death, and to the house appointed for all the living.* (Vol. 3, pp. 522-523)

And so, of course, she triumphs. However, the cost is loss of substance, dissolution. It needs to be said, I think, that Clarissa is a frightening vision of woman. Richardson wants us to hear her triumphal cry: "*O Death! where is thy sting?*" (Vol. 4, p. 346) and believe that she is pleased to be losing consciousness. Her power is absolute, atemporal, and her posthumous letters graphically demonstrate that her influence will live on. Richardson makes inordinate claims for her; not only having the power to transform others, she has the power to transform herself—but this takes place within a context of self-destruction. She has been called so many times a mythic figure, but it must also be said that she is a very terrible one. We are asked to see her as an affirmation, but of what? The power of closure, rejection, death—and she is at its core.

Obviously everything I have said about Clarissa implies very little distance between herself and the voice of the author. Distance in the novel is provided to some extent by the other correspondents, all of whom comment on her in telling fashion. As the novel progresses, however, Richardson allows them to voice fewer criticisms and in the third and fourth volume she is affirmed as absolutely right and triumphant. Why does her creator picture a loss of consciousness at the moment of triumph—in fact dissolution of body and mind *as* a triumph? Probably because to imagine oneself, even if through the voice of a woman, beyond the social, psychological, and even temporal limitations given to other human beings, is a very frightening imaginative act. For this hypochondriacal little printer, whose face and form would excite Lady Bradshaigh rather to laughter than anything else, it must have been terrifying indeed. How lovingly does he imagine the punishment for this omnipotence, and how torturously does he see it enacted upon his heroine.

Notes

[1] Cynthia Griffin Woolf, *Samuel Richardson and the Eighteenth-Century Puritan Character* (Hamden, Conn.: Archon Books, 1972) p. 2.

[2] Leslie Fiedler, *Love and Death in the American Novel* (New York: Dell, 1966), p. 49.

[3] T. C. Duncan Eaves and Ben D. Kimpel, *Samuel Richardson, A Biography* (Oxford: the Clarendon Press, 1971) p. 425.

[4] *Ibid.*, p. 8.

[5] Samuel Richardson, *Pamela* (New York: Dutton, 1962), Vol. 1, p. 309. All subsequent references will be to this edition.

[6] Eaves and Kimpel, pp. 119-120.

[7] *Ibid.*, p. 120.

[8] *Ibid.*, p. 103.

[9] *Ibid.*, p. 391.

[10] *Ibid.*, p. 393.

[11] Fiedler, p. 51.

[12] Eaves and Kimpel, p. 252.

13Quoted from Eaves and Kimpel, p. 277.

14Samuel Richardson, *Clarissa or The History of a Young Lady* (New York: Dutton, 1962), Vol. 2, p. 384. All subsequent references will be to this edition.

15In a recent, provocative essay Judith Wilt labels many of Lovelace's dominant characteristics as "female." See "He Could Go No Farther: A Modest Proposal about Lovelace and Clarissa," PMLA, 92, No. 1 (January 1977), 19-32.

16Anna Laetitia Barbauld, *The Correspondence of Samuel Richardson* (London: Lewis and Nodem, 1904), Vol. 2, p. 94.

17*Correspondence*, Vol. 4, p. 233.

18*Correspondence*, Vol. 5, p. 265.

19*Correspondence*, Vol. 6, p. 59.

20*Correspondence*, Vol. 3, p. 248.

21*Selected Letters of Samuel Richardson*, ed. John Carroll (Oxford: The Clarendon Press, 1964), pp. 135-36.

22Eaves and Kimpel, p. 48.

23*The Letters of Doctor George Cheyne to Samuel Richardson* (1733-1743), University of Missouri Studies, 18, No. 1 (Columbia: University of Missouri, 1943), p. 61.

24*Ibid.*, p. 62.

25*Ibid.*, p. 83.

26*Ibid.*, p. 89.

27For an interesting discussion of Richardson's illnesses, see Elizabeth B. Brophy, *Samuel Richardson; The Triumph of Craft* (Knoxville: University of Tennessee Press, 1974), appendix A. She considers the illness not neurotic, but neurological, in fact, Parkinson's disease. Whatever the case, he felt ill, and persistently.

[28]See, for instance, Leo Braudy, "Penetration and Impenetrability in *Clarissa*." F68: 177-206.

[29]*Conjugal Lewdness*, p. 168.

[30]*Ibid.*, p. 198.

[31]Samuel Richardson, *Clarissa, Prefaces, Hints of Prefaces and Postscript* (The Augustan Reprint Society, Pub. No. 103, 1964), p. 1.

[32]*Ibid.*, p. 1.

[33]*Ibid.*, p. 1.

[34]Stanley Fish, *Surprised by Sin: The Reader in "Paradise Lost"* (New York: Saint Martin's Press), 1967.

[35]Cynthia Griffin Woolf, *Samuel Richardson and the Eighteen-Century Puritan Character*, p. 139.

[36]Samuel Richardson, *Sir Charles Grandison* (London: Chapman and Hall, 1902), Vol. 2, p. 327.

[37]Dorothy Van Ghent, *The English Novel: Form and Function* (New York: Harper & Row, 1953), p. 51.

[38]For a further comparison of *Clarissa* and *Fanny Hill* see Edward W. Copeland, "*Clarissa* and *Fanny Hill*: Sisters in Distress." SNNTS 4: 343-52.

[39]John Cleland, *Fanny Hill* (New York: Signet, 1965), p. 44.

Chapter 4

The Demands of Gender in the Nineteenth Century

To jump from the work of Samuel Richardson to that of Charles Dickens involves an interval of some one hundred years during which the use of the first-person narrative form in the novel, as well as the female voice, declined markedly. Margaret Anne Doody eloquently sums up the premises behind Richardson's *Clarissa*, a novel that says: "Interior life, the life of consciousness, is what matters above all."[1] His is an affirmation of the "superlative importance of the individual psychic life."[2] Novelists of the nineteenth century turned away from the intense psychological dramas of Defoe and Richardson to picture the social world in all its rich complexity. The social ills of Victorian England were so obvious and pressing that any image with redemptive possibilities (and there was no more handy image than that of a woman) was seized upon and exaggerated. As a result more specific social demands were made on the behavior of women, on the definition of femaleness itself, and on the female persona in the novel. These demands on what the artist could say as a woman were fed by a number of sources: from the tradition that *Clarissa* had initiated, both in England and on the continent, from the expanded reading public and hence the press for respectability in the novel (in part a result of evangelicalism), from the forces of Victorian repression, and from the influence of the number of women novelists who had begun to write.[3] Masculine identification with a woman is as old as time itself, but how openly that identification may be expressed is another matter. The gradual congealing of the image of the respectable young woman in Victorian England meant that those who chose a popular art form, with a now widened audience, had to keep careful watch over other narrative choices. It is hardly surprising that in such an atmosphere so few important novelists of the nineteenth century would create an implied autobiographical young woman.

One peculiarity of the female voice in the novel seems to be its burden of eroticism. Its use almost inevitably invites sexual imaginings, and this fact alone would prevent Victorian novelists from using it as a narrative tool. Richardson has often been accused of engaging in voyeurism, and Defoe certainly invites such criticisms in both *Moll Flanders* and *Roxana*. The spectacle of the male author using the female voice to express, even act out his sexual fantasies, is common enough in the eighteenth century to illustrate, for my purposes, the risky nature of writing as a woman in another, more squeamish age. It would seem that there is something inherently erotic about the disguise itself—women are more sexual creatures, they are defined by their biology in a way that men are not—hence to write as one involves the author in some recognition of the fact of sex.

Erotic literature has always made use of the female voice. It is ironic that the same few years should witness the publication of *Clarissa* (1747-48) and the publication of a classic of pornography, *Fanny Hill* (1748-49). These two novels contain a number of analogous scenes, especially as they depict female awe at the sexual male. Clarissa occasionally seems to faint almost at the very sight of Lovelace, as if he were the male organ, which in *Fanny Hill* also excites to faintness. There are a number of male display passages (when he shows her the scar on his arm for instance, or when he throws open his coat); these are meant to excite Clarissa through the force of the male presence. In *Fanny Hill* there are several keyhole sequences, as Fanny watches and revels in the sexual activities of others. We are treated to many forbidden glimpses of Clarissa at the house of Mrs. Sinclair—other keyholes at her house would presumably reveal scenes exactly like those we see in *Fanny Hill*, and that knowledge encourages the reader to pornographic imaginings.

Fanny Hill apparently loves sexual intercourse, is fascinated by bodies, and wants as much sex as she can get. After her initial fears, she delights in the male organ and is rapturous about this weapon, this sword, this standard, this maypole, this engine, this mountain, this machine. There are innumerable descriptions of the sizes, shapes, and colors of assorted members. She presents herself as equally fascinated with female genitals, although such descriptions are less precise and graphic than are those Cleland devotes to men:

> But what infinitely enriched and adorned them was the sweet inter-section formed, where they met, at the bottom of the smoothest, round-est, whitest belly, by that central furrow which nature had sunk there, between the soft relievo of two pouting ridges, and which in this girl was in perfect symmetry of delicacy and miniature with the rest of her frame. No! Nothing in nature could be of a beautifuller cut; than the dark umbrage of the downy springmoss that over-arched it bestowed, on the luxury of the landscape, a touching warmth, a tender finishing be-yond the expression of words, or even the paint of thought.[4]

We are here in a lovely eighteenth-century English garden. Female genitals are bowers or just bushes, or very often wounds. Sexual couplings, despite Fanny's apparent delight in them, are repeatedly characterized as forms of assault by the male. As in Clarissa, sexual imagery has its origins in the pastoral and the military.

Cleland does, I think, really glory in the human body, al-though there is much that, as Steven Marcus suggests, is repetitious and mechanical in the work, as in all pornography. According to Marcus, an extreme fascination with the male organ, the celebration of masculine sexual powers, is characteristic of a literature written almost exclusively by men for other men.[5] The power of male sex-uality in its effect on the mind and body of the heroine is endlessly extolled. Fanny sees first intercourse as a potentially death-dealing assault, and almost every act of intercourse observed through key-holes involves fainting or dying with ecstasy.

Relying on a number of elements from the conventional romance, Cleland has Fanny's career lead her ultimately back to her one true lover, Charles, the man who has taken her virginity and thus is first in her affections. But women do not fare so well at the hands of the implied authoress, her instructors in the pleasures of sex. The book displays a strong undercurrent of dislike for women; for in-stance, "Violent passions seldom last long, and those of women least of any" (*Fanny Hill*, p. 81). The machinations of Phoebe are roundly castigated and women are often shown as double-dealing—Fanny comments freely on their perfidy and untrustworthiness. The tale ends up by being rather a moral one, and near the close of Part One she purports to affirm a distinction between animal passion and true love:

> Yet oh! what an immense difference did I feel between this impression of a pleasure merely animal, and struck out of the collision of the sexes by a passive bodily effect, from that sweet fury, that rage of active delight which crowns the enjoyments of a mutual love passion, where two hearts, tenderly and truly united, club to exalt the joy, and give it a spirit and soul that bids defiance to that end which mere momentary desires generally terminate in, when they die of a surfeit and of satisfaction. (*Fanny Hill*, p. 85)

This, despite the fact that the book is a celebration of those very pleasures; merely animal indeed. Like Defoe, Cleland insists on the moral purposes to which her narrative is to be put, and he sees fit to change the tone markedly at the end of the second part, sounding more like Sir Charles Grandison than our insatiable little Fanny. Well aware that his readers might be startled, he says:

> You laugh, perhaps at this tail-piece of morality, extracted from me by the force of truth, resulting from comparing experiences: you think it, no doubt, out of character; possibly too you may look on it as the paltry finesse one who seeks to mask a devotee to Vice under a rag of a veil impudently smuggled from the shrine of Virtue: just as if one was to fancy one's self completely turning one's shoes into slippers; or, as if a writer should think to shield a treasonable libel, by concluding it with a formal prayer for the King. (*Fanny Hill*, pp. 219-220).

Most readers would say, "Oh come now, You protest too much." It is, however, something more than a tag; Cleland seems aware of the uses to which he has put the female voice and seems to be fearful about what he may have revealed of himself. Has his disguise been imperfect, he wonders.

Whatever Mr. Cleland's protestations, the book is clearly an occasion, an excuse for the author to imagine a variety of sexual pleasures. That he chooses the female voice is our main interest. One can hardly imagine this work presented to us through a male voice. Although Cleland shows men who do some of these things, they do not express them fully. The constant and total preoccupation with sex seems merely the distaff side of Clarissa's obsessive fears of men. In each case the author reflects back a male figure larger than life. Cleland seems positively enamored of such a figure; Richardson is terrified.

The kind of erotic invitation offered by the female voice should indicate why writing as a woman would pose problems for the novelists of the mid-nineteenth century. In an age so wedded to appearances of propriety an imaginative pose that might encourage an open confrontation with sex would almost of necessity be rejected. In addition, during the latter half of the eighteenth century a bitterly misogynistic tendency began to show itself in the English novel. If it had not been for Tristram Shandy's mother, who inquired about the winding of the clock, the homunculus might have developed into a less quirky lad. Sophia Western and Molly Seagrim are charmingly changeable in *Tom Jones* (1749). In *Amelia* (1751), Fielding indulges in bitter diatribes against the false face of woman. Alluding to the acting capabilities of Miss Matthews, he finds her; "a lady in whom we had remarked a most extraordinary power of displaying softness could, the very next moment after the words were out of her mouth, express sentiments becoming the lips of a Dalila, Jezebel, Medea, Semiramis . . . or any other heroine of the tender sex, which history, sacred or profane, ancient or modern, false or true, hath recorded."[6] Fielding has some really horrifying visions of a beautiful, sweet girl whose face can suddenly turn ugly and whose speech can become obscene and fearful. These feelings found release in the gothic fictions of writers like William Beckford and "Monk" Lewis—both of whom mixed a brew of disguise, torture, threatened rape, and threatened death with which to drench the heroine.

The most direct expression of this obscene hatred of women in late eighteenth century letters can be found, of course, in the writings of the Marquis de Sade, and I quote him here:

> "Now, what do I observe upon coolly proceeding to this investigation? A puny creature, always inferior to man, infinitely less attractive than he, less ingenious, less wise, constructed in a disgusting manner

entirely opposite to what is capable of pleasing a man, to what is able to delight him . . . a being three-quarters of her life untouchable, unwholesome, unable to satisfy her mate throughout the entire period Nature constrains her to childbearing, of a sharp turn of humor, shrill, shrewish, bitter, and thwart; a tyrant if you allow her privileges, mean, vile, and a sneak in bondage; always false, forever mischievous, constantly dangerous; in short, a being so perverse that during several convocations the question was very soberly agitated at the Coucil of Macon whether or not this peculiar creature, as distinct from man as is man from the ape, had any reasonably legitimate pretensions to classification as a human; but this quandary might be merely an error of the times; were women more favorably viewed in earlier ages? Did the Persians, the Medes, the Babylonians, the Greeks, the Romans honor this odious sex we are able to dare make our idol today? Alas! I see it oppressed everywhere, everywhere rigorously banished from affairs, contemned everywhere, vilified, sequestered, locked up; women treated, in a word, like beasts one stables in the barn and puts to use when the need arises. Do I pause a moment at Rome? then I hear the wise Cato exclaim from the heart of the ancient world's capital: 'Were women lacking to men they would yet hold conversation with the Gods.' I hear a Roman censor begin his harangue with these words: 'Gentlemen, were we ever to find a means to live without women, thereupon unto us should true happiness be known.' I hear the Greek theater resound to these lines intoned: 'O Zeus! what reason was it obliged thee to create women? couldst not have given being to humankind by better devices and wiser, by schemes which in a word would have spared us this female pestilence?' I see this same Greek race hold that sex in such high contempt legislation was needed to oblige a Spartan to reproduce, and one of the penalties decreed in those enlightened republics was to compel a malefactor to garb himself in a woman's attire, that is to say, to wear the raiments of the vilest and most scorned creature of which man had acquaintance.

"But without inquiring for examples in ages at such a great remove from ours, with what sort of an eye is this wretched sex still viewed upon the earth's surface? How is it dealt with? I behold it imprisoned throughout Asia and serving there as slave to the barbarous whims of a despot who molests it, torments it, and turns its sufferings into a game. In America I find a naturally humane race, the Eskimos, practicing all possible acts of beneficence amongst men and treating women with all imaginable severity: I see them humiliated, prostituted to strangers in one part of the world, used as currency in another. In Africa, where without doubt their station is yet further degraded, I notice them toiling in the manner of beasts of burden, tilling the soil, fertilizing it and sowing seed, and serving their husbands on their knees only. Will I follow Captain Cook in his newest discoveries? Is the charming isle of Tahiti, where pregnancy is a crime sometimes meriting death for the mother and almost always for the child, to offer me women enjoying a happier lot? In the other islands this same mariner charted, I find them beaten, harassed by their own offspring, and bullied by the husband himself who collaborates with his family to torment them with additional rigor.

"Oh, Therese! let not all this astonish you, nor be more surprised by the general pre-eminence accorded men over their wives in all epochs: the more a people is in harmony with Nature, the better will be its use of her laws; the wife can have no relation to her husband but that of a slave to his master; very decidedly she has no right to pretend to more cherished titles."[7]

De Sade's views are of course outrageous in their extremity. Close to beasts, women drain man of his creative powers and as such are the deserving recipients of all destructive masculine energies; they are base creatures whom man needs but hates for that need. De Sade's writings display a pathology that does not disappear with the triumph of the angel in the house.

The erotic imagination of the ninenteenth century is also one of extremes—extremes displayed in the figure of the child, in the figure of a saintly virgin, or a degraded woman who uses men to her own advantage. The spectrum is narrow and at each end grossly exaggerated. For every Little Nell or Amelia Sedley, there is a Becky Sharp or a Lizzie Eustace. Dante Rossetti, painter and poet, favored images of ladies sickly or even dead, like Millais's floating Ophelia. Robert Browning's chronicle of bodily humiliations to Pompilia in *The Ring and the Book* is another Victorian work that displays startling contradictions in its attitudes toward women. John Ruskin, himself a victim of the extremes of sexuality (impotence and the love of young girls) articulated something like the official view in *Sesame and Lillies* (1865). He offers this account of the true role of woman:

The man's power is active, progressive, defensive. He is eminently the doer, the creator, the discoverer, the defender. His intellect is for speculation and invention; his energy for adventure, for war, and for conquest, wherever war is just, wherever conquest necessary. But the woman's power is for rule, not for battle; and her intellect is not for

invention or recreation, but for sweet ordering, arrangement, and decision. She sees the qualities of things, their claims, and their places. Her
great function is praise; she enters into no contest, but infallibly adjudges
the crown of contest. By her office and place, she is protected from all
danger and temptation. The man, in his rough work in the open world,
must encounter all peril and trial,—to him therefore must be the failure,
the offence, the inevitable error; often he must be wounded or subdued;
often misled, and always hardened. But he guards the woman from all
this; within his house as ruled by her, unless she herself has sought it,
need enter no danger, no temptation, no cause of error or offence. This
is the true nature of home—it is the place of peace; the shelter not only
from all injury, but from all terror, doubt, and division. In so far as it
is not this, it is not home; so far as the anxieties of the outer life penetrate into it, and the inconsistently—minded, unknown, unloved, or
hostile society of the outer world is allowed by either husband or wife to
cross the threshold, it ceases to be home; it is then only a part of that
outer world which you have roofed over and lighted fire in. But so far
as it is a sacred place, a vestal temple, a temple of the hearth watched
over by household gods, before whose faces none may come but those
whom they can receive with love,—so far as it is this, and roof and fire
are types only of a nobler shade and light, shade as of the rock in a weary
land, and light as of the Pharos in the stormy sea,—so far it vindicates the
name and fulfils the praise of home.

    And wherever a true wife comes, this home is always round her. The
stars only may be over her head, the glow-worm in the night-cold grass
may be the only fire at her foot, but home is yet wherever she is; and for
a noble woman it stretches far round her, better than ceiled with cedar or
painted with vermilion, shedding its quiet light far, for those who else
were homeless.[8]

Here woman is just as outrageous an object of veneration, and
through her the universe is ordered. No longer De Sade's beast of
burden, she is here a place of shelter. Ruskin's woman has literally
become an abode, and she seems very large indeed.

    Victorian repression and the celebration of the angel in the
house have received a great deal of critical attention.[9] To put Ruskin
and De Sade side by side is merely to give some indication of the
intensity of feeling around stereotypes of women. Women had to
seem pure, the center of a moral universe that was losing both its

morality and its purity. At the very same time women were part of a virtual slave class, and as Houghton suggests, in a single year (1851), "42,000 illegitimate children were born in England and Wales; and on that basis it was estimated that 'one in twelve of the unmarried females in the country above the age of puberty have strayed from the path of virtue.' "[10] That women were enshrined on the one hand (so pure that they were the spiritual salvation of mankind) or that they were beasts (figuratively or literally) whose bodies were available for the gratification of debased male instincts are extremes repetitively dramatized in Victorian fiction. There are a number of novels of the time that present the good and the bad twin moving side by side through a novel—one moving ever upward, the other down.

What we see in the mid-nineteenth century is the dissemination of stereotypes. There have always been views of women, attitudes toward them formed by their bodies and enshrined in myth. Women certainly occasion, at least in the eighteenth century novel, a great deal of speculation. Clarissa claims to be an extended meditation on the true nature of woman. Fielding, in what is often called a very masculine book, *Tom Jones,* speculates continuously on the behavior of women—on their foibles, their mysteries. In either case the question is one of absorbing interest and at the center of the novel tradition. By the nineteenth century, an answer of sorts had been formulated, and it was stamped on the public mind by cheap novels and the poetry of Coventry Patmore and by the spectacle of Queen Victoria—moving along with her century into the rotund denial of passion and impulse. Virginia Woolf, in her spoof on changes of sex through the centuries in *Orlando*, envisions the universal dampness and depression that settled over consciousness in the triumph of mid-Victorianism:

> This great cloud which hung, not only over London, but over the whole of the British Isles on the first day of the nineteenth century stayed, or rather, did not stay, for it was buffeted about constantly by blustering gales, long enough to have extraordinary consequences upon those who lived beneath its shadow. A change seemed to have come over the climate of England. Rain fell frequently, but only in fitful gusts, which were no sooner over than they began again. The sun shone, of course, but it was so girt about with clouds and the air was so saturated

with water, that its beams were discoloured and purples, oranges, and reds of a dull sort took the place of the more positive landscapes of the eighteenth century. Under this bruised and sullen canopy the green of the cabbages was less intense, and the white of the snow was muddied. But what was worse, damp now began to make its way into every house— damp, which is the most insidious of all enemies, for while the sun can be shut out by blinds, and the frost roasted by a hot fire, damp steals in while we sleep; damp is silent, imperceptible, ubiquitous. Damp swells the wood, furs the kettle, rusts the iron, rots the stone. So gradual is the process, that it is not until we pick up some chest of drawers, or coal scuttle, and the whole thing drops to pieces in our hands, that we suspect even that the disease is at work.

Thus, stealthily, and imperceptibly, none marking the exact day or hour of the change, the constitution of England was altered and nobody knew it. Everywhere the effects were felt. The hardy country gentleman, who had sat down gladly to a meal of ale and beef in a room designed, perhaps by the brothers Adam, with classic dignity, now felt chilly. Rugs appeared, bears were grown and trousers fastened tight under the instep. The chill which he felt in his legs he soon transferred to his house; furniture was muffled; walls and tables were covered too. Then a change of diet became essential. The muffin was invented and the crumpet. Coffee supplanted the after-dinner port, and, as coffee led to a drawing-room in which to drink it, and drawing-room to glass cases, and glass cases to artificial flowers, fortes, and pianofortes to drawing-room ballads, and drawing-room ballads (skipping a stage or two) to innumerable little dogs, mats, and antimacassars, the home-which had become extremely important—was completely altered.

Outside the house—it was another effect of the damp—ivy grew in unparalleled profusion. Houses that had been of bare stone were smothered in greenery. No garden, however formal its original design, lacked a shrubbery, a wilderness, a maze. What light penetrated to the bedrooms where children were born was naturally of an obfusc green and what light penetrated to the drawing rooms where grown men and women lived came through curtains of brown and purple plush. But the change did not stop at outward things. The damp struck within. Men felt the chill in their hearts; the damp in their minds. In a desperate effort to snuggle their feelings into some sort of warmth one subterfuge was tried after another. Love, birth, and death were all swaddled in a variety of fine phrases. The sexes drew further and further apart. No open conversation was tolerated. Evasions and concealments were sedulously practised on both sides. And just as the ivy and the evergreen rioted in the damp earth outside, so did the same fertility show itself within. The life of the average woman was a succession of childbirths. She married at nineteen and had fifteen or eighteen children by the time she was thirty; for twins abounded.[11]

I do not want now to run through a catalogue of the qualities marked out as belonging either to the good or the bad woman. But to choose to write as if the author were either puts *a priori* limits on what he can say. Women with whom one would care to identify publicly had a severely restricted consciousness. They were supposed to know only that which would elevate and refine. Erotic impulses expressed through them would take strange forms, would of necessity be more hidden than would ever have been the case during the eighteenth century. Since the nature of woman was so fully defined, the state of mind of the child became the locus of nineteenth-century eroticism. For male as well as female authors, childhood offered the only period on which categories of consciousness did not have to appear fixed. That Heathcliff and Cathy (of *Wuthering Heights*) can long for their time as abandoned playmates on the moors offers the only humane alternative to the prospect of a sexless, hate-filled marriage, like that of Heathcliff and Isabella or of Catherine and Edgar.

Despite all of these cultural demands on the female sex, the figure of woman was still imaginatively inviting. Alfred Tennyson imagines some better part of himself as a woman, everywhere from "The Palace of Art" to *In Memoriam*. Poetic forms, even the most novelistic like the dramatic monologue, allow for a briefer, more provisional commitment to the speaker than does a novel. Such a speaker may, according to Robert Langbaum, "dramatize a position to which the poet is not ready to commit himself intellectually."[12] The third-person form of narration also disguises authorial commitments much more thoroughly than the confessional stance of the "I." Charles Baudelaire aptly summed up the Victorian novelist's proscriptions; ". . . let us beware above all of giving away our real feelings and of speaking in our *own* name. In narrating passions and adventures which would tend to kindle sympathetic fires in the ordinary reader, we will remain icily detached. We will remain objective and impersonal as the realists tell us."[13] Never so formalist as the creators of French fiction, English novelists of this time were intent in adopting, if not an objective, then at least a distant, apparently controlled stance toward their creations. Thackeray's use of an eighteenth century mode in *Henry Esmond* accomplishes this, and even more so does his use of the cynical, worldly-wise puppeteer in *Vanity Fair*. He controls his characters' movements for his readers' edification. Anthony Trollope's frequent announcements that, dear reader, all will work out in the end, put us on notice that his creations are a matter of will, not identification. Nevertheless books like Carroll's *Alice in Wonderland* or Dickens's *The Old Curiosity Shop* or *Little Dorrit* signal the strained alliance between the socially progressive and the erotic that coalesced in a child-woman. Much of the cheap literature of the period celebrated being a real little girl, or growing up maintaining one's girlish ignorance and vulnerability. However severely restricted the expression of eroticism, at least in "acceptable" literature, the diminutive figure of the girlish child (Oliver Twist) or the childish girl testifies to the necessity, for male authors, of imaginative identification with the weak, helpless, and sexually-socially vulnerable.

Writing as a woman became even more difficult when so many real women were writing novels. A Mary Shelley or a Fanny Burney was sufficiently unusual that one marvelled, as once had Doctor Johnson, that the trick was done at all. But Jane Austen, George Eliot, the Brontës, and the myriads of Mrs. Lynn Lintons—all gave the novelist's art to women. There were still problems in writing under a female name (the Brontës and Eliot chose neutral or male names), but the number of women of genius from 1800 to 1848 must have led to a richer sense of the female sex altogether. For male authors to adopt the female voice when in fact so many women themselves were writing opened up the possibility of being utterly wrong, creating someone who would suffer by contrast with her more "authentic" counterparts. Looking about them, male authors must have seen the necessity of taking into account their female literary friends as well as their vast female readership.

It would be the subject of another book altogether to discuss the nature of fiction written by women and the specific effects they may have had on male artists.[14] Women authors were often more explicit than men about their debts to artists or mentors of the opposite sex. Jane Austen emphasized her indebtedness to Richardson's *Sir Charles Grandison;* Charlotte Brontë acknowledge the importance of Thackeray to her own work when she dedicated the second edition of *Jane Eyre* to him in 1847. To what extent women authors may deal with the same content, adopt the same tone, or reenact stereotypes in their fictions created for them by male authors are questions to which I can give only tentative answers here. I think, however, that even a brief examination of two important English women writers of the age, Charlotte Brontë and George Eliot, will reveal two central points: both writers were concerned to find a voice that would transcend sexual stereotypes of the age and both treat sexuality, power, and personal integrity in a much more positive fashion. The differences are sufficiently dramatic that they underscore the distorted face and figure of woman adopted by the male author.

The problem of the sex of the author occupied Charlotte Brontë in several ways. She herself had experimented with writing as a man in *The Professor*. When she adopts the voice of William Crimsworth she exaggerates, in the words of Winifred Gérin, "the cynical look and the license of language which she believed essential at that time to the masculine character she assumed."[15] Her male voice is full of inflated rhetoric and the verbal equivalents of aggressiveness. But Crimsworth is so unbelievable that the narrative almost grinds to a halt. While she observes male characters very acutely, not only in the case of Edward Rochester but also Paul Emanuel in *Villette* and the curates in *Shirley*, she finds picturing an entire fictional world from their perspective difficult indeed. Both Charlotte and her sisters Anne and Emily initially, at least, cultivated anonymity, and wrote under the masculine or just neutral names Currer, Ellis, and Acton Bell. In addition to their concerns about their father, they believed that knowledge of the sex of the author would damage the reception of their books. Such ruses were successful at first. Kathleen Tillotson remarks that,

> Most readers scarcely knew Thackeray's name when they met it on the cover of *Vanity Fair*. Nor had they any idea who were Currer, Ellis,

and Acton Bell—men or women, one or three. Again this did not restrain them from wild guesses; the rumour ran that *Jane Eyre* was the work of a discarded mistress of Thackeray.[16]

In point of fact, Brontë's most successful fictons, *Villette* and *Jane Eyre*, are those in which the narrative voice is given to a character readily identifiable as the author herself.

In *Jane Eyre* (subtitled "An Autobiography") the author presents a thinly disguised self-portrait: as a girl at a bad, inadequate school, as a governess who suffers the humiliations of servitude, as a woman who falls hopelessly in love with her master. Such are the details of Brontë's own life—and these belong also to her narrator. This book has a number of faults, but the narrative voice of Jane Eyre reveals, I think, the distortions that may arise when the male author takes upon himself the same task. Jane begins by being almost excessively self-assertive, but she grows up. Mastery of her situation does not demand domination at the price of disintegration, themes dear to the hearts of both Defoe and Richardson. Jane participates in soul-shattering events and emerges intact. As a young girl, she begins by announcing herself passionately committed to the truth. In the midst of the brutality of Lowood school, Brontë shows Jane a healthy little pagan who asserts her own independence and autonomy. When Mr. Brocklehurst raises the rather grim possibility that she might go to hell, where things are unpleasant indeed, Jane says, "I must keep in good health, and not die."[17] Constantly in trouble with the harsh, hypocritical moralizers who surround her, she continues against all wisdom and diplomacy to call attention to herself as someone not like anyone else, as radically and distinctively her own. Jane is a woman who can and does announce, "*I* care for myself" (p. 404).

Jane Eyre chronicles a movement away from childish passions and rages into adulthood. Such growth addresses the great Victorian dilemma—how to integrate childhood eroticism and aggression into a culturally constrained and repressive definition of the adult personality. Since Victorian novelists often see childhood as the only time in which one can legitimately experience joy and heedlessness, there is a celebration of this very state, a celebration of arrested personal development, obvious in a book like *Wuthering Heights*. Charlotte Brontë allows growing up to appear in a more positive light. The passions and impulses of childhood can be maintained and modified through understanding and reflection. She shows Jane Eyre in the act of comprehending these impulses:

> Children can feel, but they cannot analyze their feelings; and if the analysis is partially effected in thought, they know not how to express the result of process in words. Fearful, however, of losing this first and only opportunity of relieving my grief by imparting it, I, after a disturbed pause, contrived to frame a meagre, though as far as it went, true response. (p. 23)

Jane is shown to be passionately aware of true right and wrong, and tells Mrs. Reed in no uncertain terms what she thinks of her treatment:

> 'How dare I, Mrs. Reed? How dare I? [affirm that she has been miserably treated.] Because it is the *truth*. You think I have no feelings, and that I can do without one bit of love or kindness; but I cannot live so: and you have no pity. I shall remember how you thrust me back—roughly and violently thrust me back into the red room, and locked me up there—to my dying day; though I was in agony; though I cried out, while suffocating with distress, "Have mercy! Have mercy, Aunt Reed!" And that punishment you made me suffer because your wicked boy struck me—knocked me down for nothing. I will tell anybody who asks me questions, this exact tale. People think you a good woman, but you are bad; hard-hearted. *You* are deceitful!' (p. 39)

One of the most painful fears about these overwhelming feelings is that one may indeed win all and then somehow be punished for it:

> I was left there alone—winner of the field. It was the hardest battle I had fought, and the first victory I had gained: I stood awhile on the rug, where Mr. Brocklehurst had stood, and I enjoyed by conqueror's solitude. First, I smiled to myself and felt elate; but this fierce pleasure subsided in me as fast as did the accelerated throb of my pulses. A child cannot quarrel with its elders, as I had done, cannot give its furious feelings uncontrolled play, as I had given mine; without experiencing afterwards the pang of remorse and the chill of reaction. A ridge of lighted

> heath, alive, glancing, devouring, would have been a meet emblem of
> my mind when I accused the menaced Mrs. Reed: the same ridge, black
> and blasted after the flames are dead, would have represented as meetly
> my subsequent condition, when half an hour's silence and reflection had
> shewn me the madness of my conduct, and the dreariness of my hated
> and hating position. (pp. 40-41)

Aflame and powerful, then blasted and destroyed; these images
echo Richardsonian themes—only here they are understood. And
these fears are also recognized as essentially those of childhood.

Early in the novel Jane talks about her need for love:

> '. . . if others don't love me, I would rather die than live—I cannot
> bear to be solitary and hated, Helen. Look here; to gain some real affec-
> tion from you, or Miss Temple, or any other whom I truly love, I would
> willingly submit to have the bone of my arm broken, or to let a bull
> toss me, or to stand behind a kicking horse, and let it dash its hoof at
> my chest,—' (p. 80)

But this urgent and pressing need for union does not, in fact, pre-
cipitate her into an illicit relationship with Rochester. When she finds
out that the marriage must be broken off, she characterizes her own
agony: "Conscience, turned tyrant, held passion by the throat, told
her, tauntingly, she had yet but dipped her dainty foot in the slough,
and swore that with that arm of iron, he would thrust her down to
unsounded depths of agony" (p. 379). Despite the overblown, ro-
manticized language, she here presents herself in the act of bending
passion to values and judgment. Growing up for her involves inte-
grating these two, and love relationships in the book, no matter how
much temptation rests on either side, must represent a balance between passion and morality.

The pivotal incident in trying to integrate their often conflicting claims is her relationship to St. John Rivers. The exalted
religious passion of the hero, in certain of its aspects very appealing
to her, threatens at the sexual level to destroy her:

> I comprehended all at once that he would hardly make a good hus-
> band: that it would be a trying thing to be his wife. I understood, as by

inspiration, the nature of his love for Miss Oliver: I agreed with him that it was but a love of the senses. I comprehended how he should despise himself for the feverish influence it exercised over him; how he should wish to stifle and destroy it; how he should mistrust it ever conducing permanently to his happiness, or hers. I saw he was of the material from which nature hews her heroes—Christian and Pagan—her law givers, her statesmen, her conquerors: a steadfast bulwark for great interests to rest upon; but, at the fireside, too often a cold cumbrous column, gloomy and out of place. (pp. 501-502)

To deny her own need for passion for the sake of a moral commitment, even though she would have the love and companionship that she so desires, would lead to terrible inner anguish:

... but as his wife—at his side always, and always restrained, and always checked—forced to keep the fires of my nature continually low, to compel it to burn inwardly and never utter a cry, though the imprisoned flame consumed vital after vital—*this* would be unendurable. (pp. 520-521)

The fire that is passion would here be turned into a disease of self-consumption.

Charlotte Brontë sees the integration of passion into a moral system as the crucial adult act. Hence Rochester is punished by the fire, not, however, castrated, as some critics would have it. His sexuality (as well as economic pride and class consciousness) must be subjected to limitations. Jane now sees Rochester in possession of new potency:

"You are no ruin sir—no lightning-struck tree: you are green and vigorous. Plants will grow about your roots, whether you ask them or not, because they take delight in your bountiful shadow; and as they grow they will lean towards you, and wind round you, because your strength offers them so safe a prop." (p. 568)

It is the very same potency now possessed by Jane herself.

In this novel sexuality and the recognition of its existence and power is essential to personal integrity. This is not to say there is no ambivalence about the matter, however. Let us compare two fire scenes, one that appears in Richardson's *Clarissa* and one that appears in *Jane Eyre*. In each scene a fire breaks out that frightens the heroine and places her in a half-dressed state at the mercy of the strong male figure. Each case involves an unexpected event, an eruption meant to signal the metaphoric expression of the power of sexual desires. Reactions to fire and force will serve, for both Richardson and Charlotte Brontë, to dramatize the feelings of the woman when so confronted. I make this comparison to point out the fear and horror that Clarissa is made to express around the violence of Lovelace's passion, and at her own role in exciting it, to point out also the marked difference between Richardson's depiction of the scene and Charlotte Brontë's. Lovelace recounts racing to Clarissa's door to save her:

> I clasped her in my arms with an ardor she never felt before: My dearest life! fear nothing: I have been up—the danger is over—the fire is got under. And how, foolish devil! [to Dorcas] could you thus, by your hideous yell, alarm and frighten my angel!
>
> O Jack! how her sweet bosom, as I clasped her to mine, heaved and panted! I could even distinguish her dear heart flutter, flutter, flutter against mine; and for a few minutes I feared she would go into fits.
>
> Lest the half-lifeless charmer should catch cold in this undress, I lifted her to her bed, and sat down by her upon the side of it, endeavouring with the utmost tenderness, as well of action as expression, to dissipate her terrors. (Vol. 2, p. 501)

Note first that Richardson is using the scene as an occasion for erotic display. Fearful supplication is Clarissa's most frequent pose, and here the fright allows Richardson to display her body, her "limbs" twisting and turning:

> But, oh, the sweet discomposure! Her bared shoulders and arms, so inimitably fair and lovely: her spread hands crossed over her charming neck; yet not half concealing its glossy beauties: the scanty coat, as she rose from me, giving the whole of her admirable shape, and fine-turned limbs: her eyes running over, yet seeming to threaten future vengeance: and at last her lips uttering what every indignant look and glowing feature portended; exclaiming as if I had done the worst I could do, and vowing never to forgive me; wilt thou wonder if I resumed the incensed, the already too much provoked fair one? (Vol. 2, p. 502)

The protest is voluptuous indeed and Lovelace points out that "we had both already forgotten the occasion, dreadful as it was, which had thrown her into my arms. . ." (Vol. 2, p. 501). Clarissa immediately assumes that rape is imminent or in fact has already happened:

> 'Consider me, *dear* Lovelace (*dear* was her charming word!) on my knees I beg you to consider me, who has no protection but you; has no defence but your honour; by that honour! by your humanity! by all you have vowed! I conjure you not to make me abhor myself!—not to make me vile in my eyes!' (Vol. 2, p. 503)

How she would become vile is rather confusing, unless we are to think that she sees herself as responsible for the sexual feelings directed towards her—in other words, sexuality is emanating from her rather than from him. Otherwise, why should she abhor herself? In fact her supplications become hysterical, as she exhorts him even to kill her, since he must hate her to be subjecting her to this treatment:

> 'See, Mr. Lovelace!—Good God! That I should live to see this hour, and to bear this treatment!—See at your feet a poor creature, imploring your pity, who, for your sake, is abandoned of all the world! Let not my father's curse thus dreadfully operate! Be not *you* the inflicter, who have been the *cause* of it: but spare me, I beseech you, spare me! For how have I deserved this treatment from you? For *your own sake*, if not for *my sake*, and as you would that God Almighty, in your last hour, should have mercy upon *you*, spare me!' (Vol. 2, p. 504)

Shortly thereafter Clarissa threatens to do herself in with a pair of scissors. Self-defilement is for her the continuous response to threatened defilement by others. She responds this way because her author sees her femaleness at fault. Perhaps Richardson is here simply reflecting a phenomenon even more obvious in Cleland's *Fanny Hill*. Cleland depicts women as "spending" the way men do in sexual intercourse. Steven Marcus records this belief as one of the oddities of Victorian pornography and the hallmark of a literature written by men; they believe women *are* men, biologically, that is.[18] In the same fashion Richardson imagines Clarissa literally giving off sex.

Fire comes from her as much as it comes from Lovelace. It is her own sexuality that is violation, and she is bad because of it.

For Richardson fire is both a dramatic event that will throw his heroine into inviting postures and an intense emotional reality. Sexuality is fearful and terrible; its effects are enacted in locked rooms under pain of death. He has Anna Howe advise that "love is a fire that is not to be played with without burning one's fingers" (Vol. 3, p. 8). Unconcerned in the entire sequence with the reality or unreality of this plot, Richardson seems intent on dramatizing the enormous destructive force of passion. Lovelace's intense preoccupation with rape, even to burning down the house to achieve it, his endless ruminations on the near-nudity of his victim indicate the evil Richardson sees at the heart of passion, even of physical love.

Charlotte Brontë gives us a similar scene in which physical passion, however, is handled very differently. In her own love for the Belgian schoolmaster Constantin Heger, the author had struggled with the need to suppress her passion for a married man. Her attitudes toward suppressed passion changed during the course of her writing career, and she moved from exploring the union of sexuality and love in *Jane Eyre* to a nun-like renunciation, in which Lucy Snowe (In *Villette*) cultivates her love for Paul Emanuel through three winters of celibacy. Rochester's maiming by fire does involve a reduction of his potency, or at the very least a punishment for his sexual transgressions. And the mad Bertha in the attic can be identified as the powerfully destructive side of Jane's passions. However, Charlotte Brontë allows Jane Eyre to experience sexual passion, and one notable instance of this occurs in a fire scene similar to the one that subjects Clarissa to such tortures. Once again a helpless, dependent woman (the governess, a powerful sexual image in the minds of Victorian readers) finds herself alone in a bedroom on fire. Just before the fire breaks out she thinks of her feelings toward the male hero:

> And was Mr. Rochester now ugly in my eyes? No, reader: Gratitude, and many associations, all pleasurable and genial, made his face the object I best like to see; his presence in a room was more cheering than the brightest fire. Yet I had not forgotten his faults: indeed, I could not; for he brought them frequently before me.

I thought there were excellent materials in him; though for the present they hung together somewhat spoiled and tangled. (p. 181)

As the fire breaks out, Jane hears a demonic laugh, and she runs in to douse him with water:

'Wake! wake!' I cried—I shook him, but he only murmured and turned: the smoke had stupified him. Not a moment could be lost: the very sheets were kindling. I rushed to his basin and ewer; fortunately, one was wide and the other deep, and both were filled with water. I heaved them up, deluged the bed and its occupant, flew back to my own room, brought my own water-jug, baptised the couch afresh, and, by God's aid, succeeded in extinguishing the flames which were devouring it. (p. 183)

Undressed and soaked, he hurriedly puts on a robe, making Jane wait for him while he disappears up the staircase. He tells her to return to her room, but then "inconsistently" will not let her go: "He paused; gazed at me: words almost visible trembled on his lips,—but his voice was checked." To his "strange energy," "strange fire," Jane says "I am cold" (p. 187). But she recognizes the source of his intensity and becomes, once back in her bed, feverish herself:

I regained my couch, but never thought of sleep. Till morning dawned I was tossed on a buoyant but unquiet sea, where billows of trouble rolled under surges of joy. I thought sometimes I saw beyond its wild waters a shore, sweet as the hills of Beulah; and now and then a freshening gale, wakened by hope, bore my spirit triumphantly towards the bourne: but I could not reach it, even in fancy,—a counteracting breeze blew off land, and continually drove me back. Sense would resist delirium: judgment would warn passion. Too feverish to rest, I rose as soon as day dawned. (pp. 187-188)

I quote this passage at such length to demonstrate the speaker's relationship to her own feelings. She has a clear sense of what they are, even if her metaphoric expression of them is melodramatic. Lovelace rescues Clarissa, and the rescue is perceived as an assault. For Clarissa every physical touch precedes violation. Despite the fact that the author uses her to articulate fear and trembling, he also makes her affirm herself as the source of sexuality in Lovelace. Jane saves Rochester, arouses him sexually and in the act of declining affirms the nature of her own sexuality. The contrast here involves not simply an attitude toward sex—clearly very different in Richardson and Brontë. The point, more specifically, involves distortion. A male author, afraid of his own sexuality, identifies himself with a woman and allows her to express horror at herself. But Jane Eyre comprehends her own passionate experiences. To feel others' passions aroused, even those with the ability to rape, is not necessarily an invitation to suicide.

George Eliot was, if anything even more concerned with problems of identifying the sex of both author and narrator than was Charlotte Brontë. Mary Ann Evans cherished her anonymity and was much distressed when, near the publication of *Adam Bede* in 1859, it seemed that her real name would become known. To her friends she wrote, " 'Do not guess at authorship—it is a bad speculation.' "[19] Her wish to be identified as a George came from her belief that a book identified as written by a woman (and by a woman who lived, unmarried, with the critic George Henry Lewes) would be valued less: " 'When *Jane Eyre* was finally known to be a woman's book, the tone noticeably changed. Not that I believe the possibility of anything adventitious permanently hurting a *good* book, but there is always something temporary in the success of a novel, and one may as well secure all adventitious aids.' "[20] Yet she had a high opinion of her sex, believed in a special feminine nature, and assigned to women unique talents because of that nature: " '. . . women can produce novels not only fine, but among the very finest;—novels, too, that have a precious speciality, lying quite apart from masculine aptitudes and experiences.' "[21] In a letter to Miss Davies, she became more explicit about the nature of the differences between the sexes:

> And there lies just the kernel of truth in the vulgar alarm of men lest women should be 'unsexed'. We can no more afford to part with that exquisite type of gentleness, tenderness, possible maternity suffusing a woman's being with affectionateness, which makes what we mean by the feminine character, than we can afford to part with the human love, the mutual subjection of soul between a man and a woman—which is also a growth and revelation beginning before all history.

The answer to those alarms of men about education is, to admit fully that the mutual delight of the sexes in each other must enter into the perfection of life, but to point out that complete union and sympathy can only come by women having opened to them the same store of acquired truth or beliefs as men have, so that their grounds of judgment may be as far as possible the same.[22]

Yet she was long reluctant to appear as a female voice herself. Some of the more obvious difficulties Eliot had with creating a believable narrative voice come from her attempt to sound like a male author. Indeed, this male persona may have served the important function of distancing her somewhat from her own creations: " '... if George Eliot turns out a dull dog and an ineffective writer—a mere flash in the pan—I, for one, am determined to eat him on the first intimation of that disagreeable fact.' "[23] Clearly she did not in any way wish the controlling narrative voice of her fictions to appear connected to Mary Ann Evans. In *Scenes From Clerical Life*, George Eliot injects herself in the story to act as moral guide and interpreter, to make unmistakable her point of view—to sound as if she were weighing and balancing:

But, my dear madam, it is so very large a majority of your fellow-countrymen that are of this insignificant stamp. At least eighty out of a hundred of your adult male fellow-Britons returned in the last census are neither extraordinarily silly, nor extraordinarily wicked, nor extraordinarily wise; their eyes are neither deep and liquid with sentiment, nor sparkling with suppressed witticisms; they have probably had no hairbreadth escapes or thrilling adventures; their brains are certainly not pregnant with genius, and their passions have not manifested themselves at all after the fashion of a volcano. They are simply men of complexions more or less muddy, whose conversation is more or less bald and disjointed.

Depend upon it, you would gain unspeakably if you would learn with me to see some of the poetry and the pathos, the tragedy and the comedy, lying in the experience of a human soul that looks out through dull grey eyes, and that speaks in a voice of quite ordinary tones. In that case, I should have no fear of your not caring to know what farther befell the Rev. Amos Barton, or of your thinking the homely details I have to tell at all beneath your attention. As it is, you can if you please, decline to pursue my story farther; and you will easily find reading more to your taste, since I learn from the newspapers that many remarkable novels, full of striking situations, thrilling incidents, and eloquent writing, have appeared only within the last season.[24]

The sermon-like tone is oppressively formal here, although the call for sympathy to those whom we normally ignore epitomizes Eliot's work. She does seem to be putting herself forward here as a masculine presence, claiming seriousness and high novelistic intentions quite apart from more "remarkable" novels.

Though she wanted to create a narrative voice that would not of necessity be attached to a specific sex, she still wanted one that would forcefully direct the reader's attentions and sympathies. Her choices were dictated, apparently, by the wish to gain control over her own sympathies, for which in her life she was celebrated. Herbert Spencer found her " 'so tolerant of human weaknesses as to be quickly forgiving; and indeed, was prone to depreciate harsh judgments. This last trait was I doubt not in part caused by constant study of her own defects.' "[25] In the autobiographical *The Mill on the Floss* (1860) she makes her personal commitment clear, for Maggie Tulliver surely embodies the deepest sympathies of the author. She begins the book with a personal hymn to lush water and land as she watches by Dorlcote Mill:

> Now I can turn my eyes toward the mill again and watch the unresting wheel sending out its diamond jets of water. That little girl is watching it too; she has been standing on just the same spot at the edge of the water ever since I paused on the bridge. And that queer white cur with the brown ear seems to be leaping and barking in ineffectual remonstrance with the wheel; perhaps he is jealous, because his playfellow in the beaver bonnet is so rapt in its movement. It is time the little playfellow went in, I think; and there is a very bright fire to tempt her: the red light shines out under the deepening gray of the sky. It is time, too, for me to leave off resting my arms on the cold stone of this bridge. . . .[26]

Waking from what seems a dream, the narrator prepares to tell us the story, and the rest of the novel is a conventional third-person narration, with Maggie, however, as its center of interest and feeling.

Middlemarch, perhaps more than any of her other novels, manages a tone both serious and sympathetic, weighted toward the question of female heroism, but strongly interested in maintaining a balanced though critical view. She opens this book with the story of Saint Theresa of Avila and goes on to speculate on the possibilities of heroism for the modern woman. Observing what seem to be the lapses of the modern would-be heroine, she says:

> Some have felt that these blundering lives are due to the inconvenient indefiniteness with which the Supreme Power has fashioned the natures of women: if there were one level of feminine incompetence as strict as the ability to count three and no more, the social lot of women might be treated with scientific certitude. Meanwhile the indefiniteness remains, and the limits of variation are really much wider than any one would imagine from the sameness of women's coiffure and the favourite love—stories in prose and verse.[27]

For Eliot the Saint Thersa of her day is liable to diffuseness and frustration because of all those things that impede the pilgrimage. Dorothea Brooke's visions of noble fulfillment through marriage to the scholarly Casaubon come crashing down about her. For men too, dreams of the great work or the great life lead to a burning inner sense of failure. The *Key to All Mythologies* is destined to remain unwritten, and Lydgate does not become a great man of science because he has been brought low by his love for that evocation of the Victorian stereotype of the pure woman, Rosamond; she possesses, he mistakenly thinks, "that feminine radiance, that distinctive womanhood which must be classed with flowers and music, that sort of beauty which by its very nature was virtuous, being moulded only for pure and delicate joys" (p. 121). Her portrait is a brilliant, gradually revealing one of the wiles, the callousness, and ultimately the gross insensitivity of a woman so superficially attached to realms of the ideal.

Eliot exercises much of her wit against masculine grandiosity, the wish to see oneself at the center of the great and mighty, and she even turns her satire against Henry Fielding, "a great historian, as he insisted on calling himself," one given to comments "over that tempting range of relevancies called the universe" (pp. 104-105). Her own task she takes to be that of the more humble weaver of the

threads of the story. Like Fielding, however, she makes frequent
appearances as manager of our sympathies. She rather regularly
breaks the narrative to inject a note of sympathy for those whom she
has taken pains to expose in their fraudulent view of themselves.
Here she asks us to think for a moment of the poor, shivering inner
state of the reverend Casaubon:

> One morning, some weeks after her arrival at Lowick, Dorothea—
> but why always Dorothea? Was her point of view the only possible one
> with regard to this marriage? I protest against all our interest, all our
> effort at understanding being given to the young skins that look bloom-
> ing in spite of trouble; for these too will get faded, and will know the
> older and more eating griefs which we are helping to neglect. In spite of
> the blinking eyes and white moles objectionable to Celia, and the want of
> muscular curve which was morally painful to Sir James, Mr. Casaubon
> had an intense consciousness within him, and was spiritually a-hungered
> like the rest of us. (p. 205)

Part of this man's problem, as she sees it, is his spiritual and
bodily frigidity. Ultimately no idea, no position, no action, no love
can warm him to passionate rapture. His coldness and timidity come
from self-distrust and dislike and certain "swampy ground" in which
his soul mucks about (p. 206).

> For my part I am very sorry for him. It is an uneasy lot at best, to
> be what we call highly taught and yet not to enjoy: to be present at this
> great spectacle of life and never to be liberated from a small hungry
> shivering self—never to be fully possessed by the glory we behold, never
> to have our consciousness rapturously transformed into the vividness of
> a thought, the ardour of a passion, the energy of an action, but always to
> be scholarly and inspired, ambitious and timid, scrupulous and dimsight-
> ed. (pp. 206-207)

Sympathetic and personal, this narrative "I" gives people their due
even while seeking to expose their limitations. Like a number of
other men and women in the book, Casaubon's sexual desires (or
lack of them) are unknown to him. Failure to take that fact into
account has let him into a very bad mistake, as it has Dorothea, and
again Lydgate. Dorothea's reflections in Rome are ironic reflections
on the status of pleasure in her own life—pleasures she ultimately
does find in marriage to Will Ladislaw. But Lydgate compromises

himself professionally to remain at home with his sexually appealing but manipulative wife. In all cases Eliot is as direct as she can be about the importance of physical love to a true marriage. This acknowledgment distinguishes her from her male cohorts like Dickens, Trollope, or Thackeray—all of whom seem themselves enthralled by the idea that good women were sexless and that the desire for sex itself was a sign of badness.

Women authors of the time simply were not supporting the stereotypical canons of the age, and no doubt writing under a neutral or male persona helped them to write more freely. As Elaine Showalter remarks; ". . . they could use a masculine name to represent everything in their personalities that transcended the cramping feminine ideal."[28] Sooner or later all of them were known to be women, and a Catherine Earnshaw, Dorothea Brooke, Gwendolen Harleth, or Jane Eyre hardly reinforced a view of woman as passive, passionless, and the principle of Goodness in human form. Elaine Showalter indicates that reviewers of the time were noticing new kinds of heroines and new ideals being expressed as a result of all the women novelists writing.[29] None of these facts were lost on male authors, though they persisted in having many a bloodless heroine. The force of social strictures was strong indeed and of such dimensions that to take the point of view of a young, good woman for a significant part of a novel would have been to muffle oneself up in endless layers of clothing. It did not have to be so, as Thomas Hardy and Henry James were later to demonstrate, yet such extreme views on sexual identity and sexuality itself made it more difficult to identify with a thing, whether an object of veneration or a bestial creature.

George Eliot, who worked so hard to create a morally serious yet sympathetic narrator, one that would appear consistently disinterested, almost sexless, insisted, however, on the importance of the female consciousness to the novel and to history itself:

> Could there be a slenderer, more insignificant thread in human history than this consciousness of a girl, busy with her small inferences of the way in which she could make her life pleasant?—in a time, too, when ideas were with fresh vigour making armies of themselves, and the universal kinship was declaring itself fiercely: when women on the other side of the world would not mourn for the husbands and sons who died

bravely in a common cause, and men stinted of bread on our side of the world heard of that willing loss and were patient: a time when the soul of man was waking to pulses which had for centuries been beating in him unheard, until their full sum made a new life of terror or of joy.

What in the midst of that mighty drama are girls and their blind visions? They are the Yea and Nay of that good for which men are enduring and fighting. In these delicate vessels is borne onward through the ages the treasure of human affections.[30]

She did not mean the sainted, sweet vision of a childish woman, but the claims of the inner life, the realm of personality and its beneficent development. Henry James, as we know, picked up this remark and made it famous in his preface to *The Portrait of a Lady*. But he also pointed out the problems of allowing the world of the novel to filter through the eyes of a woman and took to task Walter Scott, Robert Louis Stevenson, and Charles Dickens for their decision to forego this imaginative challenge.

James must have forgotten Esther Summerson, though it is difficult to dismiss the insistent, constantly self-abnegating narrator of half of *Bleak House*. The odd fact is that while, on one level, this woman seems merely the reiteration of a stereotype, she is on the other hand, an exploration of the same themes so evident in the much earlier work of Defoe and Richardson. She is very oddly got up indeed; good, sweet, yet somehow untrustworthy, the victim of a sexual stain erased by smallpox, the expression of a fantasy of personal and social omnipotence. It is to her we now turn.

Notes

[1]Margaret Anne Doody, *A Natural Passion, A Study of the Novels of Samuel Richardson* (Oxford: The Clarendon Press, 1974) p. 151.

[2]*Ibid.*, p. 152.

3For the Details of Clarissa's influence, see Leslie Fiedler's *Love and Death in the American Novel* (New York: Dell, 1960). Cynthia Griffin Woolf remarks that what was imitated in *Clarissa* was the plot, the outline of the situation, rather than the psychological complexities and minute dissection of character Richardson himself favored. *Samuel Richardson and the Eighteenth-Century Puritan Character* (Hamden, Conn.: Archon Books, 1972) pp. 233-235.

4John Cleland, *Fanny Hill*, Intro. J. H. Plumb, (New York: Signet, 1965), p. 142.

5Steven Marcus, *The Other Victorians: A Study of Sexuality and Pornography in Mid-Nineteenth-Century England* (New York: Basic Books, 1964).

6Henry Fielding, *Amelia*, 2 Vols. (London: Dent, 1962) Vol. 1, p. 28.

7Donatien Alphonse François Sade, Comte, *Justine or Good Conduct Well Chastised* in *The Marquis de Sade* trans. Richard Seaver & Austryn Wainhouse (New York: Grove Press, 1965), pp. 647-49.

8John Ruskin, *Sesame and Lilies* (Chicago: Conkey & Co., orig. publ. 1865), pp. 143-145.

9See Walter Houghton, *The Victorian Frame of Mind, 1830-1870* (New Haven: Yale Univ. Press, 1957), pp. 341-94. See also Martha Vicinus, ed. *Suffer and Be Still, Women in the Victorian Age* (Bloomington: Indiana Univ. Press, 1972).

10Walter Houghton, p. 366.

11Virginia Woolf, *Orlando, A Biography* (New York: Harcourt, Brace and Company, 1928) pp. 227-229.

12Robert Langbaum, *The Poetry of Experience, The Dramatic Monologue in Modern Literary Tradition* (New York: Norton, 1957) p. 105.

13Charles Baudelaire, "*Madame Bovary* by Gustave Flaubert," in Gustave Flaubert, *Madame Bovary*, ed. Paul de Man (New York: Norton, 1965) pp. 338-39.

14See, for instance, Patricia Meyer Spacks, *The Female Imagination* (New York: Knopf, 1975).

[15]Winifred Gérin, *Charlotte Brontë, The Evolution of Genius* (London: Oxford Univ. Press, 1967), p. 88.

[16]Kathleen Tillotson, *Novels of the Eighteen-Forties* (London: Oxford Univ. Press, 1961) p. 12.

[17]Charlotte Brontë, *Jane Eyre* ed. Jane Jack and Margaret Smith (Oxford: The Clarendon Press, 1969) p. 34. All subsequent references will be to this edition of the text.

[18]Steven Marcus, p. 113.

[19]Gordon S. Haight, *George Eliot, A Biography* (New York: Oxford Univ. Press, 1968), p. 267.

[20]*Ibid.*, p. 268.

[21]*Ibid.*, p. 210.

[22]*Ibid.*, p. 397.

[23]*Ibid.*, p. 223.

[24]George Eliot, "The Sad Fortunes of the Rev. Amos Barton," *Scenes from Clerical Life,* ed. David Lodge (Harmondsworth: Penguin Books, 1973), pp. 80-81.

[25]Quoted by Haight, p. 119.

[26]George Eliot, *The Mill on the Floss* (New York: The Century Company, 1910) pp. 3-4.

[27]George Eliot, *Middlemarch* (Boston: Houghton, Mifflin, 1956), pp. 3-4. All subsequent references will be to this edition.

[28]Elaine Showalter, *A Literature of Their Own, British Women Novelists from Brontë to Lessing* (Princeton: Princeton Univ. Press, 1977) p. 58.

[29]*Ibid.*, p. 123.

[30]George Eliot, *Daniel Deronda* (Harmondsworth: Penguin, 1967), pp. 159-60.

René Magritte, *Le Viol*, 1934
© Menil Foundation, Houston
Photographer: A. Mewbourn
(see text reference, p. 17)

William Hogarth, *The Harlot's Progress*, Plate 3,
Apprehended by a Magistrate, 1732
reproduced by permission of
The Lewis Walpole Library,
Yale University,
Farmington, Connecticut
(see text reference, p. 36)

Jean-Baptiste Greuze, *Girl with Dead Canary*, 1765
reproduced by permission of
The National Gallery of Scotland
Edinburgh, Scotland
(see text reference, p. 85)

Antoinette Cecile Hortense Haudebourt-Lescot, *Self-Portrait* 1825
reproduced by permission of
Musée du Louvre
Palais du Louvre, Paris
(see text reference, p. 103)

Sir John Everett Millais, *The Blind Girl*, 1856
by courtesy of
Birmingham Museum and Art Gallery
Birmingham, England
(see text reference, p. 137)

Henri Matisse, *Persian Nude with Fruit and Flowers*, 1923
by courtesy of
The Art Institute of Chicago
(see text reference, p. 206)

Chapter 5

*Charles Dickens and Esther Summerson: The
Author as Female Child*

In 1869 Charles Dickens jokingly toasted the Mayor at a banquet in his honor at St. George's Hall, Liverpool and remarked that he himself was enslaved by not one woman, but by all of them. And then he made a slip of the tongue: " 'Speaking for the ladies, and for myself as one of them. . . .' "[1] Certainly Dickens has never been celebrated for creating great female characters as have Defoe and Richardson. There are indeed a great many women in his work, ranging from the mad old harridans like Mrs. Clennam or Miss Havisham, to the childlike halfwits like Little Nell, to the more complicated and moving women like Fanny Dorrit or Estella Provis. But all of his women, the good and the bad alike, labor under the burden of Victorian sterotypes and under the even heavier burden of the powerful and largely intractable feelings for women hanging about him from his childhood. Dickens really was a slave to women in such a way that he mars great long sections of his work with hymns to the angel in the house or heaps upon them the vituperation of the rejected child—angry at the evil mothers relentlessly destroying their children. In these women is placed the creative rage of someone who said about his own mother (in relation to the blacking warehouse episode): " 'But I never afterwards forgot, I never shall forget, I never can forget, that my mother was warm for my being sent back!' "[2]

Charles Dickens's fiction often seems really childish, especially when he attempts to present female characters, as opposed to caricatures. I do not refer to the deliberately childlike in his work. His is indeed a fictional world of fantasy, dream, and nightmare. But his emotional enslavement to women is something we feel as the aching response of the child engaged in intense pursuit of the one thing he can never have. This feeling pervades his work and obviously accounts for moments of great genius. *Oliver Twist* derives much of its brilliance from his recreation of childhood longing. As John Carey puts it: "Dickens goes on writing this fragment of his autobiography in novel after novel. The bright, pure child in the moldering house is an image to which his imagination constantly returns. But after *Oliver Twist* the child is always a girl."[3] Unfortunately, when the girl child is meant also to be an adult and also the heroine, the effect is of a peculiar series of contradictions, awkwardly but insistently linked.

Defoe and Richardson created towering women figures, but Charles Dickens certainly failed at his only sustained attempt at using the female voice, in the figure of Esther Summerson. I am even more interested in this failure because when Dickens narrated his novels as a man in *Great Expectations* and *David Copperfield* he created striking, important voices who shape remarkable fictions. The most obvious problem with Esther results from the constricting effects of a sexual stereotype, and these I have already discussed in Chapter Four. This stereotype will crucially affect what Esther may appear to know, and in her it is possible to see a schematic diagram of the nineteenth-century version of the mind of a good young woman. Much more to my purpose, however, will be to analyze Esther in relationship to Pip and David, on the one hand, and to Roxana and Clarissa, on the other. To do so will show how strikingly like her eighteenth century counterparts she is in the thematic uses to which she is put, and how clearly she has become a debilitated, even crippled, version of her author. The role she plays for him is one of identification, even over-identification, since the feelings expressed through her are so intense. But hers is a point of view he decided not to continue; he chose only one other time to write strictly from the female point of view. Miss Wade in *Little Dorrit* (given only a brief chapter) hates and torments herself. Like Esther, she is an illegitimate child given to grave doubts about what people think of her. She becomes a voice through which to express rage at both herself and at others who cannot learn to love. With Esther Dickens indulged in the voice of perfect love, with Miss Wade, in that of perfect hate. After that time (1857), Dickens never wrote another sustained narrative in the female voice.

In 1842 at a banquet in Boston, Dickens said, "I believe it may be said of an author's attachment to the creatures of his own imagination, that it is a perfect model of constancy and devotion, and is the blindest of all."[4] Unfortunately for this study, serious comments on both art and women are rare in Dickens's letters. But the devotion he described here is clearly central to his work. He does not make comments on the nature of fiction like those of Henry James because he was not able, or more precisely, was not interested in alleging intellectual distance between himself and his fictional creations. When he wanted to write about someone, he seemed to become that person. When he wrote about social problems, he seemed to immerse himself in an exemplary situation, situations that became prose poems and famous in themselves. Jails, laws, sewage—these too became characters in a drama intended to influence living people directly. In his later life he traveled extensively giving readings of his works. His characters were real to him, so real that he could read their lines as if in a play. He could hear them, could literally speak as if he and they were one.

This total immersion in the "minds" of his characters makes him seem closer to his more primitive eighteenth century predecessors than to Trollope or Thackeray, or George Eliot, all of whom were concerned with distancing themselves from those they observed fictionally. They adopted specific rhetorical strategies to claim their lack of identification with the people and events they described. Because Dickens rarely made such claims himself and because of what appears to be the unmediated force of his work as it confronts us on the page, the author creates the feeling of being embedded in his own fictions. We know from his number plans that the structure of his novels was often planned carefully. But what he has said about his art suggests that he intended to achieve a complete masquerade in his novels. This meant that his own voice was to appear a natural part of the world he presents. And he is largely successful at this endeavor. He saw himself as much more the recorder of experience than its judge and its rational shaper. I do not want to dismiss the peculiar, idiosyncratic personal voice, often so overwhelming in his work about which Robert Garis has written extensively.[5] Nor do I want to dismiss his role as social critic. Whatever the stance of his narrative voice, it seems infused with the voice of Dickens himself. We feel him everywhere and inhabiting everything. That person who tells us about the fog at the beginning of *Bleak*

House, or the prison in *Little Dorrit*, seems the voice of the elements he himself describes. Just as the view from Todgers is teeming and alive, Dickens' third-person narrator is that thing come alive and even speaking.[6]

Dickens believed that characters should not appear too separated from their own worlds. He wrote to Wilkie Collins in 1859 in response, apparently, to a criticism of the way Dr. Manette was presented in *A Tale of Two Cities:*

> This is quite apart from the peculiarity of the Doctor's character, as affected by his imprisonment; which of itself would, to my thinking, render it quite out of the question to put the reader inside of him before the proper time, in respect of matters that were dim to himself through being in a diseased way, morbidly shunned by him. I think the business of art is to lay all that ground carefully, not with the care that conceals itself—to shew, by a backward light, what everything has been working to—but only to *suggest*, until the fulfillment comes. These are the ways of Providence, of which ways all art is but a little imitation.[7]

It would not do to have the Doctor appear too self-aware. Experience is enigmatic, but suggestive. Dr. Manette comes to know slowly and then finally sees. He wrote to Collins in 1860 on *The Woman in White* and criticized him for investing his characters with too much authorial judgment: "Perhaps I express my meaning best when I say that the three people who write the narratives in these proofs have a DISSECTIVE property in common, which is essentially not theirs but yours; and that my own effort would be to strike more of what is got *that way* out of them by collision with one another, and by the working of the story."[8] To represent those in a fiction as thinking too carefully or as being able at all to separate themselves from the forces of their own world opposed Dickens's view of how fiction works. Forces like accidents and coincidence may seem to some readers artificial and contrived, but for Dickens they were integrally connected to character and to the way the world worked. He wrote to Bulwer-Lytton about the death of Madame Defarge:

> I am not clear, and I never have been clear, respecting that cannon of fiction which forbids the interposition of accident in such a case as Madame Defarge's death. Where the accident is inseparable from the

passion and emotion of the character, where it is strictly consistent with the whole design, and arises out of some culminating proceeding on the part of the character which the whole story has led up to, it seems to me to become, as it were, an act of divine justice.[9]

In large measure, then, what the reader often feels to be unconscious about Dickens's fiction or what seems to grow organically almost is really central to a view of the world that Dickens renders poetically. The death of Krook by spontaneous combustion is outrageous, were it not for the fact that a man so besmeared by the chemical filth of his lair could, in Dickens's world, literally go up in smoke. In such a world a Jamesian definition of irony or authorial distance simply does not work. For most Dickensian characters, the possibility of consciousness at all is nil; in fact in such a world self-awareness would be undesirable. To understand such a world fully would be to become as mad as the world itself. Hence it was extremely unusual for Dickens to adopt the first person voice at all. He did so in a sustained way only three times, with David, Pip, and Esther. These narratives are instantly recognizable as attempts at thinking about the world quite differently. These are voices of the author as an "I" who reflects on experience and who achieves that rare detachment from the teeming nightmare world from which other Dickensian figures cannot escape. With their obsessive gestures or their wild, demented repetitions, most of his other characters are prisoners.

Peter Coveney comments that "David Copperfield, and Pip in *Great Expectations*, are among the most remarkable evocations of childhood in the whole range of the century's literature..."[10] Rarely does such praise grace the head of Esther Summerson. She may be explained in her thematic significance, she may be dismissed, or be rationalized as a serious part of Dickens's aims for the book; but she is always a problem.[11] The "I," when it belongs to a young man growing up, is one of the strongest fictional articulations Dickens ever managed. When it belongs to a young woman, also apparently growing up, it fails hopelessly. Why did he choose the female voice at all, and why did he fail at its creation?

So much is known about the facts of Dickens's relationships with women and, in some ways, so little about his real feelings that

further discussion seems on the one hand superfluous, on the other
essential. All of his romances, from that with Maria Beadnell to that
with Ellen Ternan, seem a reflection of what Dickens named to
Forster as the " 'desperate intensity of my nature.' "[12] He was
referring to his youthful infatuation with Maria Beadnell and further
remarked that " 'No one can imagine in the most distant degree what
pain the recollection gave me in *Copperfield*,' " a book in which he
relived the connection.[13] His need to worship seems to have next
fallen on his wife's sister, Mary Hogarth. When she died in his arms
at seventeen Dickens was crushed and wished to be buried beside
her: " 'I cannot bear the thought of being excluded from her dust. . .
(for I don't think there ever was love like that I bear her).' "[14]
Georgina Hogarth soon enough became the keeper of this odd and
morbid flame (a flame celebrated in the almost necrophiliac Little
Nell). Six years after Mary's death he wrote to her mother celebrat-
ing her resemblance to Georgina (who was to be his housekeeper
almost for life):

> I trace in many respects a strong resemblance between her mental fea-
> tures and Georgina's—so strange a one, at times, that when she and Kate
> and I are sitting together, I seem to think that what has happened is a
> melancholy dream from which I am just awakening. The perfect like of
> what she was, will never be again, but so much of her spirit shines out in
> this sister, that the old time comes back again at some seasons, and I can
> hardly separate it from the present.

He dreamt of her frequently and ended the same letter by saying
that "she is so much in my thoughts at all times (especially when I
am successful, and have prospered in anything) that the recollection
of her is an essential part of being, and is as inseparable from my
existence as the beating of my heart is."[15] This idealization of the
woman who was not the wife must have made life miserable for the
less competent Kate. The intensity of feeling given over to the non-
sexual figure of sister-in-law clearly influenced permanently how
women were to be portrayed in Dickens's fiction. About his own
marriage he felt a miserable sense of failure:

> I believe my marriage has been for years and years as miserable a
> one as ever was made. I believe that no two people were ever created,
> with such an impossibility of interest, sympathy, confidence, sentiment,

tender union of any kind between them, as there is between my wife and me. It is an immense misfortune to her—it is an immense misfortune to me—but Nature has put an insurmountable barrier between us, which never in this world can be thrown down.[16]

When the young actress Ellen Ternan appeared on the scene we get, in his fiction at least, a picture of the hard, unloving woman of mystery. Dickens's desperate intensity (his daughters said that he behaved like a madman during the early years of the affair) is clear in Pip and in *Edwin Drood*.

This sense of being permanently unloved never left Dickens: " 'Why is it, that as with poor David, a sense comes always crushing on me now, when I fall into low spirits, as of one happiness I have missed in life, and one friend and companion I have never made?' "[17] Dickens tended to see himself as a rejected, utterly unloved child, especially when he described his personal situation to others. Much of his desperation must have come from the sense that he could never get what he wanted from women. In fact, however, he was also ruthless in his personal life; even his early letters to Maria Beadnell are peremptory and often corrective. His behavior toward his wife, what with walls between rooms, forced visits to Ellen Ternan, and public letters explaining his position (consistent apparently with much of his earlier treatment) was worthy only of someone who called himself "the inimitable." In trying to describe his personality Forster talked about "something even hard and aggressive" and then "a stern and even cold isolation of self-reliance side by side with a susceptivity almost feminine and the most eager craving for sympathy. . . ."[18]

Even this brief summary of his relationships with women indicates where his difficulties lay in putting them into his fiction. They became the vehicles for idealization in the supernaturally good and pure young women, and objects of rage in the murderous, death-dealing old harridans. Both Lionel Trilling and Edmund Wilson have concluded from Dickens's life that he often appeared to be divided between his love for the saintly figure and his identification with the criminal and the rebel.[19] This dichotomy is obvious in his female creations also. The figure of the child, being relatively sexless, seemed to solve some of his difficulties with the sex of the protagonist. In his early work it matters little whether the saintly figure is a boy or girl. Oliver Twist and Little Nell are equally threatened by rape; one by Fagin, the other by Quilp. And they are equally the vulnerable, unknowing child of holiness. Dickens often desexualized his adult heroines by making them both woman and child—Amy Dorrit, for instance. Stunted in height and deformed in appearance, they are saintly victims of life's aggressions. He can thus, artistically at any rate, have it both ways; he can worship (by making them so good) and punish (through crippling effects). Only then can they be candidates for heroism.

It is then especially important to consider why Dickens would have chosen at all to speak as Esther. Even the choice deserves our attention. Pip and David are clearly autobiographical, one about the unloved beginnings of Dickens's life, the other about that continuing failure to find the one special companion. In the beautiful and heartfelt preface to the Charles Dickens edition of *David Copperfield* he attests to this autobiographical relationship between himself and his hero:

> It would concern the reader little, perhaps, to know how sorrowfully the pen is laid down at the close of a two-years' imaginative task; or how an Author feels as if he were dismissing some portion of himself into the shawdowy world, when a crowd of the creatures of his brain are going from him forever. Yet, I have nothing else to tell; unless, indeed, I were to confess (which might be of less moment still,) that no one can ever believe this Narrative in the reading, more than I believed it in the writing.

> So true are these avowals at the present day, that I can now only take the reader into one confidence more. Of all my books, I like this the best. It will be easily believed that I am a fond parent to every child of my fancy, and that no one can ever love that family as dearly as I love them. But, like many fond parents, I have in my heart of hearts a favourite child. And his name is DAVID COPPERFIELD.[20]

Once again he asserts his imaginative closeness to his creations, but here he attempts to see something about his own life through someone he presents as "I." This novel relives Dickens's early life and the abject misery of the child abandoned by his parents to become a little drudge with low companions and no prospect of escape. *Great Expectations* involves again the violence of a certain kind of up-bringing and then the struggle to understand why one can love another who deliberately wishes not to love anyone at all. *Bleak House*, written between the other two novels, is much less a *bildungsroman* than the others—it is a scathing denunciation of the legal system in England. It is also, however, a full artistic statement by Dickens of the nature of psychological and social connection. On this level, despite the failure of Esther, it is a successful articulation of Dickensian ideas of interrelatedness. It is our business to understand what Dickens wanted to learn about himself when he gave over half the narrative to a young woman also apparently growing up. How does she reenact the dramas of childhood so precisely set out in David and Pip?

The worlds of all three of these novels are similarly violent, ugly, grotesque—and often outrageously funny. Murdstone and Grimby's, the marshes in which Pip encounters Magwitch, Tom All-Alone's—these are filthy places, literally full of slime and ooze. The task of the child is, in large measure, just to survive his world. Growing up for Dickens means in the simplest sense lifting oneself up and out. Perhaps the gravest threat to these figures is that of mutilation. The world is often so terrible that some violent physical act threatens to mark the child for life. Mutilation may come at the hands of the parent, or at least of the false parent, and it is the threat that is least amenable to control. In addition these children all must deal, both directly and symbolically, with bad and good parent figures. Here is the central strength of *Great Expectations,* that the parent-child confrontation is fully presented and finally consummated. I use this last word intentionally, first because *David Copperfield* and *Bleak House* are only partial treatments of this problem, but also because the central parent-child conflict in Dickens always has an explicitly sexual component.

Death or some other sudden loss of the parent most often initiates the parent-child problem. When this happens, the child feels intense guilt followed by a sustained period of torture at the hands of a false parent. This bad relationship is terminated often by some form of recognition, sometimes symbolic, of the true worth of the protagonist. For the most part Dickens sees "adult" love as the solution to the parent-child problem, although the components of this love are often a variant of the above. This struggle to get love, always as a form of rescue from apparently insoluble dilemmas, occupies much time and space in these novels. Love, in a variety of dimensions, will restore the hero/heroine to a state of wholeness, like that of childhood (an idealized one) but now as an adult. Throughout this journey, obviously not the same in all Dickens's novels and here only roughly schematized, a form of self-awareness is sought. Dickens does in these figures (as he almost never does in other characters) demand that they try to understand and know their own worlds. This nightmare world that offers the possibility of annihilation is too terrible to make complete sense of, and so neither David nor Pip nor Esther can completely comprehend or even see what is going on around them. Hence Dickens lets their voices fade from the narrative periodically. Though these figures participate and comment on their own experience, they do so with marked differences in sensitivity and intelligence. But it is clear that through each, Dickens confronts that intractable knot of rage at the heart of the abandoned child. And what he allows himself to say (and *how* he says it) as a woman differs markedly from what he says as a man.

There is of course a central structural difference between the way Dickens writes in the first person as a man and then as a woman. David and Pip control the world as we know it in those novels, even though they may occasionally slide away from our view. But Esther is an *alternative* view of the world. The other half of the narrative is controlled by a third-person narrator speaking in the present tense. This voice engages in the repetitive, rhetorical exhortation that Dickens reserves for profound meditations, or sometimes just tone poems, on what are often the bleakest and most depraved elements in society. There is often in these long passages, whether they concern railroads, prisms, or fogs, a sense of driving inevitability. Their existence is a fact that Dickens wants to recreate in prose—their essence and their permanence. The use of the present tense obviously makes us feel that the fog will go on and on. Esther's narrative concerns mainly the love that everyone else bears her and her growing recognition that she may love others, in the past tense. And so one consciousness is pitted against another; one that records the real nature of the world, as it exists in process, the other a human attempt at order, control, and change.

Esther cannot support the weight of her own world, as can David and Pip. Nor is she supposed to. There are many artistic choices Dickens seems to make about her because she is a good woman. Defoe's women appear unfettered by propriety—the sense of any social conventions, restrictions on how a woman should or should not act, operates weakly and sporadically in their minds. Richardson on the other hand, is obsessed with social forms, and much of the excess verbiage in Clarissa's language is traceable to the kind of language he thinks women should be using. But Dickens is obviously working within the demands of the female stereotype of the 1850's. Let us for a moment look at how David speaks and then compare him to Esther. In the justly famous beginning of the book David announces himself:

> Whether I shall turn out to be the hero of my own life, or whether that station will be held by anybody else, these pages must show. To begin my life with the beginning of my life, I record that I was born (as I have been informed and believe) on a Friday, at twelve o'clock at night. It was remarked that the clock began to strike, and I began to cry, simultaneously. (p. 49)

He begins by questioning his own potential heroism, in that peculiar and characteristic blend of stiff self-assertion and childlike faith. Indeed there is never any real doubt in his mind that he is the hero and deserves to be so. Dickens feels comfortable enough with this voice to give it resonance and strength and to speak through it as a worthy "I."

How different then appears Esther's wearying and inveterate self-apology. Dickens's narrative voice as it now appears in the feminine form undergoes a radical transformation:

> I have a great deal of difficulty in beginning to write my portion of these pages, for I know I am not clever. I always knew that. I can remember, when I was a very little girl indeed, I used to say to my doll, when we were alone together, "Now Dolly, I am not clever, you know very well, and you must be patient with me, like a dear!" And so she used to sit propped up in a great arm-chair, with her beautiful complexion

and rosy lips, staring at me—or not so much at me, I think, as at noth-ing—while I busily stitched away, and told her every one of my secrets.[21]

One can hardly imagine an introduction less calculated to raise the interest or even confidence of the reader. The endearing reticence of David is replaced here by coyness that clearly is meant to denote the female speaker. This tone should alert us instantly to the inordinate amount of censorship of this voice. The author simply will refuse to let her appear to know too much about what goes on around her; she will have to remain in ignorance about great chunks of what she sees. We should recognize also the double level of the disguise. Dickens writes as David, as a fictionalized version of himself. With Esther Dickens writes as Woman and also as himself. By putting so many conventional poses into her language he points out how overwhelmingly conscious he is that he is writing as a woman. To take on this voice is to take on for him a number of elements of a predetermined role. Furthermore, as she keeps on verbally dismiss-ing herself from the narrative, Dickens also asserts her overwhelming importance. She is after all, the summer sun, and we are living in *Bleak House*.

But she is not merely a collection of the mouthings of the angel in the house. She is Dickens's way of exploring what growing up would be like as a woman, what residing in the feminine con-sciousness would involve. But the fact that her "I" is one constantly engaged in denying itself gives Dickens a great deal of latitude in what he may assert through her. If she is indeed so unimportant, then are we not being lulled into ignoring much of what Dickens wants to explore through her? He can get away with a great deal more forbidden material than were we to take her too seriously:

> I don't know how it is, I seem to be always writing about myself. I mean all the time to write about other people, and I try to think about myself as little as possible, and I am sure, when I find myself coming into the story again, I am really vexed and say, "Dear, dear, you tiresome lit-tle creature, I wish you wouldn't!" but it is all of no use. I hope any one who may read what I write, will understand that if these pages contain a great deal about me, I can only suppose it must be because I have really something to do with them, and can't be kept out. (pp. 102-103)

Dickens creates this grotesquely false voice (and it was false even to readers at that time) to hide the nature of the fantasy he plays out through her. For she, like the female narrators in Defoe and Richardson, is invested with the will to dominate and control those around her.

Dickens believes, I think, that fearful infantilism should be the mark of the female consciousness. But he has great trouble maintaining a consistency of tone since he needs her to comment on people and events in a wry, cynical, even biting tone. Some critics would like to say that he very consciously wants to show a divided mind at work.[22] They would give him the gift of objectivity about her. Her unconsciousness is an element in her character so insistently presented, however, that even when the novel first appeared, John Forster criticized "the two conscious unconsciousness of Esther. . . ."[23] The contradictory tones in her voice become particularly noticeable when she makes observations on the shortcomings of others. So she describes Mr. Skimpole rather freely and adds:

> Of all his playful speeches (playful, yet always fully meaning what they expressed) none seemed to be more to the taste of Mr. Jarndyce than this. I had often new temptations, afterwards, to wonder whether it was really singular, or only singular to me, that he, who was probably the most grateful of mankind upon the least occasion, should so desire to escape the gratitude of others. (p. 67)

I think here that Dickens is simply inconsistent as a female speaker. He cannot really keep it up because he wants her to be both a good woman and on occasion a commentator on others. He solves his narrative problem by sliding in and out of the stereotypical ways of speaking whenever he feels like it. Far from being the distant portrayer of pathology, he identifies with her to an alarming degree, but, when convenient, forgets her.

Dickens sets up two other linguistic peculiarities around Esther. Very frequently he allows other people to speak to her in the third person. Instead of being questioned directly, things often are said about her, but to her face. Her guardian looks at her and says: "There never was such a Dame Durden . . . for making money last." (p. 734) Earlier in the novel, when he speaks of his developing feelings for her, he says:

> "I saw my ward oftener than she saw me" he added, cheerily making light of it, "and I always knew she was beloved, useful, and happy. She repays me twenty-thousand-fold, and twenty more to that, every hour in every day!" (p. 214)

These awful nicknames (the second peculiarity), Dame Trot, Dame Durden, among others, make it possible for everyone to lapse into sing-song hymns to her loving nature, and as often as not in ways exceedingly indirect.

I go into such detail about Esther's linguistic peculiarities because these mark her great distinguishing feature from David and Pip. Through his male speakers Dickens adopts the compassionate, occasionally elegiac tone of a man grown older and wiser. Their lives have had a history, and he accepts the task of recounting it. But Dickens wants Esther to gaze at the world with a sacred stupidity. Pip is an even richer character than David, and as Edward Said puts it: "*Great Expectations* reposes upon Dickens's portrayal of Pip as at once the novel's condition for being, the novel's action, and the character in it. The first-person narration adds to the purity of Dickens's achievement."[24]

I would like to consider how Dickens deals with the threat of mutilation, so omnipresent in the Dickens world, as a male speaker, then as a female. At David's first meeting with Mr. Murdstone, he perceives his own danger:

> I gave him my hand. After a moment of suspense, I went and kissed my mother: she kissed me, patted me gently on the shoulder, and sat down again to her work. I could not look at her, I could not look at him, I knew quite well that he was looking at us both; and I turned to the window and looked out there, at some shrubs that were drooping their heads in the cold.
>
> As soon as I could creep away, I crept upstairs. My old dear bedroom was changed, and I was to lie a long way off. I rambled downstairs to

find anything that was like itself, so altered it all seemed; and roamed
into the yard. I very soon started back from there, for the empty dog-
kennel was filled up with a great dog—deep-mouthed and black-haired
like Him—and he was very angry at the sight of me, and sprang out to
get at me. (p. 93)

The violence that both Pip and David are subject to comes from bad
parents (or their doubles, like the dog), intent upon bringing a child
up by hand. Dickens relates these acts of violence as if they come out
of nowhere and fast. Mrs. Joe, Pip's sister, will move from placid
kneading of dough to rage in an instant. One moment Pip stares
reflectively at the family gravestones, the next is hanging upside
down. Orlick's rage is fatal and unpredictable. But both these men
fight back; they do not lie passive in its wake. Pip decides to help
the convict, thus becoming a little liar himself. David, after all, bites
Mr. Murdstone's hand:

> He had my head as in a vice, but I twined round him somehow, and
> stopped him for a moment, entreating him not to beat me. It was only
> for a moment that I stopped him, for he cut me heavily for an instant
> afterwards, and in the same instant I caught the hand with which he held
> me in my mouth, between my teeth, and bit it through. It sets my teeth
> on edge to think of it. (p. 108)

Speaking as a male child Dickens allows violence to beget violence.
The child must put up a tremendous fight—help may not come from
anywhere but inside.

Evil is personal in *David Copperfield* and *Great Expectations*.
The hand is really out there and really belongs to someone. But in
Bleak House, the hand is metaphoric; the ultimate threat belongs to
the social system, exemplified by the legal structure of Chancery.
Esther's mutilation comes from the complexities of social linkages—
she has a social disease, and she is made to suffer from it extensively.
Looking back to Defoe and Richardson's female masquerades, I
said that a significant portion of these narratives were given out to
exploring emotional and physical disintegration. In each case the
author investigates a prolonged loss of boundaries between self and
other. This seems to be an inviting turn of mind, a chance to view
the world utterly anew, in an altered state of consciousness. In this

novel, Esther's physical disintegration has a special thematic point. The opening pages of this novel, so famous for the evocation of London shrouded in fog, show society melting into itself. All people are connected by virtue of the fog and the law, so murky, limitless, blurred is the content of this world. Such social blurring is evident in Jo's death, which itself spreads to more exalted homes. His is a disease which melts the features and changes one from what she was before. The death of Krook by spontaneous combustion is only a quasi-comical representation of a self destroyed by its own evil and by that of society. The fog, the diseases, the change in looks due to smallpox—all are various manifestations of the disintegration which results from social evil.

Her mutilation is clouded by the fact that Esther starts out with no face, no looks, no body, the wrong age, assorted nicknames. Granted that self-description is difficult for the first-person narrator, we at least are given enough physical sensation from David and Pip that they appear to reside in bodies. What is even more odd is that Esther's looks are crucial as evidence against her mother, as the erstwhile suitor Guppy is the first to recognize when he sees Lady Dedlock's portrait:

> Mr. Guppy has no eyes for either of these magnates. "It's unaccountable to me," he says, still staring at the portrait, "how well I know that picture! I'm dashed!" adds Mr. Guppy, looking round, "if I don't think I must have had a dream of that picture, you know!" (p. 82)

Later Dickens makes very explicit the significance of the resemblance:

> "Though a young man, I have ferreted out evidence, got up cases, and seen lots of life. Blest with your hand, what means might I not find of advancing your interests, and pushing your fortunes! What might I not get to know, nearly concerning you? I know nothing now, certainly; but what *might* I not, if I had your confidence, and you set me on?" (p. 114)

But the thematic significance of her face is thoroughly undercut by Dickens's refusal to let her experience herself as a person of flesh and blood. Dickens would have it that Esther is an attractive young woman of twenty-one, judging from the illustrations in the original edition. But he also takes care to desexualize her through her grand-motherly behavior—we are not to feel that she herself could possibly have a face that would excite desire. In fact, most of the illustrations present her with her back towards us. But he then proceeds to make her looks the center of her personal drama, as she suffers through smallpox.

She very melodramatically announces the onset of the illness: "And now come and sit beside me for a little while, and touch me with your hand. For I cannot see you, Charley: 'I am blind'" (p. 391). Her narrative becomes a record of her dreams and her enfeebled attempts to keep Ada from the room. When she finally does recover, her features have melted away:

> My hair had not been cut off, though it had been in danger more than once. It was long and thick. I let it down, and shook it out, and went up to the glass upon the dressing-table. There was a little muslin curtain drawn across it. I drew it back: and stood for a moment looking through such a veil of my own hair, that I could see nothing else. Then I put my hair aside, and looked at the reflection in the mirror; encouraged by seeing how placidly it looked at me. I was very much changed—O very, very much. At first, my face was so strange to me, that I think I should have put my hands before it and started back, but for the encouragement, I have mentioned. Very soon it became more familiar, and then I knew the extent of the alteration in it even better than I had done at first. I was not like what I had expected; but I had expected nothing definite, and I dare say anything definite would have surprised me.

> I had never been a beauty, and had never thought myself one; but I had been very different from this. It was all gone now. Heaven was so good to me, that I could let it go with a few not bitter tears, and could stand there arranging my hair for the night quite thankfully. (pp. 444-45)

As a result of the loss she resolves to send Woodcourt's flowers back to him, thereby indicating the final end to her youth and appeal.

Dickens is really insisting on the physical mutilation, and moreover he is going to allow this change to stand for something important and good about Esther. Like Richardson he posits a bodily disintegration with ethical significance. It is an essential part of her sainthood, and her reaction to this loss is disturbingly deprecating:

> . . . I had scarcely any time to think about that little loss of mine,
> and was almost always cheerful. If I did think of it at odd moments now
> and then, I had only to be busy and forget it. I felt it more than I had
> hoped I should, once, when a child said "Mother, why is the lady not a
> pretty lady now, like she used to be?' But when I found the child was
> not less fond of me, and drew its soft hand over my face with a kind of
> pitying protection in its touch, that soon set me up again. (p. 447)

As Joseph Gold remarks; "There is almost an outrageous courage,
a willful assertion of meaning in Dickens's creation of this character,
a woman, who can lose her looks and speak of 'that little loss of
mine.' "[25] Certainly the author makes much of assorted reactions to
Esther's changed face, as she becomes a sort of moral bellwether. The
most common reaction is weeping, as Miss Flite does for ten minutes.
The moral turpitude of Guppy is evident when she puts up her veil
and he begins to cough and act nervous. He also makes the decision
to "repel and repudiate" his declaration. Ada Clare on the other
hand bathes her face in kisses. Allan Woodcourt notices, but gently;
and she says: "I felt as if he had greater commiseration for me than
I had ever had for myself. . . While we were talking, and when I was
glad to believe that I had alleviated (if I may use such a term) the
shock he had had in seeing me, Richard came in" (p. 549). Dickens
seems to be delighting in imagining a female speaker who is the victim of a terrible disfigurement. To be marked in the face is to be set
apart as the victim. While David Copperfield is born with a caul,
Dickens allows Esther to become the emblem of permanent childhood suffering. There seems also to be a strong experiential component here, as well, however. Just as Richardson indulged himself in
the fainting and dying of Clarissa, Dickens seems to be playing at
debility and sickness. It is an inviting posture, one that, under the
right circumstances, will elicit sympathy and love. The erasure of the
self is both a punishment (like the deformation of a number of his
other female characters) and a triumph.

Why would Dickens have taken such pains to damage Esther's
selfhood? Such measures are clearly not necessary with Pip and
David (though they too suffer)—why with a woman? Perhaps the

most compelling explanation lies in the fact that Esther succeeds at what Pip and David really fail at, and for that overwhelmingly infantile success, she must be punished. Dickens indulges himself in imagining the fulfillment of his childhood fantasies as a woman. The male figures are viewed more objectively, no matter how much he loves them. They derive strength from the reconciliation of their fantasies with the world of real possibilities and limitations. But with Esther he may imagine a kind of unearthly success story that transcends all the pressing and sordid circumstances of the world as it is depicted in the novel. At the heart of Dickensian fiction, as I said earlier, is the problem of the child's reconciliation with the parent. This can sometimes be the weak center of the novel, the spiritualized and seemingly irrelevant story of an Oliver Twist or a Little Nell. The strongest novels with this theme are the narratives of David and Pip. But the greatest insight of these heroes is that they cannot resolve their childish agony of separation. Through Esther, however, Dickens imagines a complete triumph over the guilt and crippling inability to love that results from the abandonment by the true parent and the child's subjection to the false one. This triumph, however, is a very threatening one for the author. With such radical disfigurement of the heroine, he obviously reduces the threat of the victory.

In November of 1842 Dickens commented to John Forster on Browning's play, *A Blot on the 'Scutcheon*: " 'I know nothing that is so affecting, nothing in any book I have ever read, as Mildred's recurrence to that 'I was so young—I had no mother.' "[26] Children like David and Pip and Esther must deal with a profound act of abandonment by the true parent, an abandonment that is either deliberate or due to death. This leave-taking involves the child in a heavy sense of guilt, represented dramatically and often quite literally. David's father has died, and his mother fails to love him strongly and with resolve. David's problems with his lessons cause his mother to be hurt: "I had perception enough to know that my mother was the victim always; that she was afraid to speak to me, or to be kind to me, lest she should give them some offence by her manner of doing so, and receive a lecture afterwards; that she was not only ceaselessly afraid of her own offending, but of my offending, and uneasily watched their looks if I only moved" (p. 171).

The drama of torture by the Murdstones is ended when Clara Copperfield dies—a death which takes David's infancy to the grave also: "The mother who lay in the grave, was the mother of my infancy; the little creation in her arms, was myself, as I had once been, hushed for ever on her bosom" (p. 187). Now David will be left to resolve somehow the problems his mother has escaped, especially the burden of being abandoned in both life and death.

Great Expectations begins with a boy child like David contemplating his parents and his five dead siblings' gravestones. Abruptly he is yanked upside down, and here begins a guilty association that will lead Pip to be disloyal to his one true parent in the novel—Joe. He steals to feed the convict:

> Since that time, which is far enough away now, I have often thought that few people know what secrecy there is in the young, under terror. No matter how unreasonable the terror, so that it be terror. I was in mortal terror of the young man who wanted my heart and liver; I was in mortal terror of my interlocutor with the ironed leg; I was in mortal terror of myself, from whom an awful promise had been extracted; I had no hope of deliverance through my all-powerful sister, who repulsed me at every turn; I am afraid to think of what I might have done, on requirement, in the secrecy of my terror.[27]

Pip feels such terrible guilt because he is stealing from his sister, Mrs. Joe, a woman who constantly brags about the quality of her motherhood but who is actually abusive and violent. Having replaced his real parents, Mrs. Joe demands gratitude, even though her mean, cruel behavior forces Pip to fear her. Once again Dickens opposes the child to a set of bad parents, Magwitch and Mrs. Joe, against whom he feels tremendous anger, but whom he must propitiate, on pain of physical attack. These bad parents are often vividly, comically bad, but are truly dangerous, nevertheless. Mr. Murdstone and Mrs. Joe really do aim to hurt—they are life-denying and irrational— one can merely do obeisance and stay out of the way.

Esther Summerson is, herself, the victim of two bad mothers in *Bleak House*, Miss Barbary and Lady Dedlock. They mistreat her even though she herself has committed no sin:

"Your mother, Esther, is your disgrace, and you were hers. The time will come—and soon enough—when you will understand this better, and will feel it too, as no one save a woman can. I have forgiven her;' but her face did not relent; "the wrong she did to me, and I say no more of it, though it was greater than you will ever know—than any one will ever know, but I, the sufferer. For yourself, unfortunate girl, orphaned and degraded from the first of these evil anniversaries, pray daily that the sins of others be not visited upon your head, according to what is written. Forget your mother, and leave all other people to forget her who will do her unhappy child that greatest kindness. Now go!"

"Submission, self-denial, diligent work, are the preparations for a life begun with such a shadow on it. You are different from other children, Esther, because you were not born, like them, in common sinfulness and wrath. You are set apart." (p. 19)

The sin of illegitimacy is slightly different from the simple absence of parents that David and Pip suffer. Lady Dedlock has absented herself and done it out of a double evasion: an illicit sexual relationship and fear of its consequences. Esther's mother is bad in a way that the missing parents in the other novel are not. And her father has absented himself from life—he is no one (Nemo). Not even her birthday is a cause for celebration:

It was my birthday. There were holidays at school on other birthdays—none on mine. There were rejoicings at home on other birthdays, as I knew from what I heard the girls relate to one another—there were none on mine. My birthday was the most melancholy day at home, in the whole year.

I have mentioned that, unless my vanity should deceive me (as I knew it may, for I may be very vain, without suspecting it—though indeed I don't), my comprehension is quickened when my affection is. My disposition is very affectionate; and perhaps I might still feel such a wound, if such a wound could be received more than once, with the quickness of that birthday. (p. 18)

Her sin here is felt as a wound, something residing inside her rather than a fact involving accident and fate. Guilt comes to David and Pip for what they do, to Esther for what she is. Now the Dickensian speaker is a victim in a way that she cannot possibly control. This will mean that the only possible resolution will have to be done to or *for* her. No action is possible. Clearly this form of victimization leads to self-indulgence for Dickens. The tone of the passage I quoted above is one of coy self-pity. As a woman Dickens allows himself the luxurious basking of the helpless victim.

But Dickensian children must enact a reconciliation with the parent through that same person appearing in an altered, younger form. Dickens recognizes that the child repeats the problems of the past—he can love only in the way he has been taught. Dickens makes no secret that Clara Copperfield's childishness is responsible for her relationship with someone cruel and dangerous. That she is a fool and irresponsible exists barely below the surface of David's feelings for her. The admirable competence and independence of Miss Betsey Trotwood is a continual reproach. She of course feels that David is the wrong child altogether—a girl would have grown up to be like her. David's way of exorcising this erring parent is to marry another, his child bride Dora. Dora is sweet and appealing, a part of her that derived from her closeness to Mary Hogarth in Dickens's mind (indeed he named one of his daughters Dora). But she is also stupid and incompetent, attributes he very definitely attached to his wife, Kate. Dickens allows David to speculate on the failure of his feeling for Dora in a way that closely resembles what the author apparently thought and said about his own marriage:

> The old unhappy feeling pervaded my life. It was deepened, if it were changed at all; but it was as undefined as ever, and addressed me like a strain of sorrowful music faintly heard in the night. I loved my wife dearly, and I was happy; but the happiness I had vaguely anticipated, once, was not the happiness I enjoyed, and there was always something wanting.

> In fulfillment of the compact I have made with myself, to reflect my mind on this paper, I again examine it, closely, and bring its secrets to the light. What I missed, I still regarded—I always regarded—as something that had been a dream of my youthful fancy; that was incapable of realization; that I was now discovering to be so, with some natural pain, as all men did. But that it would have been better for me if my wife could have helped me more, and shared the many thoughts in which I had no partner; and that this might have been; I knew. (p.765)

The writing of this book involves a compact with himself, obviously to know as much and as well as he can about himself. There is a strong sense in this novel of the failure of this childlike view of love. But David must do it, must live with it to know it.

In *Great Expectations* Dickens is even more acutely aware of the effects of deprivation of love on the child. Joe puts up with the "government" meted out by Mrs. Joe because: "I see so much in my poor mother, of a woman drudging and slaving and breaking her honest hart and never getting no peace in her mortal days, that I'm dead afeered of going wrong in the way of not doing what's right by a woman, and I'd fur rather of the two go wrong the t'other way, and be a little ill-conwenienced myself" (p. 80). The misery of Joe's mother has made him into a slave too. Dickens recognizes that Pip has been deformed by the childhood abuse visited upon him, and part of the intense sorrow of the novel grows out of the protagonist's coming to terms with this fact. Pip is caught up with a series of women who do not care and who are asking him to "play" with them. He is literally to reenact Miss Havisham's past as she would have liked to have it played out. And he most gratifyingly does. He falls in love with a woman who cannot love—like his sister, but with the realization now that this is a kind of sickness in him. Estella does not finally offer the possibility of the good, sweet, loving, princess— he comes to see her for what she is. As for Miss Havisham, Pip wrestles her to the ground and puts out the flames—those which finally destroy her. This is a scene with many primitive resonances— but it is finally a way, for Dickens, of dramatizing the force that is sexuality—a force exacting and ugly in its manifestations. Pip finally repudiates the claim of the bad parent, while still recognizing its consequences in his love for Estella; David, however, is rescued from the dilemma through Agnes, a figure much like that of Georgina Hogarth in Dickens's own life. Both of Dickens's male speakers do, however, attempt to understand the nature of their romantic dilemmas. The possibilities of adult love have been warped by parental deprivation, a loss the growing person confronts by re-enacting it with another, younger version of the cruelly unjust parent.

When Dickens lives out this dilemma through a woman, the

reenactment and final confrontation take place only indirectly. Esther's reconciliation with the bad father, Nemo, comes in part from her relationship to Jo, the crossing sweep. Like him, her father has become a piece of social trash, diseased, living in a hovel, knowing "nothink." She lives out through her body the disease of the past. Esther's replacement parent is ostensibly very good indeed, the all-wise Mr. Jarndyce. Though usually described in benevolent terms, Jarndyce is morally obtuse (in his dealings with Skimpole), uses baby talk when dealing with Esther or Charley and her family, and has to distance himself so far from emotion as to fall into metaphors about the wind. This foolishness is often rather dangerous and makes him appear, at least in the beginning of the novel, as eccentric and untrustworthy. It is he who gives Esther her nicknames:

> "You are clever enough to be the good little woman of our lives here, my dear," he returned, playfully; "the little old woman of the Child's (I don't mean Skimpole's) Rhyme
>
> " 'Little old woman, and whither so high?'—
> 'To sweep the cobwebs out of the sky.' You will sweep them so neatly out of *our* sky, in the course of your housekeeping, Esther, that one of these days we shall have to abandon the Growlery, and nail up the door."
>
> This was the beginning of my being called Old Woman, and Little Old Woman, and Cobweb, and Mrs. Shipton, and Mother Hubbard, and Dame Durden, and so many names of that sort, that my own name soon became quite lost among them. (p. 90)

There is an edge to this acceptance of an age much closer to his own, but also much ambivalence. Jarndyce does in fact present the same sexual threat to Esther that Dora and Estella do to the male figures. He offers to her a life and love that would be clearly unsatisfactory, but for which she longs. Just before he asks that they be married, Dickens emphasizes that for her he is the father, clear and simple:

> "And oftener still," said I, "she blesses the Guardian who is a Father to her!"

At the word Father, I saw his former trouble come into his face. He subdued it as before, and it was gone in an instant; but, it had been there,
and it had come so swiftly upon my words that I felt as if they had
given him a shock. I again inwardly repeated, wondering, "That *I* could
readily understand. None that I could readily understand!" No, it was
true. I did not understand it. Not for many and many a day. (p. 214)

Dickens would like to see a reaffirmation of the father-child
role here. He is sufficiently uneasy to emphasize that, though Esther
will accept the job if necessary, she should not really be asked to.
In rejecting the older father, Dickens substitutes Allan Woodcourt,
merely a younger version of Jarndyce. He solves the matter of reconciliation by allowing the older man to become a fairy godfather of
sorts and give her as a gift to Woodcourt. She certainly cannot confront Jarndyce, as Pip does Miss Havisham (and Jarndyce is in a
state of arrested development also); she has to let all this be done to
her and for her. Jarndyce is no Quilp, but he probably wants sex
just as badly.

Everything about Woodcourt and Esther demonstrates how
important that this be a magical rescue by a young father. Dickens
almost never allows her to register him as an adult, physical presence.
"I have omitted to mention in its place, that there was some one
else at the family dinner party. It was not a lady. It was a gentleman.
It was a gentleman of a dark complexion—a young surgeon. He was
rather reserved, but I thought him very sensible and agreeable. At
least, Ada asked me if I did not, and I said yes" (p. 163). The phrase,
"it was not a lady," is a wonderful one, since it shows graphically
the kind of indirection that plagues Dickens. Later references to
Woodcourt are in this same vein. He is not even allowed to bring his
own flowers—they are handed to her by Caddy. After her illness,
and with very little warning, she announces that Woodcourt might
have once loved her. Not only is this revelation rather startling but
with it comes the assertion tht she releases him from any bond he
might have made. Releasing him from his imaginary bond seems
freeing to her and she announces that she can go, "please God, upon
my lowly way along the path of duty,and he could go his nobler
way upon its broader road; and though we were apart upon the
journey, I might aspire to meet him, unselfishly, innocently, better

far than he had thought me when I found some favour in his eyes, at the journey's end" (p. 443).

Since there has been no interaction between them, at least nothing visible to the reader, Esther's intensity comes as a shock. We have not been allowed to see any of it. When we finally do get to see Woodcourt in action, declaring his love, he speaks to her the way Jarndyce does: " 'Heavens knows, beloved of my life;' said he, 'that my praise is not a lover's praise, but the truth. You do not know what all around you see in Esther Summerson, how many hearts she touches and awakens, what sacred admiration and what love she wins' " (p. 731). Through Esther, Dickens indulges himself in the childhood fantasy of the rescuing parent, the rescuing sexual parent. We sense, I think, that here is his most profound wish—that adult life will replay the good fantasies of childhood. There is no sense in Esther, as in David and Pip, that that one dear companion is forever to be missed. As a female child Dickens gets exactly what he would want in his childish fancy. And her relationships, indeed her consciousness, remain just that—of a child. The greatest problem for us as readers of *Bleak House* is that Dickens wants it this way; he insists.

Dickens indulges an even stronger fantasy through Esther and that is of her power to transform the lives and minds of other people. Here I think we come to an important similarity in the way Defoe, Richardson and Dickens use the female voice. Both his eighteenth century predecessors explore through female speakers what complete power over others would be like. The power, as I have said, is gained with extreme loss, disintegration. Esther's disintegration is metaphoric, as well as physical and psychological, and the impulses toward domination and control explored through her are as strong as those that appear in Roxana and Clarissa. As she loses her individual identity, the collective, symbolic role takes over. As if by magic, Esther is lifted from the grim horror of what her life would surely have been had she not been pronounced one of the wards in Jarndyce. Dickens records very poignantly his own feelings (in *David Copperfield*) of being abandoned to the work in the blacking warehouse:

> No words can express the secret agony of my soul as I sunk into this companionship; compared these henceforth everyday associates with those of my happier childhood—not to say with Steerforth, Traddles, and the rest of those boys; and felt my hopes of growing up to be a learn-ed and distinguished man, crushed in my bosom. The deep remembrance of the sense I had, of being utterly without hope now; of the shame I felt in my position; of the misery it was to my young heart to believe that day by day what I had learned, and thought, and delighted in, and raised my fancy and my emulation up by, would pass away from me, little by little, never to be brought back any more; cannot be written. (p. 210)

Dickens's despair was so intense, his shame and horror at what he might have become such that it was only late in his own life that he told even his children about the incident. No feeling was so painful as I said at the beginning of the chapter, as that of having been abandoned by his parents. The rescue of the child, as if by magic through some benevolent outside intervention was to fascinate him all his life. To a large extent *Great Expectations* is a careful look at the consequences of really being rescued, but in Esther Summerson the author tries on another solution. He invests her with the power of love. It is through feelings that come from her and create love in others that she will prevail.

Dickens demonstrates the binding power of this love through the structure of the plot. Esther links everybody through herself. She is the way they are connected—and therefore resides at the center of the consciousness of a great many people. The scope of *Bleak House* is vast—all the way from Tom All Alone's to Chesney Wold. There are families of varying success: the Jellybys, the Par-diggles, the Bagnets, the Smallweeds. There is the whole class of legal men and their hangers-on: Tulkinghorn, Guppy, Krook, and Bucket. And there are those who form the domestic circle of interest in the book: Ada Clare and Richard Carstone, Mr. Jarndyce, Caddy and Prince Turveydrop. Esther literally keeps these people together—she provides psychic glue. She is the *secret* center of interest in the legal sphere, as she is in the world of Chesney Wold. She is the one every-one else wants to get hold of or get possession of. In fact to find her becomes either a legal, a moral, or emotional imperative. Love as a

way of holding people together is evident in the speed with which
Peepy attaches himself to her. In finding out about their visit to the
Jellybys, Jarndyce asks if it should perhaps have rained sugarplums
or tarts:

> "It did better than that. It rained Esther."
> "Ay?" said Mr. Jarndyce. "What did Esther do?"

> "Why, cousin John," said Ada, clasping her hands upon his arm, and
> shaking her head at me across him—for I wanted her to be quiet: "Esther
> was their friend directly. Esther nursed them, coaxed them to sleep,
> washed and dressed them, told them stories, kept them quiet, bought
> them keepsakes"—My dear girl! I had only gone out with Peepy, after
> he was found, and given him a little, tiny horse!—" and cousin John, she
> softened poor Caroline, the eldest one so much, and was so thoughtful
> for me and so amiable!—No, no, I won't be contradicted, Esther dear!
> You know, you know, it's true!" (pp. 61-62)

Containing in herself not only the sun but the rain, Esther has the
ability to generate love wherever she goes.

Dickens uses Esther as an agent of social transformation. It is
through her consciousness that those around her, at least, are to be
saved. Here is undoubtedly one of the most problematic aspects of
her character. Her ability to be loved seems often instantaneous,
magical; at other times she is shown laboring for love. Her attempts
to get love come at a cost, the housekeeper's cost. Through these
costs she can expiate the guilty birth and atone for her bad past:

> I went up to my room, and crept to bed, and laid my doll's cheek
> against mine wet with tears; and holding that solitary friend upon my
> bosom, cried myself to sleep. Imperfect as my understanding of my sor-
> row was, I knew that I had brought no joy, at any time, to anybody's
> heart, and that I was to no one upon earth what Dolly was to me.

> Dear, dear, to think how much time we passed alone together after-
> wards, and how often I repeated to the doll the story of my birthday,
> and confided to her that I would try, as hard as ever I could, to repair
> the fault I had been born with (of which I confusedly felt guilty and yet
> innocent), and would strive as I grew up to be industrious, contented,
> and kind-hearted, and to do some good to some one, and win some love

to myself if I could. I hope it is not self-indulgent to shed these tears as I think of it. I am very thankful, I am very cheerful, but I cannot quite help their coming to my eyes.

There! I have wiped them away now, and can go on again properly. (pp. 19-20)

To get love sometimes involves a struggle, one that is as painful and exacting as those carried on by Roxana and Clarissa. Because Dickens wants her to be a good woman, she must remain passive, to a certain extent, in the struggle. Yearning, a certain emotional hunger can be strongly felt in her voice. Much like Clarissa, she seems driven by the contradictory impulses played out in her. Love is certainly the only real form of power in the decayed and rotting world of *Bleak House*. People are changed through love—they are brought into consciousness of their real responsibilities to other human beings. Dickens first presents Jarndyce as a crusty, eccentric old gentleman unable to tolerate the slightest disagreement or bad feeling. Esther's ministrations turn him into a benevolent quasi-god figure. Jo, Ada, Richard, Allan's mother (a snobbish lady who worships someone called Morgan Ap Kerrig), all are ushered into the consciousness of love through her. Even her erring mother, Lady Dedlock, comes under her spell. It is Esther, or we should say more precisely her looks, that brings the downfall of Lady Dedlock. The bad woman must be brought low and made conscious of her sins in order for her to be redeemed. Dickens emphasizes that the retreat into the castle of security made of money will not help against Tulkinghorn, and he makes it no secret that this revelation will be through Esther:

As no one present takes any special interest in Mr. Guppy's dreams, the probability is not pursued. But he still remains so absorbed by the portrait that he stands immoveable before it until the young gardener has closed the shutters; when he comes out of the room in a dazed state, that is an odd though a sufficient substitute for interest, and follows into the succeeding rooms with a confused stare, as if he were looking everywhere for Lady Dedlock again. (p. 82)

When Lady Dedlock sees her in church, Esther describes her look; "Shall I ever forget the rapid beating at my heart, occasioned by the look I met, as I stood up! Shall I ever forget the manner in which those handsome proud eyes seemed to spring out of their languor and to hold mine!" (p. 224). Not only her face but her emotional intensity generate similar, reciprocal feelings in her mother. But when she meets with her mother after the illness, her mother responds to no change in her looks. It is the force of her inner being, her inner self, that her mother responds to. In experiencing radical disfigurement Esther is glad that she cannot bring disgrace upon her mother, and yet this proud, cold woman is made to fall on her knees before her: "O my child, my child, I am your wicked and unhappy mother! O try to forgive me!" (p. 449). Lady Dedlock was a type, like Rosa Dartle in *David Copperfield*, or Estella, or Rosa Bud, in *The Mystery of Edwin Drood*, that fascinated Dickens, in his later life even obsessed him, undoubtedly because of their resemblance to Ellen Ternan. How to force this kind of woman to see, to care, to love was a question that interested him deeply. When in Paris, Dickens wrote to Wilkie Collins (April 22, 1856):

> Some pretty faces, but all of two classes—wicked and coldly calculating, or haggard and wretched in their worn beauty. Among the latter was a woman of thirty or so, in an Indian shawl, who never stirred from a seat in a corner all the time I was there. Handsome, regardless, brooding, and yet with some nobler qualities in her forehead. I mean to walk about tonight and look for her.[28]

Esther at least succeeds in getting some striking, almost apocalyptic recognition from her proud, erring mother. Once again, however, Dickens refuses to allow her to register the full significance of the event. With the announcement: "I proceed to other passages of my narrative" (p. 615), she gives a short, edifying speech on the virtues of not dwelling on sorrow. Because the author refuses to allow her to understand her experiences, she comes to sound peculiarly invulnerable and monolithic, if childish too. But her lack of understanding is, for her author at least, an important element in her transformative power.

Esther very definitely triumphs in the terrible world of *Bleak House*. In fact the book ends on a note of almost supernatural praise for the little housekeeper. One of the final chapters of the book is called "Beginning the World." Esther has become the perfect adjunct to a perfect husband: "The people even praise Me as the doctor's wife. The people even like Me as I go about, and make so much of me that I am quite abashed. I owe it all to him, my love, my pride! They like me for his sake, as I do everything I do in life for his sake" (p. 769). She is beloved by everyone, having retired to a bower of bliss. Old Chesney Wold, the pride of its house reduced and disgraced, lies overgrown and dismal. Dickens did often end his books on a note of domestic happiness and social continuity, but the ending of *Bleak House* is positively rapturous. *David Copperfield* ends on a somewhat similar note, much shortened however, as the hero looks into the shining face of his Agnes. But David is not given to the ecstatic, obtuse narcissism that so marks Esther. The ending of *Great Expectations* (indeed whichever ending one chooses) is an elegiac farewell to the sense of love as Dickens had youthfully apotheosized it. With both of these male speakers, the attempt has been really to understand the nature of love and how one comes to terms with it. But Esther is idealized love in action, and she sweeps all before her. Dickens uses his female voice as the generative social conscience and consciousness. Through her the world will be saved if it can be. And yet she is a nonperson, passive, unreflective, never learning from experience. I do not think we should call Esther untrustworthy in quite the same way we can the female voices of Defoe and Richardson. But there is a fundamental problem in believing her to be what her author claims her to be. Her voice carries with it neither conviction nor authority, and scholars have been hard at work somehow reconciling all the contradictions she represents. Surely one of the most potent sources for these contradictions comes from her place in an intensely private fantasy of her author (a fantasy singularly in keeping with Victorian notions of woman as an object of veneration). This most heartfelt wish of an abandoned child, (at least he felt himself to be so for a time), was to be played out in a number of female characters during the course of his career, but nowhere with such intensity as in Esther Summerson.

It seems likely that when Dickens wanted to learn something about himself, he wrote autobiographical novels from a male point of view. It is difficult to believe that he could have learned much from his female speaker, since he indulged himself in such childish feelings of helplessness and weakness and equally childish visions of total triumph over the minds and hearts of others. A certain self-indulgence marks the female voices of Defoe also, who seemed to idealize the male role of strength and self-sufficiency and therefore used women to express his own fears about the lack thereof. Clarissa certainly expresses the fears of Samuel Richardson, and through her the author advanced a view of true power and strength (as opposed to the fraudulent kind in possession of the male hero). But her power comes through determined weakness, and this is true of Esther also. As the voices of their authors' fear, these women are weak, but they give voice to another fantasy—the King of the Mountain fantasy, if you will. The strange woman that results is an oddly costumed creature on a distorted mental stage.

After *Bleak House* Dickens grew somewhat less hopeful about the redemptive properties of saintly women. The heroine of *Little Dorrit* (1855-57) cannot transform the consciousness of an imprisoned and imprisoning society, but she can give love to her family. Other later heroines, like Louisa Gradgrind (of *Hard Times*) and Bella Wilfer (in *Our Mutual Friend*) show Dickens attempting to see women who are good in some respects—and not so good in others. In some measure, Dickens came to see the necessity, for men, of the adoption of womanly traits like compassion and self-sacrifice in order to be fully human (although the fully human was never the strong point of Dickens's work), and that is one of the reasons why *Great Expectations* is such a fine book. Pip grows into a remarkable mixture of strength and compassion. The integration of an essentially female point of view was the major hope, for Dickens, of a caring human society. As dreary as Esther is, she carries love and feeling through the world, and it is in this light that later in the century Henry James would have been interested in her. For the Dickensian vision of the saving human consciousness was shared by the expatriate American master, although now the "saving" has taken on more profound, even sinister dimensions. The women James charged with such a task are invested with extraordinary complexity of heart and mind, a complexity profoundly his own.

Notes

[1]K. J. Fielding, ed. *The Speeches of Charles Dickens* (Oxford: The Clarendon Press, 1950), p. 392.

[2]John Forster, *The Life of Charles Dickens*, Ed. and Annotated by J. W. T. Ley (London: Cecil Palmer, 1928), p. 35.

[3]John Carey, *The Violent Effigy, A Study of Dickens' Imagination* (London: Faber & Faber, 1973) pp. 149-50.

[4]K. J. Fielding, *Speeches*, p. 19.

[5]Robert Garis, *The Dickens Theater: A Reassessment of the Novels* (Oxford: Clarendon Press, 1965). Albert J. Gucrard in *The Triumph of the Novel: Dickens, Dostoevsky, Faulkner* (New York: Oxford Univ. Press, 1976) discusses a variety of tones discoverable in Dickens's "personal voice." See pp. 136-149.

[6]See Dorothy Van Ghent, *The English Novel, Form and Function* (New York: Harper & Row, 1953), pp. 125-39.

[7]*Letters of Charles Dickens to Wilkie Collins* (New York: Kraus, 1969) p. 95.

[8]*The Letters of Charles Dickens, ed. by his sister-in-law and his eldest daughter* (London: Chapman-Hall, 1880), Vol. 2, pp. 110-11.

[9]*Ibid.*, p. 117.

[10]Peter Coveney, *Poor Monkey, The Child in Literature* (London: Salisbury Square, 1957), p. 116.

[11]The literature on this problem is extensive. See Crawford Kilian, "In Defense of Esther Summerson," *D. R.* 54: 318-28. Tom Middlebro; "Esther Summerson: A Plea for Justice," *Queen's Quarterly* LXXVII (Summer 1970), p. 259. Martha Rosso, "Dickens and Esther," *Dickensian* LXV (May 1969), p. 91.

[12]Forster, p. 49.

[13]*Ibid.*, p. 49.

[14]*Ibid.*, p. 199.

[15]*The Letters of Charles Dickens,* The Pilgrim Edition, Vol. 3, ed. Madeline House, Graham Storey, Kathleen Tillotson, (Oxford: The Clarendon Press, 1974), pp. 483-84.

[16]Edgar Johnson, *The Heart of Charles Dickens, as revealed in his letters to Angela Burdett-Coutts* (New York: Duell, Sloan and Pearce, 1952), p. 354.

[17]Forster, p. 639.

[18]*Ibid.*, pp. 38-39.

[19]Lionel Trilling, *"Little Dorrit,"* The Opposing Self: Nine Essays in Criticism (New York: Viking Press, 1959), and Edmund Wilson, "Dickens: The Two Scrooges," *The Wound and the Bow: Seven Studies in Literature* (New York: Oxford Univ. Press, 1965).

[20]Charles Dickens, *The Personal History of David Copperfield* (Baltimore: Penguin, 1966), p. 47. All subsequent references will be to this edition of the text.

[21]Charles Dickens, *Bleak House* (New York: Norton, 1977) ed. George Ford and Sylvère Monod, P. 17. All subsequent references will be to this edition. David Goldknopf in *The Life of the Novel* (Chicago: Univ. of Chicago Press, 1972) compares Esther's voice to the third-person narration of *Bleak House* and also to the beginning of *Great Expectations*, with equally dramatic results. See pp. 144-46.

[22]See, for instance, Alex Zwerdling's "Esther Summerson Rehabilitated," *PMLA*, 88 (1973), pp. 429-439. John Carey thinks Dickens shrewdly draws a portrait of a young girl's sexual inhibitions. See *The Violent Effigy*, p. 173.

[23]Forster, p. 559.

[24]Edward Said, *Beginnings, Intention and Method* (New York: Basic Books, 1975), p. 96.

[25]Joseph Gold, *Charles Dickens: Radical Moralist* (Minneapolis: Univ. of Minnesota Press, 1972) pp. 193-94.

[26]*The Letters of Charles Dickens*, The Pilgrim Edition, Vol. 3, p. 381.

[27]Charles Dickens, *Great Expectations* (Harmondsworth: Penguin, 1965) pp. 46-47.

[28]*Letters of Charles Dickens to Wilkie Collins*, p. 53.

Chapter 6

Henry James: The Penalties of Action

In the fiction of Henry James, the female characters often seem much more "masculine" than the males. In all his fiction it is the women who dare to act, who move about, who dare to throw people together or pull them apart, who simply *live*. To be active in the world as demanded of an American male frightened James deeply. By temperament, by family history, he saw his own psychic situation as much closer to that of women than to the "masculine" side of the world. Social demands made women passive and often deprived them of much choice in the matter. Their struggle to influence their world, to act was by definition a heroic one. Plagued by his own passivity and fears about being a man, James acted out the more aggressive aspects of his personality through the female voice. Place John Marcher or Merton Densher or even Lambert Stretcher beside Daisy Miller, Isabel Archer, or even the governess in *The Turn of the Screw* and you place the passive, almost immobilized beside the ardent, the fascinating, the alive. James, in a number of ways similar to Samuel Richardson, allowed his deepest creative energies to flow into the women of his fiction. These possess, as Leon Edel has said, "not a little of his own power, will, and strength in imposing themselves upon the world."[1] Conjoined with this power is, however, their special status as victim, a status with which the author was also in sympathy. James felt that he was wounded physically and was condemned to live in a way that other men were not. The women who meant the most to him, his mother Mary and his cousin Minny Temple, seemed marked for sacrifice, and he identified deeply with them in both their strengths and their weaknesses. The female figures in his fiction become paradoxical voices for him; he can express through them his wish for strength and power, but he can also subject them to the destructive forces that he saw awaiting anyone who risked a strong forward stride through life.

James's identification with women was not only personal; it was artistic. He shared his cousin Minny's passion for George Eliot, and though he walked in the shadow of Dickens and greatly admired Turgenev, to his mind George Eliot had discovered principles that were to be central to his own work. For her, as for him, "the passion of the special case is surely the basis of the storyteller's art."[2] The scrutiny of the emotional life, the inner world embedded in the social reality, is the element these novelists share. In the essay in *Partial Portraits*, written in 1885 he praised her large and generous spirit, a spirit capable of contemplating the word as seriously (sometimes too seriously) as he himself did.[3] He sympathized with the reclusive life she shared with G. H. Lewes, the companion who sought to protect her from the moral and literary judgments of the world, although he thought she should have lived more (and this he thought of himself also). Very early in his career he proclaimed himself her rival. In a letter of 1873 to Grace Norton he wrote of his intention; "To produce some little exemplary works of art is my narrow and lowly dream. They are to have less 'brain' than *Middlemarch*; but (I boldly proclaim it) they are to have more *form*."[4] James announces himself more self-consciously the artist, as a great many others did at the end of the century, but he assigns to the woman artist a masculine trait, that of intelligence. The form that he was to give to his works was a single, dominant consciousness—and very often that consciousness was to belong to a woman. But in this also he followed Eliot, for, as I said in Chapter Four, he found her insistence on the importance of the young woman in agreement with his own. In the preface to *The Portrait of a Lady*, he seemed to delight in the artistic challenge of the female perspective and emphasized also "as we look at the world, how absolutely, how inordinately the Isabel Archers, and even much smaller female fry insist on mattering."[5]

Even though there are a number of so-called Jamesian centers in his novels that are female, not many of them appear in the first person. Though almost totally in the mind of Fleda Vetch in *The Spoils of Poynton*, in the mind of Maisie Farange in *What Maisie Knew*, and often in the mind of Isabel Archer in *The Portrait of a Lady*, James continues to maintain some distance from them by writing about them in the third person. His single most famous venture into "I" narration as a woman also happens to be one of the most baffling tales ever written in English. The noble little governness in *The Turn of the Screw* has spawned endless specula- tion and an apparently endless critical literature of her own. She is a rare, bold creation who has managed to create two opposing critical camps; those who think the ghosts are real, and those who think they are a figment of her imagination. Her author's intentions have been examined and reexamined for clues to the "real" meaning of the story, and his female speaker has been merci- lessly psychoanalysed. I said earlier that the other female nar- rators in this study have had difficulty in making themselves be- lieved. The governess's tale is a study of ambiguity itself. Enough snippets of information are presented to arouse in the reader's mind the possibility that Mr. Quint and Miss Jessel are real ghosts, but the overwhelming burden of evidence is that they issue solely from her mind and that they communicate solely with her. The emphasis of the tale is entirely on the intensity with which she feels their presence. Herein lies the genius of the story; we are invited to doubt the speaker at every turn, as she invites us to believe her. My interpretation is certainly not new; it is the position Leon Edel takes in his discussion of early critics who first "cracked" the tale: Harold Goddard, Edna Kenton, and Edmund Wilson.[6] It would, in some sense, be easier for me to deal with another one of James's fictions that has a woman as the center of consciousness (even though in the third person) rather than a story around which criti- cism has become narrowly focused and polarized. Nevertheless, James was intensely involved emotionally in the inner lives of women and a reluctant user of the first-person form. For these reasons, and for the controversy of the tale itself, we really cannot avoid looking upon *The Turn of the Screw* as a fascinating instance of the use of the female voice.

Viewed in relationship to his own life and to the women in the rest of his fiction, the nameless little governess becomes an astonishing exploration of the problem of obtaining power as an observer. Like other more sane aspirants toward freedom and vision, her quest demands purity and sacrifice, even death. The drama that she lives out represents the underlying dilemma in James's own life and that which underlies the social drama in the more civilized drawing rooms of *The Ambassadors* and *The Golden Bowl:* what is the nature of the power of the storyteller? If one sees more than others, what is the penalty of acting on that vision? This is an extreme tale of the manipulative force of the observer, someone who acts on her feelings. She sees herself as strong, determined, maintaining control against great odds. In fact, however, the effects of her actions are entirely equivocal. A certain kind of activity for James was fraught with difficulty, and it is obvious that this fear informs his fiction. Especially precarious are one's relationships with children, and one must be intensely on guard not to injure them. The governess's acts do hurt others. Her second preoccupation, the presumed sexual doings of others, is another Jamesian obsession shared by his male protagonists like the narrator in *The Sacred Fount* or Lambert Strether in *The Ambassadors*. The governess *acts* on her assumptions, however, and these actions cause harm. Furthermore her actions are so colored by her sexual needs that we do not trust her at all. Far from being an anomaly, this tale is of a piece with his other work and demonstrates dramatically the difference between the male and female persona for James. The author placed next to *The Turn of the Screw* in the New York Edition of his works *The Aspern Papers*, narrated by a literary man in search of the papers of a deceased poet. *The Sacred Fount* is narrated by a nameless, faceless male (we gather rather late in the tale) who speculates on the activities of the guests at a country house for the weekend. Each of these men are as prurient and as manipulative as the governess, but neither does much about anything. Each pictures himself as relatively passive (in comparison to the women who appear in the tales) and neither asserts active intervention in the lives of others. I will say more about these two men later in the chapter, but it is obvious that whereas the woman lives out her vision, these men live in the visions of others.

That men should appear passive and women active is not really surprising when we see the extent to which James felt alienated from the most masculine, active American world. He was never a part of it, in fact saw himself as more or less permanently sidelined, and wrote about these feelings in the autobiographical works of his later years. Temperamentally, he was a sensitive and observant child who realized early on that this proclivity made him appear passive and weak to other boys. In relationship to his brother William, James felt himself horribly behind. *A Small Boy and Others*, published in 1913, is full of references to the quick-witted, active pursuits of the older brother. James did not easily make friends with other boys, prompting William to say, " '*I* play with boys who curse and swear!' "[7] He wrote about his failures at Rochette in Geneva, "a deeply hushed failure," and recounts a horrible memory of being utterly inadequate at a moot court session when he briefly studied law at Harvard.[8] Even so far from the events, James recalled that his own virtues, imagination and sensibility, counted for little in the world of American boys. Feeling distinctly odd, even unnatural he contemplated his "small uneasy mind, bulging and tightening in the wrong, or at least in unnatural and unexpected, places, like a little jacket ill cut or ill sewn. . . ."[9] Even though this last reference is to his religious views, it describes a feeling that pervades whatever James chose to tell us about his childhood.

Though almost everything in Henry James's life has been extensively investigated by Leon Edel, I want to emphasize here two incidents that are symptomatic of the author's sense of physical and emotional deprivation, especially since these incidents are crucial in understanding his identification with women. At the beginning of the Civil War, when James was eighteen, something happened that made the future author feel entirely excluded from the ranks of young men fighting for the union, and this was his famous "horrid even if an obscure hurt."[10] While it appears that the hurt was something so prosaic as a back injury suffered while serving as a volunteer fireman in Newport, James writes about the injury (of course very late in his career) in terms fit for one of his most lurid ghost tales. He writes of the injury with shame, with embarrassment, with an almost agonizing indirectness. The injury made him feel as wounded as the body politic, and it established a "relation to everything occurring round me. . . extraordinarily intimate and quite awkwardly irrelevant."[11] When his illness was pooh-poohed by a specialist, James took to his bed and then later to Harvard to show that he was at least doing something, even if it was only by negation. Leon Edel takes to task those critics who have interpreted the accident as literal castration, but there is every reason to think that the hurt confirmed his sense of exclusion from the male world. He needed a specific identifying mark of his differentness. Like Ralph Touchett in *The Portrait of a Lady* he could use his illness as an occupation and an excuse for observation and passivity. This is not to say James did not feel very ill, but the illness was of a piece with his feeling of sexual vulnerability.

The second incident was the death of his cousin, Minny Temple, from tuberculosis. Her death occurred in 1870, when James was twenty-seven. His youthful infatuation with her was to be his single most ardent relationship with a woman (with the exception, perhaps of Constance F. Woolson), a relationship in which he was the passive observer of all her activity—doomed activity. She represented for him the good, the curious, the alive—and the dying. He identified her with great gifts unrealized, a victim of the swift and ruthless blotting out of human possibilities. Her death symbolized for him both the end of his own youth and the last real chance to involve himself as a man with an adult woman.

> Among the sad reflections that her death provokes for me, there is none sadder than this view of the gradual change and reversal of our relations: I slowly crawling from weakness and inaction and suffering into strength and health and hope: she sinking out of brightness and youth into decline and death.

> .   .   .   .

> She never knew how sick and disordered a creature I was and I always felt she knew me at my worst. I always looked forward with a certain eagerness to the day when I should have regained my natural lead, and our friendship on my part at least might become more active and masculine.[12]

Their sex roles are reversed here, although James looks forward to a time when he can come into his rightful masculine identity. The extent to which he saw her as a symbol is astonishing. Even in responding to the news of her death James was thinking of her spiritual and literary usefulness: "Twenty years hence what a pure eloquent vision she will be," "she the very heroine of our common scene," "What a pregnant reference in future years—what a secret from those who never knew her!", "It will count in old age, when we live more than now, in reflection, to have had such a figure in our youth."[13] Reading some of Minny's letters, I was surprised to see that, for her part, she felt only friendly and affectionate toward him. James's feelings towards her were classically adolescent in their intensity, but unusually cerebral. For him, she was an icon, reworded many times fictionally as a stand-in for the masculine self of the author.

She was so exquisitely appealing to James in death precisely because her life had been problematic, simply as her own personality was constructed. What, after all, would she have done with herself? In his later descriptions, he portrays her in very much the same terms that he uses for the artist, and we can surmise that he imagined his own psychic state to be similar to her own. Her problem was the intense wish to live actively:

> . . . she was to remain for us the very figure and image of a felt interest in life, an interest as magnanimously far-spread, or as familiarly and exquisitely fixed, as her splendid shifting sensibility, moral, personal, nervous, and having at once such noble flights and such touchingly discouraged drops. . . .
>
> She was really to remain, for our appreciation the supreme case of a taste for life as life, as personal living; of an endlessly active and yet somehow a careless, an illusionless, a sublimely forewarned curiosity about it. . . .[14]

Certainly the letters he quotes at the end of *Notes of a Son and Brother* (letters *not* written to him, but to John Chipman Gray) reveal an intelligent, witty young woman—ardently alive and wishing that she could follow the advice of William James to be manly and outwit her illness.[15] Her problem dramatized to James his own, an active intelligence housed in a recalcitrant body. Minny was a woman and ill, doomed to watch, understand, and fall. She confirmed for him his fears of the active life. To pitch headlong into life was to be at risk, and in America James felt this fear and this pressure constantly. Minny raised for him questions of gender and identity and *life*—these James felt compelled to ask and answer over and over again in his fiction.

The intensity of James's idealization of Minny, his wish to deny his own masculinity, and his subsequent fascination with women in his fiction, are all probably traceable, at the deepest level, to what Edel calls "his very experience of the over-riding female" that had "created a permanent damage within himself in his relations with women."[16] Edel is referring here to James's mother, whose treatment of the future author must, if we go by Freudian lights, have been the most serious injury to his sex. In his letters to her, James pictures her as the perfection of motherhood itself, living only for others and giving love in the purest form possible. Her strength was of the angel in the house variety, the lady with the will of iron. Certainly she would have needed such a will to manage the notoriously unruly James household. In his life, as in his art, the author was fascinated as much by older as by younger women, although they usually do not occupy the position of heroine. In fact, a good number of them are downright sinister. Beside and often in opposition to his ardent American girls appear older, world-weary women schooled in manipulative parenthood. Women like Mrs. Gereth in *The Spoils of Poynton* or Madame Merle in *Portrait of a Lady* can be alternately horrifying and funny in their persistent management of others, especially by creating a false bond of attachment. James had an ambivalent relationship to such women. During his long residence in Europe he spent a great deal of time with women who must have had their share of domineering maternity: Mrs. Kemble, Isabella Stewart Gardner, Mrs. Procter, and Mrs. Duncan Stewart. He even joked about marrying Mrs. Procter, who was eighty-two. In some sense these women too were models of action, of life lived, and they supplied much of the imaginative material on which James thrived and many of his most delightful social hours. But his fictional older women often use their considerable wit, charm, and cunning to rob life of spontaneity and joy. They often spy upon younger people, like the comically relentless Fanny Assingham in *The Golden Bowl* or even Maria Gostrey in *The Ambassadors* (though not old, she is not young). While James praises these women in round-about ways, especially in his emphasis on their narrative function, the overall effect is unpleasant—the woman becomes overwhelmingly perceptive and annoyingly omnipresent. Some such feelings James must have developed toward his mother, although he does not explicitly record them anywhere but in his fiction.

If women were in possession of the world's backbone, the elder Henry James was wayward and quirky, preoccupied as he was with the ideas of Swedenborg. He was also visibly wounded, having lost a leg in his youth. Leon Edel comments on the sex role reversal that formed the core of James's early emotional life.[17] Whatever he saw at home, it certainly confirmed his decision never to marry. He wrote to Grace Norton in 1880; "If I were to marry I should be guilty in my own eyes of an inconsistency—I should pretend to think just a little better of life than I really do."[18] His conviction here was no doubt based on his lack of sexual desire for women, although he would never have put it that way. Throughout all the letters I have read, he expresses no erotic feelings towards women at all: respect, friendship, even "love," but nothing like the intense sensual pleasure he expresses toward other men in the latter third of his life. James was mostly homosexual if sexual at all, and we have the rather silly remarks of a certain Dr. Collins, who saw the author every day for two months and was treating him for depression. He concluded:

> that James had "an enormous amalgam of the feminine in his make-up; he displayed many of the characteristics of adult infantilism; he had a singular capacity for detachment from reality and with it a dependence upon realities that was even pathetic. He had a dread of ugliness in all forms. . . His amatory coefficient was comparatively low; his gonadal sweep was too narrow.[19]

It is difficult to credit the word of anybody who talks about amatory coefficients, but then these were different times. I think we are justified surely, in seeing his creation of charming American girls as in part a result of a sexual identity closer to the female sex than to his own.

The term "masquerade" might give one a moment's pause when used in connection with Henry James. James's theories of narrative form are known chiefly for their emphasis on authorial control and distance. Though these do certainly celebrate the virtues of command, of intense concentration on form, in fact they also celebrate the virtues of ecstatic immersion in the fine consciousness that shapes every story. In his important theoretical essays on the novel, it is he who made explicit the ideal of the barely visible artist, that veiled personage who looks over the shoulder of a chosen character and views the world through his or her eyes. But the author's relationship to this central person was intense, and his finest creative energies were, if we believe his notebooks and prefaces, directed toward finding that very person who should tell the tale. He often speaks of this character as taking hold of him, as swooping down upon him so that to write his or her story becomes a way of getting hold of that specter and giving it its due. The imaginative fun then begins as James tries to penetrate this person's mind: "A beautiful infatuation this, always, I think, the intensity of the creative effort to get into the skin of the creature; the act of personal possession of one being by another at its completest. . . ."[20] That imaginative act of immersion (quite a sexual image here) had, in his view, to be fairly complete since without it the tale or novel would seem insincere and untrue, the great, failure for James. The work of art literally comes into being through its ability to produce the "illusion of life," an "air of reality."[21] And this illusion is created by holding on for dear life (as James would often put it) to that single point of view, that person who definitively *sees*. This central point of consciousness (whether appearing in third or first person) was often referred to as the narrator and became closely identified in James's own mind with the artist himself. Speaking of his shorter tales in the preface to *The Golden Bowl* he calls this person "the impersonal author's concrete deputy or delegate, a convenient substitute or apologist for the creative power otherwise so veiled and disembodied."[22]

James's struggles with point of view are sometimes almost comically intense and reveal very clearly, I think, his fears about self-revelation. For he did feel that he was himself invested in every line and that finally, even while being in one sense opaque, fiction demanded an absolute giving over of the artistic self. In his notebooks we sometimes find him prodding himself, coaxing himself into surmounting his fears about letting go:

> To live *in* the world of creation—to get into it and stay in it—to frequent it and haunt it—to *think* intently and fruitfully—to woo combinations and inspirations into being by a depth and continuity of attention and meditation—this is the only thing—and I neglect it, far

and away too much; from indolence, from vagueness, from inattention, and from a strange nervous fear of letting myself go. If I vanquish that nervousness, the world is mine.[23]

The notebooks have a number of such passages; they underscore the extent to which he lived in and through his creations. A complete masquerade was that elusive giving over of himself that he sought so assiduously. The narrative balance he usually managed has led critics, however, to concentrate on the distancing act he was often attempting.[24]

Though deeply involved in the central consciousness of his reflectors, he usually placed them in the controlled, manipulable stance of the third person. This stance gave James authorial freedom to shift his gaze, to move from behind the eyes of the central character, if only momentarily. So he moves to Mamie Pocock's hotel reflections in *The Ambassadors* or shifts from the mind of the Prince to that of his wife in the second half of *The Golden Bowl*. The third person leads to control over the form as well as a check on the author's proclivities, and in most of his theoretical writing, the extreme dangers in the use of the autobiographical form are emphasized. James used words of containment in describing the necessity of the third person, particularly in a long work: Lambert Strether is "encaged and provided for."[25] To Mrs. Humphry Ward in 1899 he enjoined the necessity of going behind a main character, and this was impossible if one used the "autobiographic dodge" as he called it.[26] To H. G. Wells he was even more emphatic. First-person narration was "accurst." "Save in the fantastic and the romantic (Copperfield, Jane Eyre. . ."Kidnapped"?) it has no authority, no persuasive or convincing force—its grasp of reality and truth isn't strong and disinterested. R. Crusoe, e. g. isn't a novel at all."[27]

From his long disquisition on first-person narration in the preface to *The Ambassadors*, it is clear that using "I" leads to looseness, to a "terrible *fluidity* of self-revelation," to a "straight and credulous gape." The first person strikes him as "the darkest abyss of romance—" through which much that is queer can be "smuggled in by a back door."[28] Note the language here—the form is dark and cursed. Revelation unchained and unchecked becomes the matter of the tale—the long novel cannot be a novel at all if written in this fashion. It is the striking freedom of the form that frightens him, and it does literally seem to frighten him. Even allowing for the portentous language of his later years, he writes about "I" narration almost as if *it* were the beast in the jungle. For an author so involved with his finely sensitive observers, to drop down into their minds alone seems to be a positively dangerous course. The form will suffer and the author may be sprawled nakedly on the page.

But James did indulge himself in this form, primarily in his shorter tales and in one longer novel, *The Sacred Fount* (a short tale that seemed to grow and grow in his mind). That he saved it for tales of the fantastic and romantic indicates the degree of license he felt he had in these works. The first person allowed for novelistic play, all sorts of personal indulgence forbidden elsewhere. That is why *The Turn of the Screw* has a place in this study. Indulging in a dangerous narrative form, in a genre loaded with conventions of excess, James creates a startling, haunting female voice. When James responded to those seeking an explanation for the meaning of *The Turn of the Screw* (and there were many, even at the time he wrote it), he always emphasized his satisfaction with the form of the story, his struggle to maintain an appropriate tone with which to reveal the horrors, and his sense of the tale as an exercise, or more pleasantly, a game. He talked of the tale with great pleasure, deprecating its mechanical aspects, but clearly pleased with a governess who is a small recorder with authority; also, however, given to interpretation. The tale is:

> a piece of ingenuity pure and simple, of cold artistic calculation, an *amusette* to catch those not easily caught (the "fun" of the capture of the merely artless being ever but small), the jaded, the disillusioned, the fastidious. Otherwise expressed, the study is of a conceived "tone," the tone of suspected and felt trouble, of an inordinate and incalculable sort—the tone of tragic, yet of exquisite, mystification.[29]

The narrator is "suppositious" and mystified, though her record "of so many intense anomalies and obscurities" is beautiful if distinct from "her explanation of them, a different matter."[30] Curiously, in his most extensive and famous unrestricted use of the female voice, he presents us with a woman who, like Moll Flanders or Clarissa or even Esther before her, turns a Janus face toward the world. She is at once an expression of the power of the storyteller, at the same moment that the psychic boundaries between herself and the world outside are almost completely indistinguishable.

In deprecating the fairly low literary class into which the tale falls, James noted to H. G. Wells; "One knows the most damning things about one's self."[31] Certainly James exposes us to the creator of a drama, a most aggressive and manipulative creator. To understand and to see—is it then to control? In this tale the act of seeing is an aggressive act, a seeing of that which others do not see, a conjuring and a recreation of the drama for those in the tale itself. Our experience of the little governess is that of being guided, controlled, directed. In his letter to H. G. Wells, James went on to emphasize how neat, firm, and clear her own voice was to be, especially in the face of the troubles she witnesses. This comment belies the reader's sense of her. It is one of real strength in the act of perception, strength in her understanding of the mystery (into which she leads us and the other characters at the same time), and the will to act on what she "knows." Therein lies her power, and it makes itself felt very much as power.

Naturally enough the governess takes pleasure in the thought of teaching two such exemplary charges as Miles and Flora. The sole authority in a great house at the age of twenty, with her only impediment in the homely form of Mrs. Grose, she feels her spirit expand and rise. Like so many of James's other young women, she finds herself suddenly confronting a new destiny that involves a move upward in the social scale. But as for Fleda Vetch and Isabel Archer, a new station demands new ethical choices. This young woman, escaping from her "small smothered life," decides to take a high, sacrificial line:

> I was there to protect and defend the little creatures in the world the most bereaved and the most loveable, the appeal of whose helplessness had suddenly become only too explicit, a deep constant ache of one's own engaged affection. We were cut off, really, together; we were united in our danger. They had nothing but me, and I—well, I had *them*. It was

in short a magnificent chance. This chance presented itself to me in an image richly material. I was a screen—I was to stand before them. The more I saw the less they would.[32]

Self-sacrifice then is the motive for her actions. She sees herself the principal actress in a heroic drama. The element of sacrifice is an important one for James; he often writes in the most ambiguous terms about the necessity of one person saving another, sometimes sexually, sometimes in a larger, more spiritual sense. The governess's claims for her own nobility are self-serving and destructive. Looked at in this light she is a sinister evocation of the all-sacrificing mother, using self-denying heroism as a justification for her mistreatment of others. Had she done her duty, the "right thing," she would certainly have left Bly and taken the children with her. Instead she goes on to do precisely the opposite of what she claims in the above quote, as she attempts to get Mrs. Grose and the children to acknowledge the ghosts.

James emphasizes repeatedly that she is working to control their responses. This control is exerted through the creation (better yet, the recreation) of characters and a tale about two dead people who have come back to haunt their former residence and the children who live there. Throughout the tale she is given to obvious embroidery of incidents, and the reader, like Mrs. Grose, is at the mercy of her interpretations. I do not now want to go through all the various spots at which such a process occurs. These moments have been thoroughly explored by the famous group of early critics I mentioned at the beginning of the chapter. But I do want to point out James's insistence on the process by which she manipulates the other members of the household. Every time one of her revelations is at hand, she watches Mrs. Grose carefully for the effect, draws her on and on. She gives meanings to incidents that are unexplained, like Miles's dismissal from school or what these ghosts are doing there at all, and what they want from the children—or even their physical descriptions. What is more, we are resolutely placed in her mind and forced to watch others suffering the effects of this tale. In describing her first male apparition (a man with no hat), to Mrs. Grose she says: "Then seeing in her face that she already, in this, with a deeper dismay, found a touch of picture, I quickly added stroke to stroke" (p. 23). She is interpreting the world for others. Reality is a blank canvas upon which the governess plays with her brush.

The story that the governess creates is a cruel one concerning perverse sexuality and involving two former servants, Mr. Quint and Miss Jessel. In life she imagines that they have initiated the children into some sort of sexual behavior, although James is careful not to specify *what* they were all doing—his famous horrors, though. Now they have begun to appear to her, though dead. They both have come back (at least to her eyes) to initiate the children into further forbidden acts, now with the added horror of necrophilia. The governess plays upon the prurient imagination of Mrs. Grose, who has herself already suggested that improper freedoms have taken place between Miles and Quint. Mrs. Grose also implies that Quint and Jessel have been having some sort of affair, with the result that the lady-like former governess went away in disgrace. The present governess seizes upon these hints and manages early on to assume that Miles has been harming others at school. Ironically, of course, it is the governess who appears to be the initiator—as she works tirelessly to convey to the children the existence of ghosts, their evil desires. These children must affirm her imagination. James remarked on the importance of the act of communication she is engaged in:

> The thing that, as I recall it, I most wanted not to fail of doing, under penalty of extreme platitude, was to give the impression of the communication to the children of the most infernal imaginable evil and danger—the condition, on their part, of being as *exposed* as we can humanly conceive children to be.[33]

The governess is responsible for the exposure; she actively seeks it, even as she blames the children, rather than herself.

This theme James had already tackled in *What Maisie Knew*, written in 1897. The innocent Maisie is shuffled back and forth between her divorced parents, only to bring together Mrs. Beale (another governess) and Sir Claude, who then also vie for her love. The sexual connections are evident to us, but only dimly available to Maisie. James gives us a picture of the world, through the girl's eyes, that is incomprehensible without the knowledge of sexuality. James was fascinated by the initiation process through which children come to know about the sexual doings of their elders.

In *The Turn of the Screw* all of this takes place in the world of darkness, stealth, and fear. The governess's mind is filled with sex. Just like Clarissa, she sees sex behind every move. An arm implies a penis, for Richardson, and for the governess a man implies a lover, as does even a little boy. Such a corrupted mind is terrifying to her charges, and we are treated to a number of scenes in which the children regard *her* with horror. When she tries to force Flora to admit that she has seen Miss Jessel, the little girl cries out:

> "I don't know what you mean. I see nobody. I see nothing. I never *have*. I think you're cruel. I don't like you!"

> .   .   .

> "Take me away; take me away—oh take me away from *her*!" (p. 73)

There are a series of ironic pairings in the tale that emphasize the consuming sexuality of her vision. The cast of the characters is presented as a series of mirrors, all of them reflecting back the governess in altered form. The governess is a slightly more sophisticated version of Mrs. Grose—the elder lady having been horrified by the real life goings on of Jessel and Quint, about whom we know only through her own prurient eyes. Jessel and Quint are a reversal of the absent master of Bly and the present governess. In their ghostly evocations the social classes are reversed, but these two have had relations that have led to dishonor and disgrace. What exactly our present governess feels for her master is unclear, but she has been charmed and overwhelmed by him, by his trust, by his absolute giving over of authority. Douglas, the first narrator of the tale, is moved to announce to the assembled company; "The moral of which was of course the seduction exercised by the splendid young man. She succumbed to it!" (p. 6). One does not know, however, how literal has been the conquest. And in yet another coupling James suggests that Douglas himself has been in love with the governess (she has entrusted her manuscript of the tale to his hands); " 'Well, if I don't know who she was in love with I know who *he* was,' " as one guest remarks (p. 3).

The governess is certainly in love with the children and often clutches them to her convulsively. Her feelings for little Miles are suspiciously hysterical and strange. We are tempted to see her acting out her sexual feelings for the master through the boy. In the younger, as in the elder master, the prerogatives of the male sex are abundantly evident, to the governess at least. She has a strong sense of them as rulers of property and people. She and Mrs. Grose have a strange conversation in which the younger woman announces her affinity for lively (sexual?) little boys. Once Flora and Mrs. Grose have gone away, the governess likens her dinner with Miles to that of a honeymoon; "We continued silent while the maid was with us—as silent, it whimsically occurred to me, as some young couple who, on their wedding-journey, at the inn, feel shy in the presence of the waiter. He turned round only when the waiter had left us. 'Well—so we're alone!' " (p. 81).

A number of James's ghost stories involve encountering one-self as an alien *other*, "The Jolly Corner" for instance, and certainly this is what is happening to the governess. She encounters her own dishonored self in Miss Jessel (a self with head in hands, like the ghostly *other* of Spencer Brydon). Unfortunately, she is forcing the children to encounter her own guilt. In fact, as the tale proceeds, she finds herself exacting from them just the names of the ghosts. The thing, the evil, must be recognized and named. When she finally does evoke the longed-for name of Quint, little Miles has died.

And here we come to the heart of the tale, the inordinately destructive force of the mind of the governess. In the debate about whether or not what she sees is real, what is lost is the fact that death is the result of her actions. This death is attributable to specific mental powers of the governess. Quint causes death only as thrown up violently by her to the mind of the boy. For the governess has the power to create in others the feeling of dead presences, and this she does by overstepping all normal mental boundaries. She can read Mrs. Grose's mind, and she knows what the ghosts want. After seeing Jessel in the school room, she tells Mrs. Grose that the woman spoke, when on the page preceding we are told that she did not. The governess remarks that "it came to that" and quotes her; " 'That she suffers the torments—!' " (p. 60). She then announces that Miss Jessel somehow wants Flora. Of course the governess had been the one to speak—not the apparition herself, who simply appeared sad. The governess excels at this apparently extraordinary knowledge of what others, even the dead, are thinking.

The governess's knowledge of the minds of other people is very carefully drawn by James so that we become confused as to whose will is being exerted. Look at this passage—it is only dimly possible to decide who is thinking what:

> Mrs. Grose's large face showed me, at this, for the first time, the far-away faint glimmer of a consciousness more acute: I somehow made out in it the delayed dawn of an idea I myself had not given her and that was as yet quite obscure to me. It comes back to me that I thought instantly of this as something I could get from her; and I felt it to be connected with the desire she presently showed to know more. (p. 23)

It is she who is trying to possess the minds of others. Everyone and everything in the tale come to be intermingled with her own manipulations. We simply lose all bearings—all bearings that is, except those of our tale-teller. By the end of the story we can see that there has been a process something like contamination of the children. Even though it would seem that Miles does utter Quint's name at the end of the tale, how are we to know whether or not all of the governess's actions haven't made it quite clear what she wants—for he has tried to please her. The brilliant ending, that I quote here, exemplifies James's refusal to give us referential signposts, referential pronouns even to distinguish the governess from those she controls:

> At this, after a second in which his head made the movement of a baffled dog's on a scent and then gave a frantic little shake for air and light, he was at me in a white rage, bewildered, glaring vainly over the place and missing wholly, though it now, to my sense, filled the room like the taste of poison, the wide over-whelming presence. "It's *he*?"
>
> I was so determined to have all my proof that I flashed into ice to challenge him. "Whom do you mean by 'he'?"
>
> "Peter Quint—you devil!" His face gave again, round the room, its convulsed supplication. "Where?"
>
> They are in my ears still, his supreme surrender of the name and his tribute to my devotion. "What does he matter now, my own?—what will he *ever* matter? *I* have you," I launched at the beast, "but he has lost

you forever!" Then for the demonstration of my work, "There, *there*!" I said to Miles.

> But he had already jerked straight round, stared, glared again, and seen but the quiet day. With the stroke of the loss I was so proud of he uttered the cry of a creature hurled over an abyss, and the grasp with which I recovered him might have been that of catching him in his fall. I caught him, yes, I held him,—it may be imagined with what a passion; but at the end of a minute I began to feel what it truly was that I held. We were alone with the quiet day, and his little heart, dispossessed, had stopped. (p. 88)

As James pointed out to Dr. Waldstein; "The helpless plasticity of childhood" is at the heart of the tragedy.[34] Even at the climactic moment, there is nothing here except emphasis on what the boy gives to the governess, and on the passionate act of will that she is engaged in. The final drama is still one of ambiguous naming. Who is the beast? Who is "he"? The governess is engaged in an act of possession, disguised as exorcism, with the woman as demonic priest. Children can be made to believe and feel anything.

When Defoe pictures Roxana going mad, the reader loses a sense of the boundaries between individuals (people become figments of her imagination) and then between the individual and the outside world. In this tale James seems to be testing the limits of the imagination itself. Not only is the governess supremely prescient about other minds and other worlds, she is convinced of her right to propagate this vision. Those around her must see what she sees, but even more than that, acknowledge the central meaning of the vision. This is an extreme reworking of the problem of the artist for James, the rights of the observer to control action. James's fears about power and powerlessness are directly addressed through this female voice. On the one hand, he sees that those with extreme mental sensitivity can sometimes control others with that ability. Such a person believes herself in a position of moral authority. However, self-righteousness growing from the ability to construct a fictional world is misplaced, for one may be deluded. Action under such circumstances is fraught with difficulty. To the degree that the observer is acute, to that degree she may be wrong. In a sense James is probably justifying to himself his own relative passivity. He is also confronting sexuality rather directly, especially as it is embodied in women. Sexuality is a demanding force that, when exerted against men, can literally kill them.

What is so striking about this tale is how unlike its counterparts it is. Most of the other ghostly tales have male protagonists passively awaiting their fate. James seems to have taken to the governess with uncommon intensity and excitement. He probably was well aware what sorts of things he was revealing about himself, and this perhaps explains why he took such pains to downgrade the tale—even as it caused other readers great excitement and mystification. "The Jolly Corner" and "The Beast in the Jungle" address a number of similar issues, but they are not in the first person. Each man awaits an aspect of himself, an apparition of either of his sexual self or of the active male that he could have become, but each simply and explicitly waits. In "Sir Edmund Orme," a first-person ghost story, the perception of the narrator is never in doubt, and it does not occur to the reader, this reader anyway, to question the reality of what he observes. He simply sees an apparition come back to haunt the mother of the girl he loves. Sir Edward stands there as an icon of the hurt done to men by women, as a warning to the narrator. The mother and the narrator enter into a pact to prevent the daughter's learning of the vision, until she finally does see. With that Mrs. Marden dies and Orme disappears. While the ending is thematically close to that of *The Turn of the Screw*, it has nothing of the wild, rhetorical complication. James remarked in the preface to this story that no one seemed interested in reading the tale at the time of its publication. Surely this is because James seems to invest the male speaker with no complexity of perception, little emotion, and finally not much energy.

In *The Aspern Papers*, written ten years before *The Turn of the Screw*, the "publishing scoundrel" of the tale seeks to get hold of some old letters of the dead poet Jeffrey Aspern from a former mistress. This man is one of the more interesting and active males that James depicts. This first-person narrator is telling us a story, but James avoids emphasis on epistemological questions. Our primary interest lies in the events themselves and only secondarily in his mind. A constant ironic contrast is drawn between the lively sensual Aspern (and the glorious Juliana) and the present narrator and the pale Miss Tita. The ancient Miss Bordereau accuses the narrator of being unmanly for his cultivation of flowers, and wryly tells her niece she will have nothing to fear on a gondola ride with him. For her the man is emasculated and unnatural in his preoccupations, although he is much less peculiar than the narrator of *The Sacred Fount*.

James was preoccupied with "the finer, the shyer, the more anxious small vibrations" of a host of young women at the time he wrote *The Turn of the Screw*, and was to be so up until the time he wrote *The Ambassadors*.[35] The only male who comes remotely close to the governess is the nameless narrator of *The Sacred Fount*. This man (we do not even know his sex until well into the tale) plunges us into his absurdly irrelevant world of social observation. James keeps alive a sense of the ridiculousness of life lived on these terms: "It was absurd to have consented to such immersion, intellectually speaking, in the affairs of other people."[36] The complete passivity of this figure is striking, and it is a quality shared with a great many Jamesian males. Often observers only, they shape the fate of others through a refusal to act. This man devises a series of mental couplings for Mrs. Brissenden and Mrs. Server:

> I was positively—so had the wheel revolved—proud of my work. I had thought it all out, and to have thought it was, wonderfully, to have brought it.

> It was exactly as if she (Mrs. Server) had been there by the operation of my intelligence, or even by that—in a still happier way—of my feeling. My excitement, as I have called it, on seeing her, was assuredly emotion. (p. 129)

James emphasizes very obviously the conjuring trick of which this man is guilty and again we are plunged into his reality. The man seems aware, if subconsciously, that he is deluded, but ultimately seems not to care. There is much energy in the conjurings of the governess, but very little in this speaker. Of course, what he observes are not ghosts, but they often seem just as diaphanous. One of the central problems here is that the speaker is male. The degree of passivity this man reveals is utterly out of phase with anything manly that the reader can identify. The man is probably at once an examination of the faded, Paterian males of the *fin de siècle* as well as an astonishing look at James and his sexual fears—the life force will be drained through contact with someone of the opposite sex. That the man is so utterly without motive or activity of his own, so hopelessly not there, makes him seem pathological. His observations lead nowhere but to the fine tuning of his own mind, a mind that manages to be both insipid and sinister. The governess acts; she takes her vision very seriously indeed. She is in possession of tremendous force of will, and it dramatically inheres in her voice. At the end of *The Sacred Fount*, the narrator is pronounced crazy by Mrs. Brissenden, and it is a verdict with which it is difficult not to concur. The poor man rather limply concedes her victory, and even though he announces his own superiority as to method, "What I too fatally lacked was her tone" (p. 319). Yes, this is precisely what he lacks, the strength of definition, any strength at all. When writing as a man in this novel James indulges himelf in a vision of rather complete powerlessness.

I put myself in the way of objections, I know, in dealing with so controversial a figure as the little, benighted governess. It might be alleged that the generic pressures on a production like *The Turn of the Screw* overwhelm the question of the sexual identity of the speaker. I do not think, however, that this is the case. When writing in the first person as a woman James allowed himself to treat the extreme dimensions of self-assertion and imagination. He was supremely aware that any attempt to mold reality so that it fits the forms of one's imagination, and then to act in that belief, could lead to terrible consequences. Such people could be badly punished. This theme is central to his work, and it is most carefully considered through his female figures. Let me compare briefly another famous female consciousness in the James pantheon to the first-person lady in *The Turn of the Screw*. As I said in Chapter Four, Isabel Archer's consciousness presented itself to James as the organizing principle of *The Portrait of a Lady*. " 'Place the centre of the subject in the young woman's own consciousness,' I said to myself, 'and you get as interesting and as beautiful a difficulty as you could wish.' "[37]

James is, of course, not completely in her mind. He presents the reader with a conventional Trollopian "I" who intervenes more regularly in this novel than in most of his other fictions, but this person does not figure in the drama. He does also spend much time on the thoughts of Ralph Touchett, another passive Jamesian male, who is certainly a rather direct portrait of the author in his relationship to women. Isabel fleshes out one possible scenario that James envisioned for Minny Temple. With her sudden inheritance and her wide imagination, she possesses powers of choice not given to young ladies like the governess. But like the latter woman Isabel confronts her destiny in possession of alarming ignorance:

> Altogether, with her meagre knowledge, her inflated ideals, her confidence at once innocent and dogmatic, her temper at once exacting and indulgent, her mixture of curiosity and fastidiousness, of vivacity and indifference, her desire to look very well and to be if possible even better, her determination to see, to try, to know, her combination of the delicate, desultory, flame-like spirit and the eager and personal creature of conditions: she would be an easy victim of scientific criticism if she were not intended to awaken on the reader's part an impulse more tender and more purely expectant. (p. 54).

Isabel is a very young person and her story is to involve learning that, even for the most gifted, life does not bend to the shapes one wishes to impose on it. Human beings are pushed and pulled by forces they can neigher control nor understand, and they are particularly prone to being fooled by appearances. Visions of control appeal to her. One such vision propels her into a relationship with Gilbert Osmond, a man who is pleasing to contemplate as a person, who inhabits a certain kind of house and cultivates a certain set of aims. And Osmond succeeds, for example, in creating a daughter for effect—the perfect convent flower, Pansy. Isabel is deeply moved by this image. She sees him as a man in control of his life and more specifically his passions. Part of her love for Osmond grows from the wish to imitate Madame Merle. This lady is to Isabel "a woman of strong impulses kept in admirable order. This commended itself to Isabel as an ideal combination" (p. 152). The appeal of Osmond is his ability to appear indifferent to her choices about him, and hence he becomes less frightening. He gives every sign of being the passive recipient of her generosity.

Isabel is terrified of sexuality in its most strident, striking form. Her refusal of Lord Warburton is incomprehensible to those around her, but he does represent largeness and a hearty passion that she cannot envision embracing. Caspar Goodwood is too distinctly male and demanding in his passions. The book ends with a scene of intense passionate possession (a scene not unlike the ending of *The Turn of the Screw*):

> He glared at her a moment through the dusk, and the next instant she felt his arms about her and his lips on her own lips. His kiss was like white lightning, a flash that spread, and spread again, and stayed; and it was extraordinarily as if, while she took it, she felt each thing in his hard manhood that had least pleased her, each aggressive fact of his face, his figure, his presence, justified of its intense identity and made one with this act of possession. So had she heard of those wrecked and under water following a train of images before they sink. But when darkness returned she was free. She never looked about her; she only darted from the spot. There were lights in the windows of the house; they shown far across the lawn. In an extraordinarily short time—for the distance was considerable—she had moved through the darkness (for she saw nothing) and reached the door. Here only she paused. She looked all about her; she listened a little; then she put her hand on the latch. She had not known where to turn; but she knew now. There was a very straight path. (p. 482).

While John Marcher can only sit and await the attack of the beast in the jungle, Isabel experiences it and runs. This fear of physical passion is much more openly expressed by the governess, although it is a fear that compromises her rather than makes us trust her. She seems to wallow in a morass of sexual fears. Something horrid goes on between adults and children. The governess's impulse to manipulate people and to create order in life is an attempt to force those around her to acknowledge her own terror.

The management of others' passions demands self-sacrifice, self-denial in the face of frightening outside forces. Isabel returns to Osmond in the end, because it is somehow *right*. The governess possesses a strong sense of her own "rightness" in the face of those dangers she perceives. The tone that James so eagerly sought was a moral one, as I said earlier, to justify those sacrifices. James is ultimately most interested in the sacrifices demanded of those with heightened sensibilities, particularly when they decide to do something. Women were images of sacrifice to him: the noble motherhood of Mary James, and the blighted life of Minny Temple. Such terrible sacrifices he also saw his sister Alice undergo. She was condemned to exercise "her wondrous vigorous judgment on too small a scrap of what really surrounded her."[38] This is precisely the fate Isabel Archer confronts in her famous meditation before the fire in Chapter Forty-Two. This set piece of the book deals once again with the problem of an overlapping cycle of love relationships. The immediate question is whether or not Lord Warburton loves Pansy for herself or for her stepmother. But as Isabel continues to think, she contemplates her husband's distrust of her, his hatred really. While she recognizes her own early happiness as essentially maternal (since she wanted to control him by giving things to him), she sees Osmond's major flaw as the totally passive egotism with which he is attempting to take over her ideas and her mind. One is struck with the force and beauty of her clear, open-eyed realization of the consequences of a wrong choice, as the doors clang shut.

The wider range of choice and influence given to Isabel or to Milly Theale in *The Wings of the Dove* means only that their fall to a figurative or literal death is more spectacular. I should undoubtedly arrange the governess here with her more problematic counterparts—Kate Croy in *The Wings of the Dove* and Charlotte Stant in *The Golden Bowl*. Through superior intelligence and cunning, really, these women arrange sexual couplings with their own interests in mind. They do not die, but their wills are thwarted by other even stronger women. Like the governess, Kate and Charlotte are destined to live on, disappointed, and in deep consternation about the consequences of their own acts. They have sacrificed themselves to a belief in the manageability of life, to its controllability. Their sensitivity and intelligence have led them into complex manipulations of the feelings of others. These women are paradoxical creations, intense, intelligent, and yet choosing wrongly, again and again. As Quentin Anderson remarked about Isabel Archer "in *The Portrait of a Lady* the bearded young artist had put on skirts and become the fool of experience rather than its master."[39] But the skirts he put on as the governess led him to gargantuan mastery and gargantuan foolishness—all at once.

As James's career evolved, he found that to be masterful, for a man, meant to remain still and observant. Relatively late in his career (1903) James adopted the point of view of Lambert Strether in *The Ambassadors*. The period of 1895-1900 had been a difficult one for James, particularly in the failure of his playwriting venture. Not long after this time the author developed an intense relationship with the sculptor Hendrik Andersen and still later a friendship with the writer Hugh Walpole. Judging from the letters he wrote to these two men, James had experienced a physical awakening. The letters are effusive, full of physical touching, and obviously erotic in a way that no letter to a woman (that I have seen at least) was. Developing the strength to have such passionate friendships, he developed also the wish to write a full treatment of the man with imagination. Yet this quality the character would not have in predominance—it "wouldn't have wrecked him."[40] Neither was the story to be in the first person, and some of James's most vehement remarks on the pitfalls of such a stance appear in the preface to *The Ambassadors*. Undoubtedly he wished to avoid too close an identification with the fifty-six year old male American sent to rescue a son of New England from the clutches of a European woman.

James himself was fond of comparing *The Ambassadors* to *The Portrait of a Lady*—they were his favorites. When looking at the world through a male consciousness, however, he presents an intensely passive figure, one who undergoes an education about sex and finds it a much less fearful process than did Isabel Archer (but then his hero is not actually doing anything himself), and one who is certainly not wrecked by his decision to return to Woollett, Massachusetts. James gave up the pose of the destructive and the destroyed woman to create a male intensely aware of his own passivity, his failure to live, whose most decisive act is to tell younger men how they should act.

Like the governess and Isabel, Strether suddenly feels on the edge of a great chance, a new life, by virtue of his trip to Europe. As the ambassador of Mrs. Newsome, he has come to convince Chad Newsome to return to his mother and his filial duties. And yet Paris infects him with a sense of the richness and complexity of life. Strether seems a very passive figure indeed, one who does little but

meet Chad's friends and talk to Maria Gostrey. His activity is evident
in two ways; as a man educating young men and as a man educating
himself. The famous "center" of this novel is his exhortation to John
Little Bilham to live:

> Live all you can; it's a mistake not to. It doesn't so much matter what
> you do in particular, so long as you have your life. If you haven't that
> what *have* you had? This place and these impressions—mild as you may
> find them to wind a man up so; all my impressions of Chad and of people
> I've seen at *his* place—well, have had their abundant message for me, have
> just dropped *that* into my mind. I see it now. I haven't done so enough
> before—and now I'm old; too old at any rate for what I see.[41]

One should live as if one were free, although Strether himself has not
even "the memory of that illusion" (p. 138).

The above-mentioned phrase is reminiscent of James's remarks
to Grace Norton about never marrying—he had a view of life that
precluded even taking the chance. Strether's second revelation, at
the famous ending to Book Eleven, concerns the nature of the intimacy between Chad and Madame de Vionnet. A chance sighting
of them rowing on the river reveals to him their intimacy; they are
lovers, and their shared experience excludes him, and so do their
lies—made up on the spot to explain their tryst. And what does he
feel about this passion revealed, a passion he had long been trying
to ignore?—"lonely and cold" (p. 331). This revelation is altogether
different from the sexual fears of Isabel Archer or the terrors of the
governess. Seeing the wonderful effect this love has had on Chad,
Strether exhorts him to stay with Madame de Vionnet; " 'You'll
be a brute, you know—you'll be guilty of the last infamy—if you
ever forsake her' " (p. 354).

James still cannot allow his hero to marry, even though Miss
Gostrey so delicately offers herself. While she is the reader's friend,
the one to whom Strether explains his thoughts, she also figures as
one of the number of frightening women in the novel. She seems to
know so much more than he does; "He foresaw that Miss Gostrey
would come again into requisition on the morrow, though it wasn't
to be denied that he was already a little afraid of her. 'What on
earth—that's what I want to know now—had you then supposed?' "

(p. 331). If only a narrative convenience, we have a great deal of her, primarily of her cloying knowingness. Her name makes her sound like a sort of goose, and James uses animal imagery to describe the even more formidable women of Woollett, Mrs. Newsome and Mrs. Pocock. Jim, the latter's husband pictures them as beasts; " 'They don't lash about and shake the case . . . it's at feeding-time that they're quietest. But they always get there' " (p. 227). Strether realizes the justice of the remark and suddenly thinks of all that he has given them and how little he has received in return. He has fed them "out of the big bowl of all his recent free communication, his vividness and pleasantness, his ingenuity and even his eloquence, while the current of her response had steadily run thin" (p. 227). Mrs. Newsome remains an astonishingly present non-character. She waits for news and for the carrying out of her wishes. Sarah is indignant at Strether's passivity—he has simply failed in his mission. Only Madame de Vionnet appears sympathetic to him, and that because she now figures as a poignant victim, "a creature so fine . . . a creative so exploited" (p. 341). But he finds it frightening that she so adores Chad. "There it was again—it took women, it took women; if to deal with them was to walk on water, what a wonder that the water rose?" (p. 341). The godlike properties needed to deal with them, Strether recognizes as he prepares to leave the ease of Europe and return to the formidable Mrs. Newsome, on whom he is financially dependent. The ending of the book certainly involves a sacrifice for Strether, but nothing like the real death of Milly Theale or the prospect of suffocation for Isabel Archer, or the sudden apocalyptic visions of either the governess or Maggie Verver in *The Golden Bowl*.

Writing from the point of view of Lambert Strether, James directly addresses his feelings of exclusion from the world of action and of heterosexual love. The author himself seems to have always felt like a small boy looking in the candy shop window, and in his late memoir he noted his own "positive lack of the passion, and thereby, I suppose, a lack of spirit. . . ."[42] The spirit of *The Ambassadors* is very much resignation in the face of this fact. But when writing as a woman James does indeed plunge to those romantic abysses that he so feared. And *The Turn of the Screw* is an extreme exploration of the problem of the person with extraordinary knowledge and with the will to act. Her inordinate strivings in her dark, little universe lead only to trouble and death. A madwoman or a saint, a savior or a killer, a loving woman or full of rage and hate? Note that we have asked these questions before. When this author put on skirts he allowed himself to play the game at a fevered pitch. Through her voice flows his love for the heroic, isolated young woman and his fear of the crazed, manipulative mother figure. But above all, she stands as his most sinister vision of the power of the maker of the tale.

Notes

[1] Leon Edel, *Henry James, The Conquest of London, 1870-1881* (Philadelphia: Lippincott, 1962) pp. 393-94.

[2] "George Eliot" in Henry James, *Partial Portraits* (Ann Arbor: University of Michigan Press, 1970) p. 52.

[3] F. R. Leavis writes at length on her influence in *The Great Tradition* (New York: New York University Press, 1964) pp. 126-53.

[4] *Henry James, Letters 1843-1875*, ed. Leon Edel (Cambridge: The Belknap Press, 1974) Vol. 1, p. 351.

[5] Henry James, Preface to *The Portrait of a Lady*, ed. Leon Edel (Boston: Houghton Mifflin, 1963) p. 9. All subsequent references will be to this edition of the text.

[6] See Leon Edel's Prefatory Note to "A Pre-Freudian Reading of *The Turn of the Screw*," in *Twentieth Century Interpretations of the Turn of the Screw and Other Tales*, ed. Jane P. Tompkins (Englewood Cliffs: Prentice-Hall, 1970) p. 61.

[7] Henry James, *A Small Boy and Others* (New York: Scribner's, 1913) p. 259.

[8]Henry James, *Notes of a Son and Brother* (New York: Scribner's, 1914) p. 4, p. 293.

[9]*Ibid.*, p. 169.

[10]*Ibid.*, p. 298.

[11]*Ibid.*, p. 297.

[12]*Letters*, ed. Leon Edel, Vol. I, p. 224.

[13]*Letters*, ed. Leon Edel, Vol. I, pp. 221-22.

[14]*Notes of a Son and Brother*, pp. 77-78. James uses words like "discouraged drops" when the governess begins to tell us her story.

[15]*Ibid.*, p. 511.

[16]Leon Edel, *The Conquest of London, 1870-1881*, pp. 358-59.

[17]Leon Edel, *Henry James, The Untried Years, 1843-1870* (Philadelphia: Lippincott, 1953) see p. 51.

[18]*Henry James, Letters 1875-1883*, ed. Leon Edel (Cambridge: Belknap Press, 1975), Vol. II, p. 314.

[19]Quoted by Leon Edel, *Henry James, The Master: 1901-1916* (Philadelphia: Lippincott, 1972) p. 453.

[20]Henry James, *The Art of the Novel, Critical Prefaces*, intro. R. P. Blackmur (New York: Scribner's, 1962) p. 37.

[21]"The Art of Fiction," *Partial Portraits*, p. 390.

[22]"Preface to 'The Golden Bowl,' " *The Art of the Novel*, p. 327.

[23]*The Notebooks of Henry James*, ed. F. O. Matthiessen and Kenneth B. Murdock (New York: Oxford University Press, 1961) p. 112.

[24]See Percy Lubbock's study, *The Craft of Fiction* (New York: Viking) 1957, especially pp. 142-155.

[25]"Preface to 'The Ambassadors,' " *The Art of the Novel*, p. 321.

[26] *The Letters of Henry James*, sel. and ed. by Percy Lubbock (London: Macmillan, 1920) Vol. I, p. 333.

[27] *Ibid.*, Vol. II, p. 189.

[28] "Preface to 'The Aspern Papers,' " *The Art of the Novel*, pp. 320-21.

[29] *Ibid.*, p. 172.

[30] *Ibid.*, p. 173.

[31] *Letters*, Vol. I, ed. Lubbock, p. 306.

[32] Henry James, *The Turn of the Screw*, reprinted from the New York Edition in *The Turn of the Screw*, ed. Robert Kimbrough (New York: Norton, 1966) p. 14, p. 28. All subsequent references will be this edition of the text.

[33] *Letters*, Vol. I, ed. Lubbock, p. 308.

[34] *Letters*, Vol. I, ed. Lubbock, p. 305.

[35] "Preface to 'What Maisie Knew,' " *The Art of the Novel*, p. 149.

[36] Henry James, *The Sacred Fount* (New York: Grove Press, 1953) p. 89. All subsequent references will be to this edition.

[37] Henry James, *The Portrait of a Lady*, p. 10.

[38] *Letters*, ed. Lubbock, Vol. I, p. 221. For an interesting discussion of the relationship between James's sister and the governess, see Oscar Cargill's *The Turn of the Screw* and Alice James *PMLA*, LXXVII (June 1963), pp. 238-249.

[39] Quentin Anderson, *The Imperial Self, An Essay in American Literary and Cultural History* (New York: Knopf, 1971), p. 213.

[40] "Preface to 'The Ambassadors,' " *The Art of the Novel*, p. 310.

[41] Henry James, *The Ambassadors*, ed. Leon Edel (Boston: Houghton Mifflin, 1960) p. 137. (a reprint of the New York Edition except for correction of error) All subsequent references will be to this edition of the text.

[42] *A Small Boy and Others*, p. 175.

Chapter 7

Modern Primitives: Molly Bloom and James Joyce,
With a Note on D. H. Lawrence

Molly Bloom seems an appropriate figure with which to conclude this study. Given a relatively small space in an immense novel,
Ulysses, she yet remains the female voice best known in this work,
known probably even to those who have never managed to read
the book in its entirety. Whatever her fame, however, her author is a
male author known primarily for his interest in the dilemmas of the
male in the modern world, not the problems of women. As an Irish-
man, Joyce sometimes seems an echo of the past in his treatment of
women, not a product of the modern era at all. Guilty love, the impulse to worship, the impulse to debase oneself—these are the
products of a Catholic childhood, a primitive constellation of feeling
that Joyce was to enshrine in Molly. Looked at in this light, she
would appear to be a much less interesting creation than some of the
other women in this study, essentially written to a formula. Certainly Joyce was more explicit than the other authors we have looked at about his suspicious dislike of women, and Molly displays the
marks of a profound authorial ambivalence.

James Joyce brings us full circle back to Daniel Defoe, whose
realism he admired for its dramatic clarity and intensity. At the
Università Popolare Triestina in 1912, he remarked on the special
fascination of Defoe's women. Mother Ross, Roxana, and Moll
Flanders form "the trio of female characters which reduces contemporary criticism to stupefied impotence."[1] Editors have been
confounded, Joyce maintained, by the grossness and wantonness so
realistically portrayed by Defoe and have wondered where on earth
Defoe found his models. Joyce seems to feel wonder himself at
these creations, and he calls Moll Flanders unique and incomparable.
Yet it is Defoe's ruthless violation of decorum that so fascinated
him; "His women have the indecency and the continence of beasts;

his men are strong and silent as trees."² And in these two qualities
Joyce found English feminism and English imperialism lurking!
The indecorous, the unexpected, even the bestial—these are essential
elements of woman, affirmed by Defoe and reaffirmed by Joyce.
The sharing of Defoe's views and his recreation of them in Molly
shows the extraordinary persistence of certain themes in the female
voice.

Joyce's work, especially in his treatment of men, bears an
interesting relationship to that of Henry James. Joyce often spoke
fondly of the work of James, who was like himself, an exile from
his own country. Joyce was obviously nowhere near so feminized a
male as the American author nor does his fiction reveal the same
devotion to the fine consciousness of young girls. But Henry James
did often counterpose to his ardent young women weakened, effem-
inate young men who hardly seem in possession of any will at all.
His attitudes toward these men move from sympathy and approval
to distaste—but there is a kind of inevitability about them. They are
natural to their own setting, and rarely does their author criticize
them outright. Womanly men prey to the manipulations of others,
usually women, crowd the Jamesian drawing rooms. James Joyce
created one of this century's most famous womanly men, Leopold
Bloom, the so-called hero of *Ulysses*. Although different in class and
profession from the Jamesian artist or adjunct to the artist, we may
well imagine that Bloom's sexual proclivities and his passivity in the
face of the world and women especially, mirror the inner state (were
it ever to be revealed to us) of characters like Ralph Touchett or
Lambert Strether. Joyce is putting his womanly man, however, to a
specific social purpose, a purpose shared by other writers of the early
twenties in Europe. Like T. S. Eliot's Prufrock or D. H. Lawrence's
Paul Morel, Bloom's sexual passivity is at once a symptom of the
enervated state of Europe and a symptom of the difficulties of the
sensitive man lost in the world, an easy victim of all the other strong-
willed ones, whether male or female. In fact, in Joyce (and much
more directly in the work of D. H. Lawrence) one discerns a protest
against conventional notions of masculinity, especially as it is exemplified in the insensitive, boastful carouser and lover.

The relative brevity of Molly Bloom's appearance, indeed the rarity of sustained first-person narrations at all, during this period is characteristic of modern fiction. Faith had been lost in a single, discrete observer who could be trusted to relate what he or she sees. The world and its confusions had become too complex. The great experimental novelists of the period, like Joyce, Woolf, and Lawrence were to follow Henry James's lead in making consciousness itself the focus of the novel, but a consciousness that did not always appear in the first person. Lawrence explained this shift best when he wrote:

> You musn't look in my novel for the old stable *ego*—of the character. There is another *ego*, according to whose action the individual is unrecognisable, and passes through, as it were, allotropic stages which it needs a deeper sense than any we've been used to exercise, to discover are states of the same single radically unchanged element.[3]

Stability of the ego—therein lies the great difficulty. The period in art that produced *A Portrait of the Artist as a Young Man, Women in Love,* and *Mrs. Dalloway* produced also Cubism, Freud, particle physics, and motion pictures. Matter, space, time, visual images—all in pieces. Even the sectors of the mind appeared to have faced off into warring factions, according to Freud. "I" depends on acceptance of an observable, knowable reality and the presence of a whole person. But in every mode of thought people were discovering that one could not necessarily know the truth simply from observation, and the fiction of the period dramatically displays this epistemological problem.

Even, however, as a fragmented perspective became the norm (two or three or four points of view—sometimes unexplained ones), the individual consciousness was still celebrated as the antidote to the ills of civilization. But the antidote appeared to be weak and vulnerable. Its sphere was shorter—experimental novels took place in a day or week or month but rarely ranged through generations and even centuries, as the great Victorian novels had. The outside world was unstable, confusing, often imperfectly perceived by characters in the novel. Characters did not seem to be conceived in the same dimensionality that they once had. Often characters seemed undifferentiated versions of the author himself and became in some sense irrelevant. Only the author seems real. Lawrence creates fairly conventional characters but then allows them all to partake of a sort of hovering consciousness. Any one of the characters is liable to launch into a speech enunciating Lawrence's *idée fixe* about the ills of civilization. It is as if the author hovers over the ficiton and then swoops down upon a character, only to fly off just as suddenly. Virginia Woolf's characters may sometimes even be fragments of each other. Septimus Smith and Clarissa Dalloway are conjoined mentally in a way that suggests male and female aspects of an androgynous ideal. Those first-person narrators who do appear, like Dowell in Ford Maddox Ford's *The Good Soldier*, are untrustworthy in the extreme and seem hardly able to comprehend their world at all.

Even if the single, fixed perspective retired as a literary device for a time, the novel remained a social instrument used to proclaim the primacy of consciousness and feeling. The figure of the woman was central to this purpose. As August Comte had articulated the role of woman in the nineteenth century: "She personifies in the purest form the principle of Love upon which unity of our nature depends. . . ."4 During the early years of this century, the woman was still to perform a curative function, to restore the lost unity of the self, but how she did it was quite another matter. No matter how debased, no matter how untrustworthy, Molly Bloom is at some level a healer for Joyce. As Penelope to Leopold Bloom's Ulysses, Molly is home, rest, peace.

Positivist beliefs were transmuted during this period into primitivism, the widespread belief that what is deeper, more basic, is also, at least in the novel, better. The woman was to heal but heal through her archetypal qualities; unconsciousness, irrationality, undifferentiated acceptance, mother love, and sex. Revolutionary work in the psychology and philosophy of mind gave support to this view. In his researches on the unconscious Freud used many women patients and his emphasis on the integration of repressed material from the unconscious indirectly supported the female consciousness as the path to regeneration. What Freud had postulated as an innate bisexual disposition Jung went on to personify in the *animus* and the *anima*. The incorporation of the opposing sexual polarity was a goal, at least for the latter thinker, and though Joyce had little patience with Jungian doctrines, he seems to contemplate seriously the return to a less conscious, rational state of being, and the example of this state became for him a woman. Unfortunately a certain sort of celebration ends up as a return to what is ultimately a degraded view of the primitive female consciousness. Women are further degraded in the celebration because so closely tied in the mind of James Joyce with sin and guilt, with dirty bodily thoughts and acts.

By temperament, James Joyce seems most like Dickens in this study. His relationships to women were important to him but circumscribed. There were periods in his life of intense romantic or sexual feeling, followed by long periods of apparent indifference. Unlike Richardson or Henry James, Joyce's mental life was not absorbed with women and their concerns. Rather like Dickens, when he was concerned with them, the extremes seemed to emerge. These extremes involve his fundamental feeling of betrayal, a betrayal that belongs first and foremost to his country, Ireland. Stephen Dedalus's famous characterization, "Ireland is the old sow that eats her farrow" pictures his country as a horrifying fat old hag consuming young piglets.[5] The image of the consuming mother grew out of his hatred for the relationship women had to the primary force destroying Irish youth, the church. In *Stephen Hero*, the first draft of the *Portrait*, Joyce inveighs against the relationship women have to the church. Their religiosity binds them to hypocritical attitudes, particularly to sexual repression. His mother and Emma Clery seem to him incapable of leading an authentic life because everything they are and think was put there by the Irish church. Joyce wrote in pencil across the pages that deal with this subject; "Stephen wished to avenge himself on Irish women who, he says, are the cause of all the moral suicide in the island."[6]

But the Catholic church also supplied Joyce with his female ideal, Mary, and his early spiritual life was enacted in her shadow.[7] Throughout his fiction floats the image of the ideal spiritualized woman. As an image of radiant beauty, like the girl at the seashore in *A Portrait of the Artist*, she remains unknown and functions as an icon of inspiration. Against her image real women like Emma Clery are pale, false imitations. As his fiction develops, the idealized woman is replaced by motherly, sexual women with whom all sorts of male debasements are possible. This earthy woman (and Molly is the major example) allows the man to humble himself before her, since she herself is one of the dirty elements. This figure takes on the quality of icon also, now, however, as the mothering, the engulfing, that being who will absorb the artist and give him rebirth. Essentially women are important in his fiction only as they provide evidence of the sensitivity of the male protagonist. And they are important in leading men to a certain state of mind. But in both his fiction and his life they are ultimately untrustworthy and indifferent—and as such guilty of profound betrayals even as they are ignorant of what that betrayal means.

Toward his mother, May Joyce, the author seems to have felt guilt about his betrayal of her, rather than anger at her own betrayals of him. Her life was not a happy one, if we read the account of Joyce's brother Stanislaus and Joyce's own remarks in his early work.[8] As John Joyce drank more and succeeded less in his checkered career, his rages filled a household already overcrowded with children. One night he tried to strangle his wife and James came to her rescue by jumping on his father's back.[9] When she was fatally ill the strain became too much for the elder Joyce to bear and he yelled at her to go ahead and just die.[10] There was no doubt that the marriage was a torment for her, but the two older brothers could do nothing but look on. It was the church that bound her to her husband, and both James and Stanislaus noted this bitterly. Nevertheless, she seems to have been, in some measure, a sensitive friend to the future author. In *Stephen Hero* he has her reading Ibsen at his behest, and she actually admires the plays. Particularly affecting in this early novel is the death of Joyce's sister Isabel, whom May attends to compassionately. In *A Portrait of the Artist* she is a somewhat more shadowy figure; he remembers her kiss as a boy, she smells good. But Stephen is painfully aware that their deepest separation involves religion:

> Yet her mistrust pricked him more keenly than his father's pride and he thought coldly how he had watched the faith which was fading down in his soul aging and strengthening in her eyes. A dim antagonism gathered force within him and darkened his mind as a cloud against her disloyalty: and when it passed, cloudlike, leaving his mind serene and dutiful towards her again, he was made aware dimly and without regret of a first noiseless sundering of their lives. (pp. 164-165)

Ultimately he refuses to make his Easter duty in a dramatic repud-
iation of the faith that is so important to her.

A Portrait of the Artist ends with a diary entry recording his
mother's hopes that by going away he will learn what his own heart
is and how to love. This is the real betrayal that Joyce feared he may
have been guilty of—coldness, the inability to care. Called a woman-
hater by Emma in *Stephen Hero* and a woman-killer by Bertha in
Exiles, Joyce was haunted by his mother's spirit. How to deal with
her failure to love him perfectly and his own refusal to serve religion
and through it her—that is, his own failure of love, became the
question. *Ulysses* begins with a vision of Stephen's mother in death,
and this younger version of Joyce reflects bitterly on the uncleanness
of women. She appears to him again in Nighttown and again he
speaks of his religious rebellion. By saying no to it and hence to her,
he seemed to be turning his back on the heart and on forgiveness itself. The attempt to make his way back from this betrayal has a
great deal to do with his subsequent attitudes toward women in his
fiction. Molly Bloom and Anna Livia Plurabelle in *Finnegans Wake*
are betrayed and betrayers, but they hold the key to the heart of the
universe. To know them, to be them, is to assuage his restless mother's spirit.

Joyce found in the woman who was to become his wife, Nora
Barnacle, a blend of the spiritual and the profane, a woman who
seemed to reconcile the conflicting views he had of women. Joyce
walked out with her on the famous Bloomsday of *Ulysses*, June 16,
1904, and it seemed to him on that very day that her soul was beautiful in its simplicity; she was not full of the pretensions of better
educated girls. Nora apparently satisfied two important impulses in
Joyce: the wish to worship someone (her strange, sauntering soul)
and the wish to debase himself before her. In their passionate early
years he wrote her letters full of obeisance and a childlike need for
an all-consuming love. Her soul was to be his instructress:

> O take me into your soul of souls and then I will become indeed the
> poet of my race. I feel this, Nora, as I write it. My body soon will pene-
> trate into yours, O that my soul could too! O that I could nestle in your
> womb like a child born of your flesh and blood, be fed by your blood,
> sleep in the warm secret gloom of your body![11]

It often seemed to him that she occupied as sacred a place in his manly heart as had the Virgin Mary to his boyish heart (p. 165, *Selected Letters*). Nora was both to mother him and to be his muse. In his many letters praising her beauty Joyce seemed most taken with her innocence before the world of hypocrisy. Unlettered and simple, she seemed to him to possess an unconscious joy that lived on its own.

As much as the madonna for him, she was also the prostitute. She certainly fulfilled his need for a sexual woman. It seems that it was she who first made her sexual desire for him very clear, and he memorializes these acts in Molly's monologue. In the sexually explicit letters written to her in the fall of 1909 while Joyce was in Ireland and Nora in Trieste the tone alternates between that of the domineering husband and the childish apologetic man obsessed with, among other things, anal sex. Sometimes he wants her to whip him and imagines her a wildly aggressive female, at other times he thinks of making her submit to anal intercourse and various forms of sexual submission. He also takes care to instruct Nora on her appearance. She needs to fatten herself up and procure provocative underwear. The letters were part of a mutual masturbatory pact, and they make for shocking reading even by today's standards, I think. It seems that she returned his letters in kind, although these do not survive. What these letters show is an extraordinary level of intimacy, certainly of trust, and Richard Ellmann claims that in addition to their sexual purpose, Joyce wished "to possess his wife's soul, and have her possess his, in utter nakedness" (*Selected Letters*, p. XXV).

Joyce was indeed extraordinarily possessive and domineering despite the often submissive posture he adopted toward his wife in the letters. Having been told that she was dating (and "dating" really does seem the right word) someone else during his own courtship of her, he flew into a rage of betrayal, only to recant when he learned the truth. Nora seems to have threatened to leave him shortly after this incident (and the masturbatory letters). Joyce himself thought of leaving her several times in the early years of their marriage, and his repeated complaint was of her apparent indifference. What delighted him, her unconscious simplicity and sexuality, ultimately enraged him because it did not allow her to appreciate his work.

Though he realized immediately that she could not, this lack of interest rankled. Even the elaborately copied out verses in *Chamber Music*, done by Joyce himself, seem to have been only partially read. When *Finnegans Wake* appeared Nora remarked: " 'Well, Jim, I haven't read any of your books but I'll have to some day because they must be good considering how well they sell.' "[12] Joyce always saw this lack of interest as a profound betrayal, although it is impossible to imagine what sort of total union he sought. Submissive, sexual, faithful, interested in opera, poetry, the most advanced literary composition of the century, Nora also had to be a mother to two children, one of whom was severely disturbed, a friend to the ubiquitous brother Stannie, an adept avoider of debt collectors, an inveterate pub-crawler, always and eternally moving the whole unruly household. Through it all she seems to have moved with aplomb, saved by her sense of humor and her resolute acceptance of life with a genius. When Jung praised the "psychological peaches," the knowledge of women so evident to him in Molly Bloom's monologue, Nora had only one thing to say about her husband's supposed insights: " 'He knows nothing at all about women.' "[13]

Joyce was particularly given to meditations on the faithlessness of women, the ease with which they might betray their husbands. Conveniently forgetting his own tendency toward bizarre crushes and (whether consummated or not) infidelities, he seems to have been a rather pure instance of a man projecting his own inner state upon women. From 1912 to 1914 he was infatuated with one of his language students, Amalia Popper. When he went on to write *The Exiles* (which he set in the year 1912, though it was written later), Joyce expressed all his fears about taking Nora away from her home, but primarily his guilt at what he may have taken from her to find his art. Richard Rowan says, "Is it worth what I have taken from her—her girlhood, her laughter, her young beauty, the hopes in her young heart?"[14] His guilt at his own merely carnal infidelities makes him wish that she would betray him and he sets her up to do so. But the whole business is a mental exercise for the hero, playing off his male friend Robert and his female friend Beatrice. The play ends with his declaration of his own eternal wound of doubt and Bertha's wish for the return of the earlier love they once shared. The play seems a bizarre atonement for the very projection Joyce knows that he is guilty of. The hero of the play is perverse, suspicious, manipulative, and apologetic. Doubtless, Joyce exaggerated imagined betrayals by Nora because his own of her were serious indeed. They were infatuations that were apparently mental and spiritual, not physical. His later peculiar romancing of Marthe Fleischmann during 1918 and 1919 (peeping through windows, etc.), has her figured as Beatrice to his Dante. The curious courtship culminated in an evening of Chanukah candles, and Marthe ended up in a sanitarium, sent there by her "protector," Rudolf Hiltpold.[15] Both of these relationships were bizarre crushes on a new muse. His eternal worry over cuckoldry seems much more an indication of guilt over his own betrayals rather than a reflection of the behavior of Nora, whose own nature was preternaturally faithful.

As time went on, however, the important women in his life did turn away from him, or at least so it must have seemed to Joyce. The relationship between Joyce and Nora seems to have become more difficult after her visit to Ireland in 1922, and they appear to have subsided into a state that Joyce had always dreaded, one of mutual indifference. Though they finally legalized their relationship in 1931, Richard Ellmann mentions that their sex life had already begun to disappear.[16] In his carousing he was given more and more to a sometimes cheerful, but more often bitter misogyny. Intellectual women (a breed he claimed to dislike) began to take a serious role, however, in the promotion of his work, and the most important of these became his benefactor, Harriet Shaw Weaver. Joyce cared very much for her opinions and her later disapproval of *Finnegans Wake* was a severe blow, another female betrayal, but also another cause for guilt, since it was he, the artist, who had failed to please. But the worst source of disappointment and guilt in these later years was his daughter Lucia. As she drifted into madness, Joyce tried more and more frantically to rescue her. He came to believe that her mad sayings were actually a special language full of profound meaning. Just as the world disapproved of the bizarre linguistic games of *Finnegans Wake*, the world was not charmed by the antics of Lucia Joyce. For him she was an artist manqué. He was tireless in seeking a cure for her, moving her from hospital to hotel to sanitarium, but he could not save her. While there are many indications that Joyce identified with his daughter, saw her as another victim of the uncomprehending world, he must surely have felt betrayed, as parents of such children might, by a child who behaved outrageously to friends trying to help, who showed tremendous anger toward her mother, finally who failed to grow up at all. One's guilt would be that much deeper, precisely because of the need to suppress any expression of anger at the betrayal.

Guilt, then, and a sense of mutual betrayal pervade what relations he had with women, although these relations seem only periodically intense. On the casual level Joyce seems to have gotten along rather better with women than with men, and he saved his real confidences for Nora and for his Aunt Josephine. The frankness and charm of his letters to them is quite different from the stiff pedantic tone he adopted with men.

Clearly Joyce did have enough sympathy with women to write Molly Bloom's monologue, and this sympathy derives, in part, from his own exiled state, an exile that was in no small measure a rejection of the life of an Irish male, as it was really lived and as it was expressed in the heroic structure of Irish Catholicism. In exile not only from his country, but also from what his country stood for, he wrote to his brother in 1905: "I am sure however that the whole structure of heroism is, and always was, a damned lie and that there cannot be any substitute for the individual passion as the motive power of everything—art and philosophy included." (*Selected Letters*, p. 54) The individual passion is just what George Eliot had discovered, and substituted for a religious vision of the heroic. And Joyce was, like James, her follower in portraying the inner life of the special case. Joyce's fondness for thinking of himself as a Jew supplies another clue to his interest in adopting a female role, if only for a short time. Degraded wanderers subject to the spite or even abuse of the lowliest Christian, the Jewish man presented himself as the archetypal outsider. Joyce was proud of his exiled state; it indicated the superiority of the artist, but it made him feel vulnerable, and he really was vulnerable, financially as well as physically. Living a hand-to-mouth existence for years did not improve his health. Eye operations and ultimate blindness gradually complete what his ideological convictions had begun, something near complete personal isolation. For all of these reasons, women presented yet another way of expressing the views of the outsider, someone not chained to the old system of heroism, indeed excluded from it. Like Jews, like the Irish (for him outsiders in the universe) they are victims in a world that often ridicules their very state of mind (an isolated, hermetic state of mind), although Joyce himself was not the least of the ridiculers.

Joyce's theories of artistic creation, if we take them from the lips of Stephen Dedalus, place heavy emphasis on an identification between the artist and the mother. Joyce often remarked on the purity of a mother's love, in the abstract, and was fond of metaphors of gestation and parturition to characterize the birth of a work of art. The artist himself giving birth was the purest of all reproductions, as Stephen Dedalus asserts in *A Portrait*. Notice that it is the conjunction of the male artist with a metaphor from female physiology that accounts for creation. The new Virgin Mary is a man. Woman herself remains a highly impure creature, the creator of impure art as Stephen defines it, since Molly Bloom creates in her monologue an art that titillates and arouses. (Even though Judge Woolsey did not find that the pornography outweighed the art.) One has only to read his own obscene letters to see the similarities in tone and imagery, although in this instance Joyce puts his own thoughts into the mouth of Molly. Joyce seems to be engaged in a covert exercise at masturbatory prose, a proclivity to which male artists writing as women are particularly prone.[17]

When he adopted the voice of Molly, he did give her one great compliment; he made her a discrete identifiable voice, a character (though not an actor) as we have come to know them in the novel. The epiphanic mode in the *Portrait*, a mode that evoked sudden moments of illumination usually taking place in the mind of one character (although a number of other voices are heard as well), was replaced in *Ulysses* with several characters whose voices and minds intersperse the narrative, but in a fragmentary way. In 1931 Edmund Wilson noted a whole array of voices in the novel, some of which seem neither the author's nor any character's.[18] Hugh Kenner, in his recent book *Joyce's Voices*, claims to find in *Ulysses* essentially two points of view operating at any one time; the voice of the speaker and another voice that may poke fun at or may coincide with the voice itself speaking. The internal monologue form thus becomes at once internal and external (the external being the narrator or implied author).[19] It is very difficult, however, to assign to this narrative "other voice" a discrete being since "the person" has neither name nor wholeness. And this is where Molly Bloom differs so markedly from Stephen Dedalus and Leopold Bloom. Whereas their thoughts, words, and acts scatter through the day in fragments, Molly appears at the end, at once, with an uninterrupted narrative. She, at least, is a person whom we can recognize as a discrete presence in the drama, if not an actor.

The masculine search for identity and wholeness is the central dilemma of *Ulysses*. Most critics place too much emphasis on the search of the father for his son, and vice versa, however. Both Stephen Dedalus and Leopold Bloom also wander in search of a loving female figure on this June 16, 1904; without her they remain partial and fragmentary. Each man is guilt-ridden, one because of the death of his mother, the other because of the death of his son and the subsequent souring of his marriage. Much of the substance of their day is taken up with longing, with needy thoughts about women—each seems peculiarly in thrall to these longings, but guilt and dislike for real women prevent their finding any satisfaction. Stephen turns away from women in philosophic dislike, but he is torn by his physical desire. His primary feeling is bitterness. Leopold identifies himself too much with women; he seems to have become an odd hybrid—a womanly man. The climax of their day is reached in Nighttown, when a group of prostitutes castigate them for their failings, their shameful behavior toward women. The principal women they have betrayed appear before them in accusatory postures. For both of these men, guilt has weakened them to the point of impotence, both sexually and spiritually.

Stephen is haunted with images of woman's suffering and of her physical impurity. As she sees his sister Dilly's feeble attempt to learn French (after the other books in the house have been pawned), he senses her bitter misery and seems to feel her dragging him down to a watery grave. Looking at an old woman pouring milk into a dish he thinks with revulsion of her hideous body. This ugliness then leads him to consider the uncleanness of a woman's loins and her peculiar biblical relationship to man.

While looking at the dirty windows and the dirty fingers of the man behind the window, the lapidary, Stephen suddenly has a vision of a foul hag, dancing while her hips and huge belly flop. The climax of these visions comes in Nighttown. Stephen's mother appears, and with blackened arm points to his breast and tells him to beware God's hand. God's hand turns out to be the claw of a crab, and it closes over his heart. She continues to exhort him, and the whole episode ends with his breaking the chandelier and fleeing. Stephen is enraged and in terror—this is the vision of woman that so haunts the author, woman consumed by real disease and by the crippling effects of the church. It is a horrifying vision of both physical and spiritual corruption.

The other side to Stephen's horror is his longing for love, for sexual fulfillment and the power that fulfillment will give him. As he lies stretched upon the rocks by the sea, he aches for a woman's touch. He is sad and alone, but who will come save him? "She, she, she. What she?"[20] He mentally conjoins sexual desire to the wish to idealize the figure of the loved one. Out of this emerges his worship of a magna mater who presides over the act of pure creation. This figure appears to be a fusion of the classical weaver goddess from whose weaving the human body emerges and the Virgin Mary. As I said earlier, Joyce liked to make an analogy between the virgin birth and the work of art. Stephen is engaged with this image also. As in "woman's womb word is made flesh" so in the imagination of the artist the word is made whole and real (*Ulysses,* p. 391). All that is contained in past, present, and future coalesces at an instant of time. But the fusion requires the presence of the maker—a figure who in Stephen's mind is the great presiding goddess. What Stephen seeks, in Joyce's view, is the reconciliation of the bestial and the exalted in woman. Without such knowledge he will roam unsatisfied and waste himself on prostitutes, as Leopold observes. On this day in June he is poised between the two polarities, in comically cerebral indecision. Until he can resolve the dilemma of woman's true nature and her relationship to the divine, he knows nothing about himself.

Adulthood has done nothing but weaken the sexual identity of Leopold Bloom. Not only does Joyce make him unable to enjoy normal sexual relations, he also confuses his sexual identity—a kind of man-woman is held up to us for our admiration. Central to his sexual difficulties is Leopold's identification with women, especially in their birth pangs. Several important sections of the book are given over to the birth of Mrs. Purefoy's baby and to the question of abortion. Bloom feels great sympathy for the endlessly reproductive Irish wife who finds herself in yet another hard labor, and his imagination is such that he wonders what it would be like to feel the baby's head coming out. While the drunken medical students contemplate various forms of wenching and the propriety of doing away with the issue, Bloom thinks of the travail of his own Marion and her deep grief at the death of the eleven-day-old Rudy. Molly's grief in this novel is minuscule, however, to that of her husband. Dignam's funeral, which begins the day, calls up thoughts of death and the boy. Several times he thinks of sex with his wife, but death intervenes to sour the thoughts. The culmination of Bloom's guilt about motherhood comes in Nighttown, when an eleven-year-old Rudy appears in hilarious garb reading a book in the Jewish fashion from right to left. Joyce has made Rudy an Oscar Wildean figure, right down to his ivory cane, unaccountably dressed in a helmet and glass shoes (Cinderella?). Even the son is androgynous, a fop, a soldier, and a woman all in one. Bloom's softness in these matters has come to dominate his life. We are left to think that his sympathies with the pains and losses of motherhood have enfeebled his sex.

Sexually, Bloom has turned inward and manages for himself only partial satisfactions. His "romances" are conducted with himself and with women whom he barely knows. Catering to what he considers his wife's preferences, he purchases *The Sweets of Sin* by Mr. Paul de Kock—then *he* precedes to become sexually aroused by it. The famous Nausikaa section of the book, given over to his masturbation while watching Gerty McDowell, reveals him as a squeamish voyeur whose dominant sexual mode is one of fantasy. Joyce makes Gerty a woman of discharges and sentimentalized imagination. Her thoughts issue from cheap romances, and to her Leopold Bloom is a handsome, romantic stranger. Like nearly every woman in Joyce's fiction, her mind fuses the sacred and the profane, and with complete indifference to what that implies. She is willing, even delighted, to excite an unknown man at the beach. And

Leopold is ready to respond. His masturbation is somewhat comically linked to the exploding skyrockets. But this act allows him to meditate on women and *their* flaws. Gerty is lame, he finds, and probably due for her period. Somewhat resentful, he fears that she has taken something from him. "Tired I feel now. Will I get up? O wait. Drained all the manhood out of me, little wretch. She kissed me. My youth. Never again" (p. 377). At this moment Blazes Boylan is making a cuckold of Bloom. We know that Joyce's own extra-marital romances were given over to extensive watching, even peeping through windows. It is disturbing to think that this whole sequence may well be autobiographical (his Marthe Fleischmann romance). In relationship to the sexual practices of her husband, Molly is a model of mental health.

The various guilty obsessions that drive Leopold culminate during his visit to Bella Cohen's brothel. His father, his mother, his wife, prostitutes—all jeer at his inadequacy. He is roundly castigated for bizarre sexual behavior, including the sending of lewd letters to unknown ladies. Even though he is crowned King, he then is pronounced a virgin, a blasphemous joke on a union between God and the Virgin Mary. Bloom has now become the God Stephen had derived from Shakespeare earlier; "glorified man, an androgynous angel, being a wife unto himself" (p. 213). Bloom, Joyce is saying, is complete in himself, and the dream figure of Dr. Dixon pronounces him a "finished example of the new womanly man" (p. 493). Furthermore we learn that he is going to have a baby. This section of the book, nightmarish, comical, absurdist, shows Bloom in a posture of intense humiliation. A complex joke on religion and the eunuch-like status imposed on Irishmen by the church, the section contains a number of Joyce's own sexual fantasies—flagellation, for one. And Leopold's shame and guilt before these women is astonishing. Be limp, be weak, be ruled by women; he has taken these commands to heart. Is it his suffering at the hands of Bella Cohen that makes him "our hero"? (p. 658). If so, his nighttime vision makes him a particularly helpless hero, consumed by guilt about the nature of his own passions, such as they are. The nighttime of Molly Bloom is tranquil and healthy by comparison.

At one point in his humiliations he is informed of his cuckolding in graphic terms. Rather than castigate his wife he himself asks for forgiveness, begs for it. Even Leopold knows that it is he who is faithless, who has betrayed his wife, but one still cannot help wondering at his almost abject terror of women. The wife is in charge, and Leopold speculates on the nature of the domination of Woman in the Ithaca episode that immediately precedes Molly's monologue. Speculation on the constellations leads to the moon and thence to Woman. The reasons for her ascendancy are analyzed:

> her power to enamour, to mortify, to invest with beauty, to render insane, to incite to and aid delinquency: the tranquil inscrutability of her visage: the terribility of her isolated dominant implacable resplendent propinquity . . . (p. 702).

Woman is for Leopold a force of nature, like the moon with crags and crevasses (earth) and like the moon in her influence over the sea. As any inscrutable goddess growing from earth, she is base, elemental, and frightening. This speech prepares us for Molly's monumental appearance—a monologue that demonstrates her powers graphically. As Joyce himself said, she was meant to be "perfectly sane full amoral fertilisable untrustworthy engaging shrewd limited prudent indifferent *Weib*" (*Selected Letters*, p. 285).

Joyce thought Molly to be at the center of the book's meaning. Given his penchant for a female figure to adore, she functions as an odalisque. Like one of Matisse's ladies with her arms languidly held behind her head, she looks out at us without a flinch, waiting. *Weib*, as Heinz Wismann states, has a negative connotation, it implies someone close to prostitution, someone with distinctly animalistic traits.[21] Just as the modern Ulysses and the modern Telemachus have fallen from heroic status, the modern Penelope is awash in men, food, stockings, gloves, religion, sex—the most sacred and profane are conjoined. Her mind is a garbage dump. Because she can make no distinctions, she is ultimately indifferent. Joyce remarked to Nora that he sometimes saw her as a madonna and at other times "shameless, insolent, half naked and obscene" (*Selected Letters*, p. 167). But in fact Joyce has given to this woman a strength that neither Stephen nor Leopold possess. However, it is the strength of ignorance. Joyce invests her with an understanding that escapes guilt and impotence and fright and endless questioning of the universe—but it is know-nothingism that he recreates. Obviously he has enjoyed creating this non-stop talker, he has enjoyed peering at men through her eyes and banishing in himself the debilitating sense of sin and guilt. She is a *tour de force*, hanging about the book like a gigantic priestess, and she herself is a god of sorts, looking down on everyone about her, powerful and indifferent. To be dismantled of one's paralyzing guilt—there is a sort of peace for man in this state of mind.

Molly is easily the most disintegrated of the female voices in this study. Her thinking runs on for over forty unpunctuated pages. Her monologue is difficult to read, even harder to understand, since the reader must follow a dreamlike sequence of continuously shifting images and pronouns. Edmund Wilson called her ruminations "a long, unbroken rhythm of brogue, like the swell of some profound sea."[22] Molly is nothing if not oceanic.

The French critic and friend of Joyce, Louis Gillet, commented on the author's remarkable powers of mimicry, his love for storytelling and with it his imitations of a variety of speakers.[23] Molly's soliloquy is a sustained dramatic performance, a masquerade of extraordinary length in the voice of a middle-class Irish housewife. That anyone could be thinking in this way—entirely in language (rather than through visual images) and without pauses, even down to her describing for us her own motions onto the chamber pot, or the discovery that she is menstruating—is inconceivable, even monstrous in its implications. The endless verbal flow makes her seem feverishly active mentally for someone about to go to sleep. In fact her head seems alive in nightmarish fashion. Over forty pages of uninterrupted speech (and it is a speech) appears unnatural and highly contrived, just as Richardson's strenuous attempts to account for the fact that Clarissa can write those innumerable letters herself, is contrived. She seems overwhelming, grotesque, and she is made even more so by her position at the end of a narrative obsessively concerned with relations between men and women. There are no boundaries between anyone or anything in this monologue, between me and not-me, he, she, or it. Supposed to be the tapestry of the weaver Penelope, it seems a form of madness, a woman's tongue loosed upon the world of night.

Coming to know Molly is, even given the extremity of the form of her voice, much easier, however, than coming to know either Stephen or Leopold, since there is so much other noise and interference to cloud our sense of them. Molly has the stage to herself; she bears a closer relationship to fictional characters, at least insofar as we can always clearly identify the "I" that is speaking to us. Joyce obviously wants her to be accessible and knowable in ways that his male figures are not, and that is because she *can* be known. In this sense Molly has a fixed identity; she has been given a discrete text by the author. She also has a powerful position, the end, as Joyce gives her the definitive last word. But none of these facts about Molly, facts embedded in the form of her speech, vitiate the overwhelming experience of being driven on the waves of incoherence and irrationality; even though in point of fact she is neither incoherent nor irrational when one reads her monologue over several times. But only an academic reader would. Joyce seems to have wanted us to take her in one great gulp, to be swept along by her song. The form in which she appears defines entirely our conclusions about *what* she says, especially since it is so relentless.

If there is any word that dominates the monologue, it is "I". Thus Joyce has reinforced the cultural assumption of female narcissism. The female ego is dominant, central, but incorporates the outside world into aspects of the self. This assertion is problematic, however, since in the monologue it is Joyce who is being narcissistic, indulging himself in a rapturous and strange holding up of the mirror in two and sometimes three directions.

At one level the monologue recaptures Joyce's wife Nora. He often remarked on his wife's penchant for unpunctuated prose, and the salty humor Molly displays sounds much like anecdotes about Nora. The courtship of Bloom and Molly resembles closely that of the artist and his wife, even down to the glove she left with him one day (*Selected Letters*, p. 22). Mark Schechner calls the monologue a "sly penitential gesture" to Joyce's wife for all the years of his neglect, downright misogyny, and indifference to women in his fiction.[24] If there is much penitence here, it is difficult to find. Certainly as a recreation of her, it is a grotesque portrait of flesh incarnate. The act of homage is specifically made to her husband, to

Leopold Bloom. He is laughed at, extolled, and finally affirmed. As a great many critics have said, Molly's monologue is an affirmation of her love for her husband. Thoughts of Leopold gain gradual ascendance over those of other men, and the monologue ends with the famous rapturous retelling of their early love. The narcissist here is Joyce, looking at a version of himself through his wife's eyes.

Getting behind his wife's eyes, Joyce gives us a litany of wry, almost sardonic praise. This praise is double-edged, since Molly reduces Leopold to comical postures, praising and belittling at once. She remarks on the specialness of Leopold. He is neat and clean, wipes his feet on the mat. Once he was intensely romantic towards her and could make up all sorts of beautiful phrases for her and even gave her a book of Lord Byron's poetry. He often uses big words that she does not understand, but then he putters about the house too much. What he needs is some more steady work, perhaps even at a bank "where they could put him up on a throne to count the money all the day. . ." (p. 752). Many of the author's sexual proclivities appear, particularly in Master Poldy's fondness for drawers. For all of his neglect Molly compares him favorably with her new lover, Blazes Boylan. In fact Poldy is in a number of ways extraordinary, even to wanting to milk her into the tea when her breasts are large after the birth of their daughter, Milly; "well hes beyond everything I declare somebody ought to put him in the budget if I only could remember the one half of the things and write a book out of it the works of Master Poldy yes. . ." (p. 754). Ultimately, no matter what I do, she loves me, Joyce writes. Of course Molly makes much fun of her husband; he is laughable, but she loves him intensely despite his obvious, longstanding sexual neglect.

Much is usually made of Molly's betrayal of her husband, since she has just had a most athletic encounter with her singing tour manager, Mr. Blazes Boylan. In point of fact this infidelity diminishes considerably in significance when we note Leopold's behavior and how she feels about it. Her monologue begins with her concern that he may be unfaithful to her, for the simple fact is that they have not made love properly in ten years. These thoughts lead her to recall his pursuit of one of their servants and then later to speculate on whether he has been seeing prostitutes lately. (Joyce himself seems to have gone to a prostitute during his Ireland visit in 1909, and it apparently provoked a marital crisis.) (*Selected Letters*, p. 177) He has simply turned away from her and, in fact, indulges in much more prurient, unnatural behavior than does his wife, engaged as she is, apparently for the first time, in getting some sexual satisfaction for herself. Coldness, indifference, and ultimately betrayal—the man stands accused. The monologue once again has the air of a public chastisement, just as the Circe episode is a long fantasy of humiliation at the hands of women before all the world. At the end of her thoughts, Molly reflects on the jealousy of husbands toward wives and begins to justify her own behavior of that day. "What else were we given all those desires for Id like to know I cant help it if Im young still can I its a wonder Im not an old shrivelled hag before my time living with him so cold never embracing me except sometimes when hes asleep. . . ." (p. 777). She comments shortly thereafter that her adultery is surely his fault. The idea that even if she had not, Nora certainly *should* have betrayed him is central to the *Exiles* as well. Joyce's guilt about his own infidelities and coldness lead him to imagine woman as herself the central betrayer, and the entire day in Bloom's life is clouded by worries about his wife's sexual intercourse with someone else. Whatever accusations the monologue contains about Bloom's failures of love, hers is still the real, immediate betrayal. One can see here the uneasy mixture of self-accusation and self-justification. Whatever the degree of Bloom's own neglect, Molly's activities are worse. Nearing the end of her difficult tenure as Joyce's wife, Nora wangled a dinner invitation to a friend's house and announced, " 'There sits a man who has not spoken one word to me all day.' "[25] Joyce replied that he had nothing to say after all the years of married life. One cannot escape the conclusion that Joyce blamed women, beginning with his mother, for his own failure to love.

Joyce uses Molly's voice also to express a number of fears he had about male sexuality. First and foremost he feared that to women all men are the same. They blur together into one great *he*. This is what Kenner calls her "prenominal promiscuity."[26] Secondly when they are sexual, they look ridiculous. D. H. Lawrence often imagined that to women the sex act itself was silly, and that they could be detected laughing at men as they make love. Certainly

Blazes Boylan appears to her often as a coarse, ludicrous person who goes around singing, slapping bottoms, and lunging about in a highly excited state. In his erect condition, man looks to Molly "like a hatrack" (p. 753). Much of the sex that Molly describes (and of which she disapproves) is bestial. Men force women to do it like dogs, and they are constantly after a woman. In fact their excitement is such that their "omissions" take place everywhere except the right spot. Joyce's own feelings about sex, on the basis of the masturbatory series of letters, were deeply tied to dirtiness and bestiality, although he also can be found laughing at himself for these feelings. Molly does the same. She puts sexual men in their place—they are clowns.

But Molly Bloom is also the voice of the author, a female masquerade in which Joyce imagined the resolution of the most crippling problems confronting his male alter egos in *Ulysses* and also certainly himself. He uses her not only as a mirror to reflect back himself, but he imaginatively fuses the voice of the male artist with the voice of the woman. There are several obvious elements in Molly that identify her with her author. She is terrified of thunderstorms, and Joyce was frightened of these himself. Molly is a singer, although how good is unclear, while Joyce was celebrated among his friends for his beautiful tenor voice. As were Joyce's friends about the author himself, one is immediately struck with the act of memory being conveyed here.[27] As she mentally fuses the past and the present, she gives memory its due and brings it to bear on what is now happening. This is a talent only sporadically evident in either Stephen or Bloom, whose memories are fragmentary. Joyce allows Molly to comprehend experience through the act of remembering. A much more significant affinity is their hatred of hypocrisy and their penchant for telling the truth. Stephen and Leopold spend the day temporizing and posturing for the benefit of their fellow Irishmen. Molly talks only to herself and to us, and feels no fear of self-revelation. She is especially vehement about her dislike for the religious hypocrises of women. The monologue has her very early attacking the way Mrs. Riordan looks down on sex and wants people to be ashamed of their bodies. Molly is having none of it. She castigates Father Corrigan for his dirty mindedness and goes on to accuse him of all sorts of prurient activities. "I hate that pretending of all things" (p. 751) she says and means it. These are almost the same words Joyce himself used in discussing the drivel perpetrated by his friends and some churchmen on the subject of romantic love and sexual purity (*Selected Letters,* p. 129). In fact much of her monologue is devoted to showing up the fakeries of others who are always bent on propriety, especially sexual propriety but are themselves full of dirty thoughts.

Critics tend to find clichés about women in the monologue. Several negative remarks that Molly makes about women are often quoted to show that, just as all women are supposed to, she dislikes her own sex. Such, however, is not the case. A certain kind of hypocritical woman comes in for sarcastic dislike, but Joyce gives evidence of deep identification with women on several levels. Molly thinks that women suffer a great deal, primarily because of the way their bodies are made and the inordinate male need of them. Men think only of plunging right into the center of a woman. Compared to the curious male body, woman is beauty itself, and to prove it she recalls a statue of a woman hiding one breast with her hand. She even takes to imagining what it would be like to make love to a woman; "God I wouldnt mind being a man and get up on a lovely woman. . ." (p. 770). But more than beauty, women have character. Thinking of her old love Lieutenant Mulvey, she speculates on how changed he must be by marriage. It is the love of a woman that does it—as Joyce indicated that his love for Nora made him grow up and become a man. Molly even has a feminist moment (very reminiscent of her counterpart Moll Flanders). She remarks that it would be better if women ruled the world, "you wouldnt see women going and killing one another and slaughtering when do you ever see women rolling around drunk like they do or gambling every penny they have and losing it on horses yes because a woman whatever she does she knows where to stop. . ." (p. 778).

Woman's occasional bitchiness is due to mistreatment, not to stupidity and viciousness, qualities she lays at the door of the Irish male (she makes an exception for Leopold). Certainly the male structure of heroism is here under attack, what Joyce himself found so distasteful. Molly does show a strength of character that makes her male counterparts appear physically and psychologically impotent. It is guilt that has had so corrosive an effect on the men. Stephen is guilty about the death of his mother, trying to break free of her spirit. To do so he joins forces with male comrades and a substitute father, Leopold. Leopold himself tries to avoid all day the knowledge of his wife's infidelity, even while he is writing letters to Martha Clifford. The image of his dead son Rudy haunts him as does his father's suicide. Molly, on the other hand, is certainly not concerned with guilt. She feels justified in what she does. The images of the past she summons to mind are not threatening or abusive as they are for Leopold. Her motherhood seems less a worry to her than fatherhood does to her husband. Rudy figures only briefly in her memories, and even then only after a graphic, sexual reference to the coupling of dogs. But she has also been speculating on Stephen Dedalus's running wild; "I suppose I oughnt to have buried him in that little woolly jacket I knitted crying as I was but give it to some poor child but I knew well Id never have nother our 1st death too it was we were never the same since O Im not going to think myself into the glooms about that any more. . ." (p. 778). And she does not fall into gloomy thoughts. Her maternal feelings toward Milly are equally clear; she feels herself a rival with her husband for her affections, but knows that her daughter comes to her when there is something really wrong. This absence of the maternal in her talk contrasts sharply with the obsessional thoughts of Stephen and Leopold, both of whom are being strangled by the past. Molly has freed herself from guilt in a way that they cannot.

Molly is sexually potent in ways that the male figures are not. Leopold Bloom has not managed satisfactory sex with his wife in ten years, while Stephen is absorbed in moony reflections on the nature of motherhood, his own need for sex, and squeamishness about dirty women. Molly is the only one having any sex, and she is the only one not paralyzed by guilt. And it is she alone who understands the conflict between romance and sexuality, a conflict that has made Stephen and Leopold impotent. In *A Portrait of the Artist as a Young Man* Joyce records a squeamishness at the physical realities of the body. As Stephen and Bloom appear in *Ulysses*, this squeamishness has been transferred to women; they appear to each as organic beings with distasteful smells and constant physical reminders of the flesh. Just as it had for Dean Swift or Yeats, such reminders bear directly on the sex act, and even more potently on romantic love. Molly thinks with pleasure about oral sex and even about flatulence, although she has the usual complaints about menstruation.

Acceptance of her body allows her to rise above the problematic relationship between bestiality, human sexuality, and romantic love. Her sexual reflections often display a similar pattern. First she will think of dogs, then of Boylan and how good sex makes her feel, then of Poldy and his eccentricities, usually in a romantic vein, then of him as a lover. Not always in this order, of course, but Joyce presents a constellation of love here. It is the bestial, the human, and the romantic all at once She often does see the contradictions, but she resolves them easily. That beasts copulate, that men look silly making love fuse in her mind with the pleasure of the long kiss and the love she feels for Poldy. Because it is a blend, she does not demonstrate the debased mentality of Gerty McDowell. It is Leopold who has bought Paul de Kock's *Sweets of Sin* because his imagination is full of the titillations of sinfulness in sex (as was Joyce himself, it would seem). Alternately Molly laughs at the bestial and appreciates it. When Joyce has her say "O Jamesy let me up out of this pooh sweets of sin. . . ." (p. 769), as she menstruates, he allows his female voice to send a direct message to the world. Molly laughs also at the sentimental, sighing and dying school of romance, although she wants some of this in her life. In fact love itself is a wonder to her, and you can see love "around you like a new world. . ." (p. 758). A combination of the animal, physical, and romantic love is what she manages here—and they fuse together into her final affirmation of Leopold. As Hugh Kenner says even in such a debased world, "Her 'yes' is confident and exultant; it is the 'yes' of authority: authority over this animal kingdom of the dead."[28] Joyce thus gives to Molly a strength and potency denied to his male figures, yet she is another paradoxical female voice. Possessing will and power, she is rendered in a way that makes her frighteningly incoherent; her strength is made monstrous by the form her voice takes. Like all the female voices we have examined she is outsized, voluminous, her dimensions are frighteningly large. In fact, the rest of *Ulysses* gives the overall impression that she is omnivorous egotism in human form. Somewhere, somehow she has drawn the manhood from Leopold, because she is monstrously self-contained. The womanly man that

Leopold Bloom has become is the apotheosis of the hen-pecked male
of the first two decades of this century. His loss of maleness is a
symbol for the paralysis of the modern world. Like the impotent
Fisher King of T. S. Eliot's *Wasteland* or the hen-pecked males that
populate the work of D. H. Lawrence, Bloom's loss of power has
been made equivalent to his loss of sex. In Joyce's work women are
central to this loss of power. They have usurped it. They have deprived the male of his potency, through the absurdity of their minds
and the insatiability of their bodies.

The female masquerade has allowed Joyce to throw off
conscience and the intense demands of logic and intellection, to
abandon the male self and luxuriate in fluids, sex, and sin. This game
is in part an act of self-arousal, in part a contemplation of the *male*
essence. Joyce also looks at women and then through them at the
world. Two versions of himself, Poldy and Stephen, dance to the
tune of a third, Molly. But it is the woman who has achieved mastery, as she babbles, as she falls asleep. Molly Bloom's linguistic
peculiarities are an extreme expression of what we have already seen
in other female speakers. Molly's untrustworthiness comes not from
what she says, but from how she says it. The sense of a double vision
at work, one that looks at her, another that looks through her makes
all of her meanings ambiguous. Her bearings on the inner and the
outer world are fused, and we are consequently in doubt. How many
lovers has she really had? Do she and Leopold have some form of
sexual intercourse, even if only partial? Presented to us here between
waking and sleeping, in her own mind the world has no boundaries,
and readers are prevented from knowing where reality stops and
starts.

Molly also bears striking affinities to her forbears in the pornographic uses to which she is put. Joyce's masquerade here is at
times much like that of John Cleland as Fanny Hill, at other times
like Roxana. Imagining the world as a woman results in a world
largely concerned with men and sex, and even more in the picturing
of their sexual organs. Like Roxana, Molly seems consumed with an
inner itch, a restless yearning and longing. It becomes maniacal in
Roxana, in Molly it is both funny and voracious. Joyce refers to Moll
Flanders in the monologue, and Molly is certainly more like her than

Roxana in her lack of guilt. Defoe imagined himself in dark, horrifying postures as the lady in the *deshabille*. Moll and Molly career
along with a certain amount of obliviousness.

Joyce said that Molly was an affirmation of the flesh. (*Selected Letters*, p. 285) She is meant to be a redemptive figure, just as is
Esther Summerson. Esther's voice controls only half of *Bleak House*;
her saving consciousness is limited. Molly receives even a smaller
share of this huge novel. Placed where she is, she is in large measure
irrelevant; she is given nothing to do, she merely is. A kind of verbal
icon, her voice seems in itself an object; it cannot be torn apart.
Since the book is the record of one day, we do not know what will
happen to all of these people. Can this world be redeemed by flesh
alone, by a revolution of consciousness through the body? But surely
Joyce is recommending nothing so definite as this. He seems to be
saying that there is life in the flesh made conscious of itself. If the
flesh were to speak, this is what it would say. But at this point
Stephen and Leopold are tormented outsiders in this world. The
latter's most decisive act may have been to order an egg for the next
day's breakfast (reminiscent of Eliot's Prufrock daring to eat a
peach). Molly also contains as voice the high degree of ambivalence
that any model, any worshiped figure would. Does Joyce not hate
and degrade women for their powers of resolution just as Richardson does his Christian saint? Are her powers not achieved at the
sacrifice of form, logic, rationality? The heart finally rules out the
head, and so the compliment to woman is a backhanded one indeed.
The ambiguous quality of this voice has polarized her critics, some
of whom see her as an affirmative figure, others of whom see her as
"satanic mistress," Mr. Hugh Kenner among them.[29] Like the other
female figures in this study, she seems to issue from the twin motives
of hatred and love, and as Mr. Shechner puts it: "But for Joyce,
every gesture of hostility generated its own antithesis, and the harsh-
er his attack, the more lavish the reparation."[30] Since the narrative
pose itself, I would add, has allowed such imaginative freedom,
especially as it relates to the matter of strength and power, it has led
also to its denial and to its severe punishment.

During the last two years of his life, Joyce was preoccupied
with problems connected to speech and language, we might almost

say voice. These problems centered in the illness of his daughter, Lucia, and *Finnegans Wake*. "Work in Progress," as he called it then, was incomprehensible to most people, and disliked by his patron, Harriet Shaw Weaver. He seemed to his friends to be creating something beyond language and literature itself. Lucia was going mad, while Joyce frantically moved her from hospital to hospital. Her speech became more and more bizarre, and at least in Jung's view (with whom Joyce consulted) the author indulged himself in a destructive overidentification with her.[31] Certainly his last years were filled with a sense of his own psychological isolation, with an intense resentment at the sufferings of the misunderstood genius. So he chose to regard his daughter and undoubtedly himself. Out of his last work, the single voice that emerges most accessibly, most "authentically" according to Harry Levin, is that of the female heroine, Anna Livia Plurabelle.[32] The River Liffey winding to the sea, she is also another, less harsh exploration of his wife's psychology, a reflection on the mental death of his daughter, and the anticipation of his own death. As Nora, she still derides; "I thought you the great in all things, in guilt and in glory. You're but a puny."[33] The river herself is lonely and mournful, as she slips away, saying goodbye all the while to "you, my cold father, my cold mad father, my cold mad feary father. . ." (p. 628). Joyce never exonerated himself from the charge of not being able to love. Anna voices the movement toward loss of consciousness, the river bids farewell to the land and rushes to the Irish sea; "A way a lone a last a loved a long the" (p. 628). Joyce himself said that *Ulysses* ended with the strong word "yes" and *Finnegans Wake* with the weak, gliding "the."[34] This is the word of giving way. Nothing, of course, could be stronger or more perpetual than the river; yet the force of nature is flow, is a specific loss of boundaries—she becomes the All. Once again the woman represents eternal power and dissolution. Like Molly, Anna is meant to be both real person and monolith. What she says makes her sound real, recognizable in some sense as an Irish woman of a real time and place. Yet she herself is a place in which people wash their dirty linen. The form corroborates her dual existence; it is poetry this time, slurred, flowing. Again representing affirmation, the woman is the voice of loss of being itself, a loss of will that is total— and beautifully expressed.

James Joyce's interest in Defoe is not so surprising when we see the immediacy, the tangibility he wished to give to the voices of his drama. Consciousness that appears to be unmediated, that appears to issue from the mouth of a real person who confides in us represents a remarkably pure form of human contact, from the work of fiction to the reader. The result is that the consciousness becomes itself a sort of exemplum, a mode held up for our scrutiny. The larger purposes that Defoe may have had in mind when he wrote as a woman are unclear now, though we can guess at them. In Joyce's case a larger purpose clearly operates; the woman becomes a tool in the change of consciousness, a vehicle for the affirmation of sexuality over and against the demands of conscience, for feeling against hyper-rationality, for qualities of spirit against the deadness of the age. But it is entirely unclear here whether woman is the cause or the cure. Her strength is frightening and omnivorous, but it is also the source of life and feeling (it may even mean death, as in the case of Anna Livia). To plunge into the source is horrifying in the nothingness that results, and yet to be separated from it is a nightmare, as we can clearly see in Stephen and Leopold.

No one plunged into this dilemma with more fervor or more ambivalence than D. H. Lawrence. He probably did to death the idea of woman and the redemptive female consciousness. However, as I said earlier, he rarely wrote in the first person as a woman, preferring at least after *Sons and Lovers* to violate freely the discreteness of his characters through the third person. This is particularly the mode of *The Rainbow* and *Women in Love*, although *Aaron's Rod* and *Lady Chatterly's Lover* partake heavily of it also. Only in *The Lost Girl* and *The Plumed Serpent* does Lawrence show respect for the individual identities of the characters—leaving them to speak their piece more or less consistently. In what are usually called his masterpieces, *The Rainbow* and *Women in Love*, the predominant ethos is that of primitivism, as William York Tindall said long ago.[35] The consciousness most tied to that ethos (and this element is annoyingly consistent in his work) belongs to a woman. The female figures of Anna, Ursula, and Gudrun most often become the mouthpieces of the struggle with masculine will that Lawrence saw at the heart of the decline of the west and, at a deeper, more personal level, his own struggle with homosexuality.

I bring Lawrence up at this point because he explores most fully in his work the problems he saw as the modern reversal of the sex role. Women, to him, had become authoritative and men weak and full of sympathy. This vision issues very directly from his own deep identification with women and his rejection of the more aggressive aspects of male identity. The result is a strange fusion between himself and women. They loom as possessors of power and intensity, while most men stand by helplessly. The true male, however, wishes to recapture his lost strength and becomes a sort of womanly man. Great contradictions so glaring in Lawrence's work will serve to dramatize the paradoxical appearance of the female voice in the other works we have examined.

Lawrence was a prophetic writer and a romantic revolutionary. One of the primary objects of his fury was the male will to power; "the great serpent to destroy, is the will to Power: the desire for one man to have some dominion over his fellow-men."[36] Lawrence used several different words to embody this will; it often is synonymous with intellectuality or hyper-rationality. At other times the word seems to mean force. When this quality appears in a man, like Gerald Crich in *Women in Love,* Lawrence is ambivalent. Gerald's will to power is destructive, ultimately self-destructive, but the other male protagonist, Rupert Birkin, works hard to get in touch with this quality. For Lawrence the worship of maleness as sexual power is the other side of the coin. He wrote to E. H. Brewster in 1927; "I do this out of positive belief, that the phallus is a great sacred image: it represents a deep, deep life which has been denied in us, and still is denied. Women deny it horribly, with a grinning travesty of sex" (*Letters,* Vol. Two, p. 967). Lawrence conceived of a pure maleness (and a pure femaleness) that was, for him, the ultimate true thing in the world.

This true sexuality is confusingly represented in Lawrence's fiction, however, since the characters who embody such sexual truth are usually women who stand at rapt attention over a phallic, instructive male. Lawrence takes genuine pleasure in contemplating the dominant male through the eyes of a woman. As he remarked at length in the prologue to *Women in Love,* he felt a deep sexual attraction for men, for women (by whom he was surrounded) only a brotherly fondness.³⁷ Though he was involved with women of great force of will in his own life, his mother, his wife Frieda, and Mabel Dodge Luhan among others, Lawrence suggests that his inner life was consumed with thoughts of being overpowered by dominant, almost imperialistic males. This results in the women of his fiction being educated out of will (good and bad in men, but abhorrent in women), taught submission, as Lawrence fantasized of himself. David Cavitch remarks that "His creative self was so closely bound to his image of woman that he needed constantly to defend the genius of himself against the conscious shame of effeminacy."³⁸ Characters like Anna Brangwen or Ursula and Gudrun or Constance Chatterley grow out of the defensive identification of their author that becomes a voice appropriate for contemplation of the male essence.

Lawrence's tortuous reflections on will point up its very problematic nature in the works of other authors in this study. These male authors consistently use the female voice to confront problematic assertions of the self. Placed in a passive, weakened, outsider status in relationship to the rest of the world, a position in which artists often find themselves, how can they exert an influence? Furthermore, this problem may be confronted without the burden of abstraction laid upon a male persona. To many of the women I have discussed the possession of a strong will is a torture, and their struggle to gain control of an intractable world overwhelming. Esther Summerson's agonized self-abnegation is the flip side of an astonishing egotism. Clarissa towers like a tormented giant over the gleefully powerful Lovelace. Now using the voice of the weakened woman these authors may imagine astonishing degrees of manipulative control of others and astonishing spiritual superiority. The ability to set human beings in motion at will but then claim that ability from Olympian heights would be qualities of the artist, not the woman. That these women are so torn by their willpower testifies to the inordinate amounts of fantasy at work in their voices. Two problems appear the most pressing; the moral and the sexual. Robinson Crusoe, even though momentarily troubled by his defection from the middle state, asserts relatively untroubled kingship of his island. Moral reflections recur, but they do not overwhelm the narrative with a tortured heroic self. Beside him Moll and certainly Roxana are much more complex, self-aware, and self-denigrating about the less-than-moral acts they must undertake to get their way. Esther must keep asserting her self-righteousness in the face of the almost supernatural assumption of power she is made to bear. Tormented she sounds, because Dickens does not care to elucidate the contradictions in the fantasy that animates her. He must have her deny her control over others. Henry James's little governess is an intriguing instance of the moral contradiction in the exercise of power. James has her reflect many times on the moral role she is adopting. Only in this way is her complete assertion of emotional and spiritual domination justified.

Sexual vulnerability impedes self-assertion, and certainly Samuel Richardson and Henry James were amply provided with their own sexual vulnerability. There is considerable reason to think that both Dickens and Joyce were unhappy in their sexual lives. The utter sexlessness of the world of Crusoe, and the writing of a book like *Conjugal Lewdness*, suggest that the idea of his own sexuality was disturbing to Defoe. Possessing sexuality means that one becomes vulnerable and is tempted to sin. All of the female voices under discussion here are part of a prurient landscape. They emanate sexuality, even when (as in the case of Clarissa and Esther) their denials of it are vigorous. In their sexuality they call to mind most vividly the contradiction inherent in being both subject and object. As part of the author's pornographic fantasy, they seem inordinately concerned with sexual thoughts. Yet they are often in a position to observe the ridiculousness of the male's sexual posturing. Being sexual puts them frequently in the way of serious danger. Passion is the enemy of control and domination and a check on the assertion of will. Moral law and sexual vulnerability constantly threaten to overwhelm the power these women are made to seek.

The novelists I have discussed, even Defoe, invoke a vision of much of society as heartless and cruel. The use of the female voice is meant to infuse the dead world with life and heart. Her disintegration, whether madness or mysticism, seems to be both a punishment for the powerful position she occupies and a transitional stage to another level of consciousness. Another *idée fixe* of D. H. Lawrence's was that a change in the state of mind of human beings was essential before the world could live again. He worshipped what he called a blood consciousness, and if one had no knowledge of this, one was to all intents and purposes dead. He expounded these views in some detail in *Fantasia of the Unconscious*. Mankind must return to true knowledge, via the solar plexus, and return to a knowledge of the passional self. Forms of knowledge that impede this return, like intellectuality, are to be decried, particularly when they appear in women.[39] The blood consciousness is most acute in them, since they are connected to the moon; "The moon is the mother of darkness. She is the clue to the active darkness. And we, below the waist, we have our being in darkness."[40] Lawrence describes, several times, the modern man who has taken on the woman's role and consciousness, and he obviously is describing himself, ambivalently. To take on, whether mentally or in his fiction, the role of the woman is both programmatic and therapeutic, but also potentially destructive. Freud, he alleges, errs in making the unconscious a psychic goal. One must emerge from, issue from, this state of mind and be a real man, only to return to it and the woman at night.

Lawrence's views on the sensual awakening of the world, contradictory and even laughable, are embodied in a number of female characters. Often these women are propagandistic efforts in the furtherance of a primitive consciousness. He wrote to Lady Ottoline Morrell in 1928 (she had forgiven him for picturing her as a vile representation of female will in *Women in Love*); "But I want, with *Lady C.*, to make an *adjustment in consciousness* to the basic physical realities" (*Letters*, Vol. Two, p. 1111). This adjustment was accomplished by creating the consciousness of a woman, Constance Chatterley, coming into repeated contact with the idealized phallic male and experiencing deeper and deeper orgasmic awakenings. Writing from the view of the passive female, Lawrence rapturously observes the beauties of the male body and convincingly describes a loss of consciousness that leads one into more profound awareness. William York Tindall, in a withering study (although he modified his view later), remarked on the "bestial intuitions" Lawrence explored in relationship to women and felt that Lawrence (more than Virginia Woolf) intently recorded them "perhaps because no woman writer has been at once as feminine and gifted as he."[41] That is, he had successfully expressed the true nature of woman because he was a highly feminized male genius.

The disintegrative self explored by Defoe, Richardson, Dickens, and Joyce is quite different from this one, since there is not much pleasure in dissolution itself. But the motives may be similar. The most obvious one is punishment, disintegration as a purification of the bad. Constance is being purged of her "bad" class consciousness. Guilt and fear drive Roxana mad, as punishment for her bad acts. Defoe leaves her in this state of mind, though, unresolved. Clarissa's dying atones for her sin of pride, as Richardson wallows in the process of her weakening body. Dickens specifically uses Esther's smallpox as a rooting out of the sin of bastardy (destroying the likeness between her and her mother). The governess's punishment is external to the tale; it lies in the total ambiguity James throws upon her narrative. He pictures her mind in illicit traffic with some sordid ghosts and then refuses to verify their existence. Is Molly Bloom punished for her infidelity by being made into a broken record, a voice in which all things are conflated and confused? Or is it merely that flesh itself is incoherent?

The emphasis on the irrational and the confused may be for the artist the simple wish to explore that state of mind. While it may not be a pleasure for his heroine, it may be for the author. To observe the world with its ordinary boundaries dissolved would be an appealing artistic exercise in itself. The fear of loss of consciousness, madness, and nothingness is universal. To experience these states of mind, before the fact, may explain their appearance through the voice of the woman, as a way to allay fear. To assert a loss of self may be for the author an act of repentance for his own imaginative arrogance. Frieda Lawrence remarked in her memoir of their life together that she thought her husband dreaded women principally because they were more powerful than men.[42] Certainly these authors have imagined themselves as inordinately powerful in these narratives. Yet, they dread what they see as female power and dread even more the infusion of their own power and will into the woman. They are frightened of themselves in a new guise.

It would be simple enough to say that all of the female voices in this study are simply portraits of woman as domineering, irrational and untrustworthy. This would be in error. Combining the strengths of their authors and the weaknesses of women, these creatures are as odd as the women in Shakespeare, whom Stephen

Dedalus in *Ulysses* characterized: "But his boy women are the women of a boy. Their life, thought, speech are lent them by males" (p. 191). They should be read as glosses on the male spirit and with the same ironic perspective that Shakespeare's Cleopatra invoked when she said:

> "Antony
> Shall be brought drunken forth, and I shall see
> Some squeaking Cleopatra boy my greatness
> I' the' posture of a whore."[43]

A feminist critic like Carolyn Heilbrun praises Lawrence (earlier the victim of the deserved drubbing by Kate Millett), for the portrait of Ursula in *The Rainbow*; "In *The Rainbow* Lawrence wrote the myth of the new female creation born into a world the male spirit had despoiled."[44] Androgyny becomes an ideal for Heilbrun, although she declines to speculate on what the future great "androgynous" works will be like. In fact, we see them in their purest form in the female narratives under discussion in this study. These "women" certainly possess a complex, rich dimensionality that often their male counterparts do not. Sir Edmund Orme is a bore but James's governess probably generates another article as you read this. Roxana and Clarissa are fascinating evocations of the lioness in chains, while all seven volumes of Sir Charles Grandison languish on the shelves of even the most scholarly library. Esther Summerson has at least proved fascinating to critics, who still keep on curing her of her problems.

The use of the first-person form is only the most dramatic representation of a male author's identification with a woman, and there are numbers of heroines created by men who betray this same identification. It is difficult to believe that Becky Sharp does not represent her author's gleeful imagining of attack on the snobbisms of society or that Madame Bovary does not, as Flaubert himself claimed, represent himself in the guise of a woman. Baudelaire noted this miraculous fusion: "The most energetic and ambitious, but also the most imaginative part of Madame Bovary's personality have definitely remained masculine in kind. Like weapon-bearing Pallas issuing forth from the forehead of Zeus, this bizarre and androgynous creature houses the seductiveness of a virile soul within the body of a beautiful woman."[45] Could Roxanna or Clarissa or even Molly Bloom be called anything but bizarre, androgynous souls? Yet it is they, and the thousands of female characters, who comprise what we call the image of woman in fiction. This image has been of enormous importance to women themselves, since they have always made up the largest share of the novel-reading public. How much easier it has been for critics to say these are acute portraits of women, rather than to praise the psychological revelations of George Eliot's Will Ladislaw or Brontë's Rochester or Virginia Woolf's young men. No—these men are unreal fairy tale characters obscured by fantasy and fear. If there is such a thing as androgyny, it apparently applies only to the male ability to absorb himself into a woman. To women it should now be obvious the extent to which fear and fantasy operate in the male creation of a female protagonist. She represents the best and the worst of the man.

It would be silly to deplore the female voice created by these authors, even though this voice has influenced profoundly how women think of themselves and how other authors write about them. And, as Oscar Wilde pointed out long ago, art in itself should not be measured by the standards of reality. The wonder of fictional creations is their fusion of art and life, and to demand that "real" women be portrayed is like asking for photo-realism or for men to change their sex. Wilde's idea that "the object of art is not simple truth but complex beauty" is a persuasive one, and the beauty of these women is nothing if not complex.[46] But just as Wilde asserted the artificiality of art, he also reminded us how often people model themselves on fictional or artistic types, how often they become what they are told they represent. Pablo Picasso painted the face of his close friend Gertrude Stein a number of times and remained unsatisfied. He could finish the portrait only when he did not look at her. So he painted out her face and replaced it with an impassive, ample visage, one that James Mellow calls strange and masklike. "When friends complained that Gertrude did not look at all like his painting, Picasso was in the habit of shrugging his shoulders and saying, 'She will.' "[47] The visions of men have created the word portraits of women in this study. It is probably too late to undo these real-life reproductions, but not too late to understand their origins.

Notes

[1]James Joyce, *"Daniel Defoe,"* ed. and trans. Joseph Prescott *Buffalo Studies*, Vol. 1, No. 1, SUNY at Buffalo, 1964, p. 20.

[2]*Ibid.*, p. 23.

[3]D. H. Lawrence, *The Collected Letters of D. H. Lawrence*, 2 Vols., ed. Harry T. Moore (New York: Viking Press, 1962) Vol. 1, p. 282. All subsequent references to Lawrence's letters will be to Moore's collection.

[4]Auguste Comte, *A General View of Positivism* (New York: Robert Spiller & Sons, 1957), p. 253.

[5]James Joyce, *A Portrait of the Artist as a Young Man* (New York: The Viking Press, 1964) p. 203. All subsequent references will be to this edition of the text.

[6]James Joyce, *Stephen Hero* (New York: New Directions, 1944) p. 200. See also p. 210.

[7]*Ibid.*, see p. 112.

[8]See Stanislaus Joyce, *My Brother's Keeper* (New York: Viking) 1958.

[9]Richard Ellmann, *James Joyce* (Oxford: Oxford University Press, 1959) p. 41.

[10]Stanislaus Joyce, p. 238.

[11]*Selected Letters of James Joyce*, ed. Richard Ellmann (New York: The Viking Press, 1975) p. 169. All subsequent references will be to this edition.

[12]Quoted in Ellmann's *James Joyce*, p. 734.

[13]*Ibid.*, p. 642.

[14]James Joyce, *Exiles, A Play in Three Acts* in *The Portable James Joyce*, intro. and notes Harry Levin (New York: The Viking Press, 1947) p. 581.

[15]See Ellmann, *James Joyce*, p. 465.

[16]*Ibid.*, p. 652.

[17]Barbara Hardy first suggested to me the closeness of the language of the letters and Molly's speech in the Spring of 1978.

[18]Edmund Wilson, "James Joyce," reprinted in *Joyce, A Collection of Critical Essays*, ed. William Chase (Englewood Cliffs: Prentice-Hall, 1974) p. 57. The essay appeared originally in *Axel's Castle*, 1931.

[19]Hugh Kenner, *Joyce's Voices* (Berkeley: University of California Press, 1978). See p. 67 and 84.

[20]James Joyce, *Ulysses* (New York: Random House, 1961) p. 48. All subsequent references will be to this edition of the text.

[21]*Neitzsche Aujourd 'hui?* 1) *Intensités* (Paris: Union Generale D' Editions, 1973). This is a discussion of Derrida's remarks on the relationship between sex and style in the work of Neitzsche, p. 288.

[22]See #18, p. 56.

[23]Louis Gillet, *Claybook for James Joyce*, trans, Georges Markow Totevy (London: Abelard-Schuman, 1958). See pp. 116-118.

[24]Mark Shechner, *Joyce in Nighttown, A Psychoanalytic Inquiry into 'Ulysses'* (Berkeley: Univ. of California Press, 1974) p. 225.

[25]Quoted by Ellmann in *James Joyce*, p. 743.

[26]Hugh Kenner, *Joyce's Voices*, p. 20.

[27]See Gillet, #23, p. 55.

[28]Hugh Kenner, *Dublin's Joyce* (Bloomington: Indiana University Press, 1956) p. 262.

[29]Mark Shechner lists the two camps in *Joyce in Nighttown*, p. 200.

[30]*Ibid.*, p. 225.

[31]See Ellmann, *James Joyce*, pp. 692-693.

[32]Harry Levin, *James Joyce, A Critical Introduction* (New York: New Directions, 1941) p. 195.

[33]James Joyce, *Finnegans Wake* (New York: Viking Press, 1939) p. 627. All subsequent references will be to this edition of the text.

[34]See Ellmann, *James Joyce*, p. 725.

[35]William York Tindall, *D. H. Lawrence and Susan His Cow* (New York: Columbia University Press, 1939) p. 86.

[36]*The Collected Letters of D. H. Lawrence*, Vol. 1, p. 312.

[37]See D. H. Lawrence, *Phoenix II*, Coll. and ed Warren Roberts and Harry T. Moore (New York: The Viking Press, 1970) pp. 92-108, pp. 104-105 in particular.

[38]David Cavitch, *D. H. Lawrence and the New World* (London: Oxford University Press, 1969) p. 29.

[39]D. H. Lawrence, *Fantasia of the Unconscious* and *Psychoanalysis and the Unconscious* (Melbourne: Heinemann, 1961). See p. 22 and p. 81.

[40]*Ibid.*, p. 176.

[41]William York Tindall, *D. H. Lawrence and Susan His Cow*, p. 202.

[42]Frieda Lawrence, *"Not I, But the Wind. . ."* (New York: The Viking Press, 1934). See p. 57.

[43]William Shakespeare, *Antony and Cleopatra*, V, ii, 218-220.

[44]Carolyn G. Heilbrun, *Toward a Recognition of Androgyny* (New York: Harper and Row, 1973) p. 102.

[45]Charles Baudelaire, *"Madame Bovary*, by Gustave Flaubert,"* in Paul de Man's translation of *Madame Bovary* (New York: Norton, 1965) p. 340.

[46]Oscar Wilde, "The Decay of Lying" in *The Artist as Critic, Critical Writings of Oscar Wilde*, ed. Richard Ellmann (New York: Vintage, 1968) p. 302.

[47]James R. Mellow, *Charmed Circle, Gertrude Stein & Company* (New York: Praeger, 1974) p. 93.

INDEX

Male Novelists and Their Female Voices:
Literary Masquerades

Composed in IBM Electronic Selectric Composer *Journal Roman* and printed offset by Cushing-Malloy, Incorporated, Ann Arbor, Michigan. The paper on which the book is printed is the Northwest Paper Company's *Caslon;* the book was sewn and bound in Scottek C Vellum, *Deep Blue Burlap* by John H. Dekker & Sons, Grand Rapids, Michigan.

Male Novelists and Their Female Voices is a Trenowyth book, the scholarly publishing division of The Whitston Publishing Company.

This edition consists in 750 casebound copies.